PREACH THE WORD

Preparing Biblical Messages—Homiletics 1

Cover Photo

"Preach the Word; be prepared in season and out of season; correct, rebuke and encourage—with great patience and careful instruction" (2 Tim. 4:2).

Preach the good news, anointed by the Spirit (Luke 4:18).

Components That Complement This Book

Visit www.FaithAndActionSeries.org to see components with this book:

eVisuals—all figures in color with captions for projection in classroom. Download from our website.

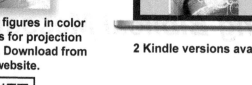

2 Kindle versions available from Amazon:

Version on right is a typical Kindle format. Suitable for your tablet or phone or computer

Teacher's Guides—To purchase a TG a person must submit our online form and be approved as a teacher, pastor, or administrator.
www.faithandactionseries.org/teachers.html

To find us on Amazon search Faith & Action Team.
www.amazon.com (search Faith & Action Team)

Contact Information

Order your copy from:

Faith & Action Team
429 U.S. Hwy 65
Walnut Shade, Missouri 65771 U.S.A

Telephone: 417-881-4698

E-mail: Orders@FaithAndActionSeries.org

Web: www.FaithAndActionSeries.org

Special thanks to BGMC for helping fund this project.

PREACH THE WORD
Preparing Biblical Messages—Homiletics 1
Student Manual

by Dr. Quentin McGhee
& Dr. Gaylan D. Claunch

Instructional Design by
Dr. Quentin McGhee,
Senior Editor

PUT YOUR FAITH TO WORK!

Faith & Action Series

Faith & Action
429 US Hwy 65
Walnut Shade, MO. 65771 U.S.A

Photo Credits

	Figure #
Berg	1.15, 4.7, 6.6
Cooley	1.14, 4.4
Corel	1.5, 4.4, 4.5, 4.8, 5.7, 6.2, 12.1, 13.1
Harris	2.4
Photos.com	1.9, 1.16, 2.1, 5.9, 6.1, 6.5, 7.1, 7.5, 7.7, 7.8, 8.13, 8.15, 8.16, 9.3, 9.4
Univ. North Texas, Dept. of Communications Studies	4.3

Copyright Information

First Edition 2005
Second Edition 2011

Faith & Action Series—Preach the Word, Second Edition
©2012 Faith & Action Team

Course # MIN1013
ISBN 978-1-60382-028-8
Item # 4432-11E0

Table of Contents

List of Charts

Faith & Action Series Overview

Bible	Theology	Church Ministries
Survey of the Old Testament	God & the Bible (Theology 1)	Evangelism & Discipleship
Survey of the New Testament	Angels, Man, & Sin (Theology 2)	Marriage & Family
Pentateuch	Christ & Salvation (Theology 3)	Pastoral Ministry
Historical Books	The Holy Spirit & the Church (Theology 4)	Ministerial Ethics
Poetic Books	General Principles for Interpreting Scripture (Hermeneutics 1)	Preach the Word (Homiletics 1)
Major Prophets	Hermeneutics 2	Homiletics 2
Minor Prophets		Principles of Teaching
Life & Teachings of Christ (Synoptic Gospels)		Biblical Counseling
John		Children's Ministry
Acts of the Holy Spirit		Youth Ministry
Romans & Galatians		Missions 1
Corinthians		Cross Cultural Communications (Missions 2)
Prison Epistles		Teaching Literacy
Pastoral Epistles		Leadership
Hebrews		Church Government & Administration
General Epistles		Church History 1
Revelation & Daniel		Church History 2

Faith & Action Series
Three-Year Bible School Plan (103 credits)

First Year

First Semester

Course #	Title	Credits
BIB1013	Survey of the New Testament	3
BIB1023	Pentateuch	3
BIB1033	Synoptic Gospels	3
THE1012	God & the Bible (Theology 1)	2
THE1022	Hermeneutics 1	2
MIN3023	Children's Ministry	3
		16

Second Semester

Course #	Title	Credits
BIB1043	Survey of the Old Testament	3
BIB1052	John	2
BIB1063	Acts	3
THE1032	Angels, Man, and Sin (Theology 2)	2
MIN1013	Homiletics 1	3
MIN1033	Evangelism & Discipleship	3
		16

Second Year

First Semester

Course #	Title	Credits
BIB2013	Romans & Galatians	3
BIB2023	Historical Books	3
BIB2072	Hebrews	2
MIN2012	Church History 1	2
MIN2023	Missions 1	3
THE2013	Christ & Salvation (Theology 3)	3
THE2032	Hermeneutics 2	2
		18

Second Semester

Course #	Title	Credits
BIB2043	Corinthians	3
BIB2052	Prison Epistles	2
BIB2063	Poetic Books	3
MIN2032	Church History 2	2
THE2042	The Holy Spirit & the Church (Theology 4)	2
THE2052	Leadership	2
MIN3073	Marriage & Family	3
		17

Third Year

First Semester

Course #	Title	Credits
BIB3012	Pastoral Epistles	2
BIB3022	General Epistles	2
BIB3033	Major Prophets	3
MIN3013	Pastoral Ministry	3
MIN3022	Church Government & Admin.	2
MIN3033	Cross Cultural Communications	3
MIN3043	Homiletics 2	3
		18

Second Semester

Course #	Title	Credits
BIB3043	Revelation & Daniel	3
MIN1032	Teaching Literacy	2
MIN3053	Biblical Counseling	3
BIB3053	Minor Prophets	3
MIN3063	Principles of Teaching	3
MIN3072	Ministerial Ethics	2
MIN3082	Youth Ministry	2
		18

About This Book

1. **The Lesson** headings divide each chapter into two to four parts. Each of these parts or lessons focuses on several principles related to one theme. We number the lessons consecutively throughout the book.

2. **The Lesson Goals** are listed at the beginning of each chapter. Also, when a lesson begins, the goal for that lesson is printed there. You will find that there is at least one goal for each lesson.

3. **Key Words** are defined in a section called "Definitions" at the end of the book. The symbol * comes before all words that are defined. To help some students, we have also defined a few words that are not key words.

4. **Teaching Method:** These courses are designed for the *guided discovery* method of learning. This method focuses on the student, rather than the teacher. When this course is used in a classroom, lectures are not intended. Rather, most of the class time should be used for students to discuss the questions in the margins and related questions from the teacher and other students. At least 25% of the student's grade should be on how faithfully the student has tried to answer questions *before* class.

   It is VERY important for each student to own his or her book. We encourage Bible schools to require students to buy their texts at the time they pay tuition. It is a shame for students to leave school without their books, because they need them for a lifetime of ministry. Owning the book enables a student to write notes in it and underline important ideas. Also, when students own their books, they do not waste class time by copying things that are already written in the text. Rather, they spend their time discussing questions related to the Bible and ministry.

   In a classroom the teacher and students should discuss key questions together. The best teachers never answer their own questions. Some students will complain at first when the teacher requires them to think, read, and search for answers. But a good teacher knows that children who are always carried never learn to walk. And students who are always told the answer learn to memorize, but not think and solve problems. In many ways, a good teacher is like a coach—guiding others to succeed.

   The questions in this course are like a path that leads straight to the goal. If the questions are too hard for a student, the teacher can ask easier questions that are like stairs toward harder questions. Also, the teacher should ask questions that guide students to apply the text to local issues. Often, a good teacher will add a story or illustration that emphasizes a truth for students.

5. **Schedule:** Most *Faith & Action Series* courses have up to 40 lessons. For a Bible school course, it is good to plan for 40 contact hours between the teacher and students. This allows 1 lesson for a class hour.

6. **The Questions.** Most questions in the margins are identified by the hammer ⟋ and nail ⟍ symbols. Questions are steps toward a goal. As a student answers the questions, he or she is sure to reach the goals. The hammer introduces *content questions* and the nail precedes *application questions*. Our logo for this book includes the hammer hitting the nail. A student must grasp content before being able to apply it. The answers to all content questions are in the text, near the question. We encourage students to answer nail or application questions from their local settings.

   In some books there is the symbol of a shovel ⟍ before certain questions. Questions beside the shovel symbol are inductive questions. The word *induce* means "to lead." These questions lead students to discover truth for themselves. The shovel symbol alerts students that it is time to dig in and discover truth for themselves. *All students studying this course alone should complete the shovel questions.* Such students miss the 40 or more hours in a classroom that resident or extension students receive. The shovel questions will help these correspondence students get more out of the course. *When this book is used in a classroom setting, students will still benefit from answering the shovel questions. Teachers may require students to answer all shovel questions outside of class, or they may guide students to complete these questions in class; or they may replace some shovel questions with other work.*

7. **The Illustrations**, such as stories and examples, are preceded by the candle symbol.

8. **Figures** include pictures, photos, charts, and maps. We number the figures in order throughout the chapter. For example, the first three figures in chapter one are numbered 1.1, 1.2, and 1.3. There is a list of figures near the front of the book.

9. **The Test Yourself** questions come at the end of each chapter and are indicated by the balance symbol. There are always ten of these questions. As a rule, there are two test questions for each goal in the chapter. If students miss any of these questions, they need to understand why they missed them. Knowing why an answer is right is as important as knowing the right answer.

10. **Essay Test Topics** are at the end of each chapter, indicated by the pencil symbol. Note that these essay topics are the lesson goals of the chapter. A student should be able to summarize these goals, writing 50-100 words on each one. These essay topics test students at a much higher level than the multiple choice, Test Yourself questions.

11. **Sample Answers** to the hammer questions, some comments on the nail questions, and answers for the Test Yourself questions and the Essay Test topics are in the Teacher's Guide. Students should answer questions so they will grow and become strong in their mental skills.

12. **Bible quotations** are usually from the New International Version (NIV). We also use the New Century Version (NCV), New American Standard Bible (NASB), and the King James Version (KJV). We encourage students to compare biblical passages in several versions of the Bible.

13. **The Scripture List** includes key Scripture references in this course. It is located near the back of the book.

14. **The Bibliography** is near the endnotes page. It is a complete list of books the author refers to in this course. Some students will want to do further research in these books.

15. **Endnotes** identify the sources of thoughts and quotes. They are listed by chapter at the end of the book.

16. **The Unit Exams and a Final Exam** are in the Teacher's Guide. In the Teacher's Guide there are also other useful items for the teacher and potential projects for the students.

17. **Course Description (MIN1013):** This study is designed to teach pastors, evangelists, missionaries, teachers, and lay persons a Five Step Method of preparing expository sermons. The course explains the problem/solution approach as a method to organize the sermon. Students are taught to develop the problem and solution parts of the sermon by stating a principle, and then explaining, illustrating, and applying it.

18. **Course Goals** for the entire course are listed below. The goals in each chapter will enable a student to reach these broader goals. By the end of this book a student should be able to:
- Explain 12 characteristics of a pastor based on 1 Timothy 3 and Titus 1.
- Describe 9 principles for preparing a biblical message.
- Analyze the 10 commandments of delivering a message.
- Explain what the anointing is and is not; relate it to a pastor's character, message, and delivery.
- Identify 14 types of illustrations.
- Give 16 reasons preachers should use many illustrations.
- Create a file for sermon illustrations, and put at least 10 illustrations in it.
- Summarize the purpose for each step of the Five Step Method.
- Explain the reason for preaching about the problem before the solution.
- Outline and preach a complete expository sermon based on principles, and organized by the Problem/Solution Method.

19. Authors

Dr. Quentin McGhee is the founder and senior editor of the *Faith & Action Series*. He earned a B.A. from Southwestern College in Oklahoma City, and a B.S. from Oral Roberts University (ORU). Later he completed an M.Div. at the Assemblies of God Theological Seminary. There he taught beginning Greek and was selected by the faculty for "Who's Who Among Students in American Colleges and Universities." He earned a D.Min. from ORU in 1987. Dr. McGhee and his wife, Elizabeth, pioneered a church in Oklahoma. They went on to serve as missionaries in Kenya for 15 years, where they helped start many churches, developed an extension Bible school for full-time ministers, and assisted in curriculum development. Currently, Dr. McGhee serves with the Assemblies of God World Missions as Director for the *Faith & Action Series* under the Latin America/Caribbean field.

Dr. Gaylan D. Claunch is known as a biblical preacher. As a professor of Biblical Preaching at Southwestern Assemblies of God University in Waxahachie, Texas, he has trained hundreds of young ministers in the principles of homiletics. His additional ministry activities include being a member of the South Dallas Sectional Committee and the Missions Committee for the North Texas District Council of the AG. He has also served as an adjunct, visiting professor of a Bible school in Brazil.

Dr. Claunch earned a B.S. degree from Southwestern Assemblies of God University; an M.Div. from the Assemblies of God Theological Seminary; and a D.Min. from Oral Roberts University. He has served in full-time ministry for over 40 years—and has been a senior pastor for 30+ of these years. He pastored the Crossroads of Life Assembly of God in Duncanville, Texas, for 17 years and currently serves as the District Missions Director for the North Texas District of the Assemblies of God. He has a great love for missions, and has led his congregation to be one of the top 100 churches in America in world ministries giving.

Gaylan and his wife, Nancy, have been married for over 35 years. They have two children, both in ministry—a daughter, Lesli, married to Rev. Dyran Deer, and a son, Loren.

20. Contributors and Consultants

Dr. James O. Davis earned his B.A. in Bible from Central Bible College and two masters' degrees at the Assemblies of God Theological Seminary. His D.Min. in Preaching was awarded by Trinity Evangelical Divinity School.

For 12 years, Davis served as the National Evangelists Representative for the American Assemblies of God. He has served on the General Presbytery for the Assemblies of God, the Two-Thirds World Missions Board, the Committee on Mission, and as an adjunct professor at several Bible colleges and seminaries. He is co-founder of Billion Soul Network, a global evangelism and church planting thrust. Internationally, he is known for providing biblical solutions to today's hard problems.

Rev. James Kirigi helped develop and field test many of the ideas in this course, and co-authored a book on preaching that laid the foundation for this volume. His ministry is a balanced blend of teaching and preaching. He has taught homiletics for nearly 20 years at East Africa School of Theology (EAST) in Nairobi, Kenya. During all of these years, he pastored the church he pioneered, and has now past 25 years as senior pastor. In addition, he served 8 years as the Assistant Principal of the Kenya Assemblies of God Extension Bible School, and continues to teach in that program.

James earned a B.A. degree in Bible and Theology from EAST. Later, he completed a Masters degree through the East Africa Graduate Studies Centre. He is an active pastor, mentor, and teacher, and is fluent in three languages: English, Kiswahili, and Kikuyu.

Rev. Terrence (Terry) B. Johnson has a B.A. in Biblical Studies from Central Bible College. He is a third-generation AGWM missionary to Brazil and began serving in 1988. Since 1995, Terry has served as president of a network of educational ministries that include: Brazil Extension School of Theology (BEST), Brazil Advanced School of Theology (BAST), Pentecostal Bible Institute, and Children Of Brazil Outreach (COBO). Currently, BEST has 17,000 students throughout Brazil and in Portuguese-language churches in the U.S., Japan, and Canada. Since its founding in 1979, BEST has graduated 13,000 students. BAST now has 800 extension students. COBO has built 12 Christian schools and daycare centers, and has a total enrollment of 4,000.

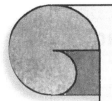

Unit 1: First Things First

Welcome to this study of homiletics. You are studying because you want to become a better preacher of God's Word. Some people have questions about the difference between a preacher and a teacher. The following definitions will be helpful:

- *Homiletics* is the study of preparing and preaching biblical messages.
- *Preaching* is declaring the Word of God through the anointing of the Holy Spirit. Its three-fold purpose is to persuade people to be reconciled to God, grow in grace, and live victoriously in Jesus Christ. Sometimes we think the only preachers are those who stand behind pulpits. But Acts 8:1-4 says that all the believers who had been scattered from Jerusalem preached the Word wherever they went. So there is a sense in which all believers may preach or declare the Word of God.
- *Teaching* is helping others gain knowledge, values, right attitudes, and skills.

to a Decision

How to live

New Testament preaching and teaching are two parts of one ministry.[1] The ministry of Jesus and the twelve apostles included both preaching and teaching (Matt. 4:23; Mark 1:21-22, 27; Luke 4:44; Acts 18:4-5, 11, 19; 19:8). All pastors have the ministry of preaching and teaching. And all laypersons may be anointed by the Spirit to preach and teach the Word.

The purpose of this course is to teach you to prepare and preach biblical messages with the Five-Step Method. As a foundation for our study, we begin with the preacher. Learn the principles of Unit 1 well. Why? Because the preacher is always more important than the method. We will divide this Unit into four parts (See below).

Chapter 1 focuses on the preacher's character. We will guide you to:
- *Explain why a pastor must be blameless and have a good reputation.*
- *Analyze five things the Scriptures say a pastor must not be. Illustrate each.*
- *Summarize seven things a pastor must be. Illustrate each.*

Chapter 2 is about the preacher's message. You will learn to:
- *Explain why devotions are essential, and give six guidelines for them.*
- *Explain and give an example of each of the nine keys for preparing biblical messages.*

Chapter 3 discusses the preacher's passion and delivery. We will enable you to:
- *Summarize the commandments on passion, neatness, posture, manners, and voice.*
- *Explain the commandments for speech, gestures, the hands, face, and eyes.*

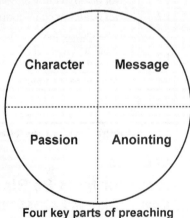

Four key parts of preaching

Chapter 4 emphasizes the preacher's anointing. In this vital chapter you will learn to:
- *Explain five things the anointing is not.*
- *Summarize five things the anointing is.*
- *Describe how the anointing affects a pastor's character, message, and passion.*

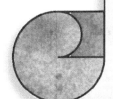

Chapter 1:

The Preacher's Character

Introduction

Figure 1.1   The handwriting on the wall said that King Belshazzar had been weighed on the scales and found lacking.

King Belshazzar gave a great banquet for 1,000 of his nobles. He drank wine with them. While drinking, he ordered the servants to bring the gold and silver cups. His father, Nebuchadnezzar, had taken these cups from the temple in Jerusalem. King Belshazzar, his princes, wives, and mistresses drank wine from these holy cups. As they drank, they praised the gods of gold, silver, bronze, iron, wood, and stone (Dan. 5:1-4).

Suddenly, the fingers of a human hand appeared and wrote on the wall. The king's face turned pale as he watched the fingers. He was so frightened that his knees began to beat against each other. His legs grew too weak to stand upon (Dan. 5:5-6).

In a short time, someone brought Daniel to interpret the handwriting on the wall. He spoke words of rebuke and judgment to the great king. Daniel said that King Belshazzar had not humbled himself (Dan. 5:22). Instead, the king had set himself up against the God of heaven. The prophet said, *"You did not honor the God who holds in his hand your life and all your ways"* (Dan. 5:23). Part of the handwriting on the wall said that the king had been weighed on the scales and found lacking (Dan. 5:27).

Q 1 *Explain: God weighs each person (Dan. 5:27).*

God weighs each person. Much will be demanded from those who have been given much (Luke 12:48). The Bible tells us that God expects certain qualities of *pastors. Study Figure 1.2. In this chapter, we will take a close look at how much a pastor should weigh.

1 Tim. 3:2	Titus 1:6-7	(-) Negative 5 Bad Characteristics to Avoid (Blameless: Not guilty of 5 accusations)	(+) Positive 7 Good Qualities to Have (Respected for 7 good reasons)	1 Tim. 3:2, 7	Titus 1:7
3:3	1:7	1. Not given to drunkenness	1. The husband of one wife	3:2,12	1:6
3:3	1:7	2. Not overbearing or quarrelsome	2. Gentle	3:3	—
3:3	1:7	3. Not quick-tempered; not violent	3. Temperate; self controlled; disciplined	3:2	1:8
3:3	1:7	4. Not a lover of money; not pursuing dishonest gain	4. Hospitable	3:2	1:8
3:6	—	5. Not a recent convert	5. One who loves what is good; upright and holy	—	1:8
			6. Able to teach; holding firmly to sound doctrine	3:2	1:9
			7. A good manager of his own family	3:12	1:6

Figure 1.2   Twelve requirements for a pastor to be blameless and have a good reputation

Lessons:

A Pastor Must Be Blameless and Have a Good Reputation
Goal: *Explain why a pastor must be blameless and have a good reputation.*

Characteristics That a Pastor Must NOT Have
Goal: *Analyze 5 things the Scriptures say a pastor must not be. Illustrate each.*

Characteristics That a Pastor Must Have
Goal: *Summarize 7 things a pastor must be. Illustrate each.*

○━━○   **Key Words**   ○━━○

homiletics	*logos*	*pneumatos*	*episkopos*	blameless
ethos	*pathos*	character	*presbuteros*	reputation

A Pastor Must Be Blameless and Have a Good Reputation

Goal: *Explain why a pastor must be blameless and have a good reputation.*

Setting

*Homiletics is based on the Greek word *homileo.* It means to "talk" or "speak." A homily is a message or sermon based on the Bible. Homiletics is the study of preparing and preaching biblical messages.

This course is designed to help you learn to prepare sermons with "The Problem/ Solution Method." One great teacher taught preaching for more than 40 years. He said the Problem/Solution Method was the easiest, yet most powerful method he had ever seen for planning a sermon.[2] We will teach you how to plan each of the five steps of a sermon. But there are important things to consider before we come to the five steps.

The ancient Greeks put great emphasis on speaking. They divided the subject of public speaking into three parts. The Greek words for these three parts are *ethos, *logos,* and *pathos.*[3] To these three we will add a fourth called *pneumatos.* Figure 1.3 summarizes these four parts or dimensions of speaking or preaching.

Greek Word	Meaning	Related English Words
1. *Ethos*	Character, behavior, lifestyle	Ethics
2. *Logos*	Word, message, speech, sermon	Theology
3. *Pathos*	Passion, feeling, delivery	Passion
4. *Pneumatos*	Anointing of the Spirit	Pneumatology: the study of the Spirit

Figure 1.3   The four parts or dimensions of preaching

We will spend a chapter on each of the four words in Figure 1.3. *Ethos,* the pastor's *character, is the theme of our first chapter on homiletics. We study the pastor's character first because it is the most important.[+]

A. A pastor is more than a preacher.

The most important part of preparing a sermon is preparing a pastor. Notice that we said *pastor,* not preacher. You see, a pastor is more than just a preacher or speaker. In the Greek New Testament there are three words for pastor. *Poimen* is a Greek word for "pastor" or "shepherd." It emphasizes that a pastor must watch over God's sheep. Jesus is the Chief Shepherd (John 10; Heb. 13:20; 1 Pet. 2:25). And other pastors should follow His example, laying down their lives for God's sheep (1 John 3:16). *Poimen* is not used often in the New Testament, but it reminds us that a pastor is a shepherd of God's sheep.[4]

Two common Greek words for a pastor are *episkopos* and *presbuteros.* *Episkopos* is the Greek word in 1 Timothy 3:2. It means "overseer" or "bishop" (1 Pet. 2:25; Acts 20:28; Phil. 1:1; Titus 1:7). *Episkopos* emphasizes that the pastor is a steward who watches over God's house.[5] The second common Greek word for pastor is *presbuteros* (Titus 1:5). It emphasizes the spiritual maturity and dignity

Q 2 What is the difference between a pastor and a speaker?

Q 3 Explain the role of a pastor, based on the words *episkopos* and *presbuteros.*

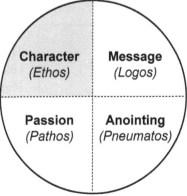

Character (Ethos)	Message (Logos)
Passion (Pathos)	Anointing (Pneumatos)

Figure 1.4   First of four key parts of preaching

+ Throughout this book, we refer to the pastor as a man rather than a woman. The Bible mentions many anointed women. Today, women serve in a variety of ministries, including pastoring. We refer to pastors as men, not to restrict women from ministry, but only for the flow of language and interaction with biblical passages, which do likewise.

Figure 1.5   A blameless pastor is as bold as a lion.

required for the office of pastor.[6] Together, these two Greek words show us that a pastor is a mature leader who watches over God's flock.

Q 4 ⋏ *Which of the 12 requirements in Figure 1.2 deal with a pastor's talent? Explain.*

Q 5 ⋏ *Is God's greatest concern for talent or character? Explain.*

A mature leader does not just appear suddenly.[7] Becoming like Jesus is a process. All of life is a spiritual journey. None of us is perfect. There is, however, a level of spiritual maturity to reach before becoming a pastor. There are certain moral and spiritual standards that qualify a person to pastor. Study Figure 1.2. It contains 12 requirements for a pastor (1 Tim. 3:1-7; Titus 1:5-9). Notice that only one of the 12 requirements relates to ability or talent! A pastor's character is more important than his ability to speak or organize. A pastor's character is more important than his abilities or education.[8] God *is not* searching for ability. He has no problem with a man like Moses who considered himself a slow speaker. Many have the ability to be good speakers. But God calls pastors on the basis of their character, not their ability to talk.

B. A pastor must be blameless and have a good reputation.

Q 6 ⋏ *What are 2 ways that blame can come?*

Paul wrote to both Timothy and Titus that a pastor must be *blameless (1 Tim. 3:2; Titus 1:6-7). To be blameless means not to be guilty of accusations. Blame can come when a person does bad or neglects to do good. In this chapter we will study the 12 characteristics or character traits of a pastor. These 12 qualities explain how a pastor can be blameless and have a good *reputation.

Pastors must be blameless in two ways.

Q 7 ⋏ *Why must a preacher be blameless in his own eyes?*

First, we must be blameless in our own eyes. A wise man said that sin makes cowards out of all of us. If a pastor does not tithe, his conscience will blame and condemn him. How then will he preach on tithing with courage? If a pastor is immoral, he must be a Pharisee to preach holiness to others. Living a high standard enables us to preach a high standard.

"The wicked man flees though no one pursues, but the righteous are as bold as a lion" (Prov. 28:1). Blessed is the pastor whose conscience does not condemn him (Rom. 14:22-23). Blameless pastors preach God's truth with boldness.

Q 8 ⋏ *Why must a preacher be blameless in the eyes of others?*

Second, we must be blameless in the eyes of others.   Hebrews 12:13 says, *"'Make level* [righteous] *paths for your feet,' so that the lame may not be disabled* [made worse], *but rather healed."* Lame people need a level, smooth path to walk on. Otherwise, they might fall and make a lame leg even worse. The pastor should make level, upright paths for his own feet to walk on. Then the weak that follow him will not stumble because of his steps. Rather, they will watch his example and their limp will be healed.[9]

Q 9 ⋏ *People from which 2 towns talked about Timothy?*

Timothy was a blameless man with a good reputation. *"The brothers at Lystra and Iconium spoke well of him"* (Acts 16:2). Notice that more than one person spoke about Timothy. People talk. News about a person travels around. People in two different towns talked about Timothy. We can always expect people to talk about others. Therefore, it is important for pastors to have a good reputation.

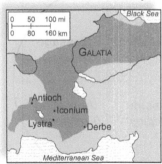

Figure 1.6   Timothy had a good reputation in the Galatian cities of Lystra and Iconium.

Q 10 ⋏ *What is the loudest and most famous sermon a pastor will ever preach?*

One cannot prevent accusations. But blame stings most when it is true! Paul told Timothy, *"Set an example for the believers in speech, in life, in love, in faith and in purity"* (1 Tim. 4:12). From the earliest days, the Church has needed leaders above reproach. Remember the seven deacons chosen in Acts 6? One of the qualifications was having a good reputation (Acts 6:3). Be blameless and have a good reputation. Why? Because you, pastor, are a sermon. Your character and daily living are the loudest sermon you will ever preach!

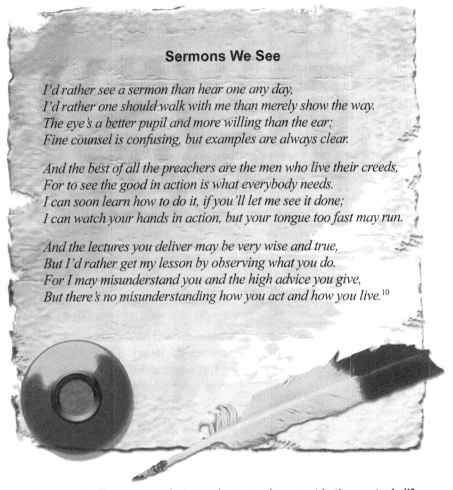

Sermons We See

I'd rather see a sermon than hear one any day,
I'd rather one should walk with me than merely show the way.
The eye's a better pupil and more willing than the ear;
Fine counsel is confusing, but examples are always clear.

And the best of all the preachers are the men who live their creeds,
For to see the good in action is what everybody needs.
I can soon learn how to do it, if you'll let me see it done;
I can watch your hands in action, but your tongue too fast may run.

And the lectures you deliver may be very wise and true,
But I'd rather get my lesson by observing what you do.
For I may misunderstand you and the high advice you give,
But there's no misunderstanding how you act and how you live.[10]

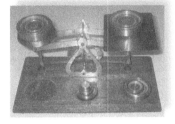

Figure 1.7   Pastors must be measured by 1 Timothy 3:1-7 and Titus 1:5-9.

Figure 1.8   The sermon that people remember most is the pastor's life.

Lesson 2 — Characteristics That a Pastor Must NOT Have

Goal: *Analyze 5 things the Scriptures say a pastor must not be. Illustrate each.*

Being blameless sifts out those branded with faults. It disqualifies those with certain weaknesses or sins. God's standard for pastors is high. We cannot reach it with our own strength. But as we depend on Jesus and walk in the Spirit, God will enable our lives to produce the fruit He desires. *"Remain in me, and I will remain in you. No branch can bear fruit by itself; it must remain in the vine. Neither can you bear fruit unless you remain in me"* (John 15:4). We will study more about depending on the Spirit in chapter 4, lesson 10.

Q 11 How can we recognize a blameless pastor?

A person living with reproach cannot be a pastor. Paul explains what he means by being blameless and having a good reputation. He gives us a list of 12 characteristics. The list includes five negative traits. Let us look closely at these five characteristics a blameless pastor cannot have.

A. A pastor must not be given to drunkenness.

Those who sell alcohol describe it as a blessing. But the Bible tells the truth about alcohol. In the beginning of the journey, alcohol sparkles in the cup. But at the end of the road, it bites like a poisonous snake.

Q 12 In what way does your culture make alcohol look inviting?

29Who has woe? Who has sorrow? Who has strife? Who has complaints? Who has needless bruises? Who has bloodshot eyes? 30Those who linger over wine, who

Q 13 Contrast the beginning and the end of the road of alcohol.

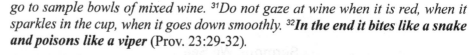

go to sample bowls of mixed wine. ³¹*Do not gaze at wine when it is red, when it sparkles in the cup, when it goes down smoothly.* ³²***In the end it bites like a snake and poisons like a viper*** (Prov. 23:29-32).

A pastor and a deacon talked about the use of alcohol. The deacon mentioned that Paul told Timothy to use a little wine as a medicine (1 Tim. 5:23). The pastor smiled and said that people should feel free to use the medicine a doctor orders. Then, the deacon reminded the pastor that Jesus turned water into wine. The wise pastor sat silently for a few moments. Then he replied, "If a person holds a glass of water up to heaven and it turns to wine, then he or she should drink it. Our problem is not with water Jesus turns to wine. Rather our problem is with grape juice that humans turn into alcohol."

Q 14 How would you respond to a person who emphasized that Jesus turned water into wine?

Q 15 Summarize the fruit of the drunkenness of Lot and Noah.

Figure 1.9   In the end, alcohol bites like a poisonous snake.

Lot defiled his own daughters after he became drunk (Gen. 19:30-38). The children born as a result were Moab and Ben-Ammi. These two sons were victims of alcohol someone else drank. They became the fathers of the Moabites and the Ammonites. Thus, two godless nations resulted from one man's drunkenness. These evil nations became bitter enemies of Israel. There will be thousands of Lot's grandchildren in hell. They would never have been born if he had not become drunk. A serpent bit Lot, his daughters, and his grandchildren (Prov. 23:31-32).

Noah cursed his grandson, Canaan. This happened *"When Noah awoke from his wine"* (Gen. 9:24). The curse would have been avoided if the wine had been avoided! Millions of children have been cursed because their fathers drank too much alcohol.

Pastor, set an example for your people. Do not lead them down a road with a poisonous snake at the end of it. It is better not to eat meat or drink wine or to do anything else that will cause our brother to stumble (Rom. 14:21). No drunkard will enter the kingdom of God (1 Cor. 6:10). Be filled with the Spirit, not with wine (Eph. 5:18).

B. A pastor must not be overbearing (bossy) or quarrelsome.

Q 16 Describe a bossy, overbearing person.

An *overbearing person is self-willed. That is, he is like a dictator. Overbearing people are proud. They think they are always right and never wrong. They insist on having their own way and act like the big boss. Bossy people may be in a family, a business, a school, an organization, a government, or in a church. They seldom like the ideas of others because these stubborn people think their way is the only way. They argue or quarrel with those who disagree with them. Bossy people do not like any authority except their own. A pastor must not be bossy!

Robert is married and has three children. He is a believer and leads his family to church. He works hard to provide for the needs of his wife and children. His family members appreciate the good things about him, but they know he is overbearing, bossy, and *domineering. Robert does not value the opinions of others. His wife and children have few choices because Robert makes all the decisions by himself. He lives like he is a king and they are servants below him. When he is home, they nod their heads and smile. But when he is not around, they have learned to do things the way they want to.

Q 17 What are 2 things that may cause a person to be bossy?

What causes a person to be bossy? We will look at two reasons. *First,* some parents spoil their children by giving them too much. These children always get their own way, so they learn to be bossy and proud.

One day, there was a child who wanted some candy at a store—but the mother said *no!* So the child got down on the floor, kicking and screaming with a loud voice. This embarrassed the mother, so she told the child, "Get up. Mama will get the candy for you." In this way, the child learned to boss his mother. Later on, when the child grew up, he continued to boss other people. Sadly, he would never admit that he made a mistake, not even when others knew it. When he tried to witness about Jesus, he gave the church a bad name. Behind his back people called him "Mr. Know-It-All."

Second, a person may become bossy after success. King Saul was like this. Before success, Saul was humble. He did not want to control others, so he hid from those wanting to make him king (1 Sam. 10:21-22). But success changed Saul from a humble man to a proud one. It changed him from a servant to a *tyrant. Before success, he was small in his own eyes (1 Sam. 15:17). But success caused him to think too highly of himself (See Romans 12:3). Then, he felt taller and more important than other leaders like Samuel. Success turns many servants into dictators.

A pastor must not be bossy. He must not act like a lord over the church members, but should instead be an example to the flock (1 Pet. 5:2-3). Pastors should clothe themselves with humility. *"God opposes the proud but gives grace to the humble"* (1 Pet. 5:5).

Examine yourself. Are you a bossy person? It is good for a leader to have a strong will. Moses needed a strong will to lead the people. Paul needed a strong will to fulfill the ministry God gave him. But neither Moses nor Paul was an overbearing, bossy leader. Moses listened to the advice of Jethro (Exod. 18:17-24). Paul submitted to the advice of Jerusalem leaders (Acts 21:17-26). It is good for a pastor to be strong-willed. Then he can hold firmly to righteousness. But it is bad for a pastor to be self-willed. Self-willed, bossy people crush others. If you struggle with being bossy, discover the cause. Did your parents give you too much? Or has success made you proud? If so, repent. Practice listening to the opinions of other spiritual people. Learn to value the Spirit's wisdom that flows through other members of the body. Ask the Lord to help you be blameless in this area. Perhaps there is a friend or elder who will help you grow in grace.

Q 18 *What 4 things should a bossy person do?*

C. A pastor must not be quick-tempered or violent.

A pastor must not be one who gives in to sudden anger (James 1:19). He must not be like the hammer that flew off of the handle. This does not mean a pastor can never be angry. All anger is not sin. Jesus was angry when He cleansed the temple. Likewise, God the Father becomes angry at times. And we know He does not sin. The Bible says that when we are angry, we should not sin (Eph. 4:26). There are some things that should cause believers to become angry. As we love what is right, we should hate what is wrong (Rom. 12:9). Therefore, angry feelings related to sin are righteous.

Figure. 1.10 Never argue with a carnal person. Others might not notice the difference between you and him!

Q 19 *When is anger sinful?*

The Bible condemns two kinds of anger. It forbids anger that lasts too long. A hen sits on her eggs until they hatch. Likewise, some meditate on offenses. These carry a grudge. They cultivate a root of bitterness. Like Herodias, they look for a chance to hurt those they do not like (Matt. 14:8-11). Instead of forgiving, they seek vengeance (Rom. 12:17-21). These have

Figure. 1.11   A pastor must not be quick tempered or violent!

Q 20 Explain the African proverb about the 2 bulls fighting.

Figure 1.12   "When two bulls fight, it is the grass that suffers" (African proverb).

a slow burning anger like hot coals. They let the sun go down on their wrath and rise on it the next day (Eph. 4:26)! Anger that lasts too long is wrong. But this is not the type of anger Paul mentions in Titus 1:7. Rather, Paul refers to fleshly anger that rises too fast. This is a sudden outburst of anger. A pastor must not be one who bursts forth with anger, like gasoline explodes when a burning match touches it.

Moto was known for his sudden anger. His name meant "fire" in Swahili. Some of his friends often referred to him as *Moto Mara Moja,* or Instant Fire. For short, they just named him *Moto.* He was the opposite of one who stayed cool, calm, or self-controlled. Moto could become upset as quickly as you could drop a hat. Sometimes he would strike his fists on the table. Often, he stood up and yelled at people. Once, he became so angry during a meeting that he stomped out of the room. Another time he threw his shoe across the room at a person who disagreed with him! Those who saw him coming tried to go in a different direction. Perhaps he was like James and John once were. They wanted to call down fire from heaven on their enemies. Jesus called them the *Sons of Thunder.* At that time, they, like *Moto,* were not ready to be pastors! It took Jesus some time to disciple them.

Man's anger does not bring about the righteous life that God desires (James 1:20).

24Do not make friends with a hot-tempered man, do not associate with one easily angered, 25or you may learn his ways and get yourself ensnared (Prov. 22:24-25).

Violence is a step beyond the quick temper. It is fighting or striking that results from hot anger. Automobiles sometimes go out of control. Then they cause injuries to people. Likewise, a violent person is out of control. He strikes out and hurts those nearby. The Greek word Paul uses is *plektes.* It occurs only two times in the New Testament (1 Tim. 3:3; Titus 1:7). Both times this word follows Paul's reference to drunkenness. Often, those who get drunk become violent. They lose control of their senses and their anger. Bars are famous for fights. A pastor must not be known for either drunkenness or striking others.

D. A pastor must not be a lover of money or seek dishonest gain.

9People who want to get rich fall into temptation and a trap and into many foolish and harmful desires that plunge men into ruin and destruction. 10For the love of money is a root of all kinds of evil. Some people, eager for money, have wandered from the faith and pierced themselves with many griefs (1 Tim. 6:9-10).

It has been falsely said that the lack of money is the root of all evil. If this were true, people would increase in holiness as they increased in wealth. Unfortunately, money does not make us godly.

Q 21 Can a person who does not pay his bills be a pastor? Explain.

All of us need some money or wealth to exist. It is a necessity. Not only do we need money, we deserve it. The laborer is *worthy* of his wages (1 Cor. 9:9-11; 1 Tim. 5:18). Nonetheless, we are to seek first the kingdom of God and the right relationship with Him, knowing that He will meet our material needs (Matt. 6:33).

Demosthenes was a famous Greek speaker who lived in Athens. He used to practice speaking with small stones in his mouth. As he walked along the seashore, he raised his voice above the roar of the Mediterranean waves. He was the people's favorite. They did what he counseled them to do. "All the gold in Macedon could not bribe him," said one philosopher. Yet what were the facts?

Q 22 How did Demosthenes lose his influence?

Alexander the Great went to war and entrusted his riches to Harpalus. Harpalus misused the wealth and fled for his life to Athens. At first, Demosthenes advised the Athenians to dismiss Harpalus and have nothing to do with him. Demosthenes himself, however, did not refuse to attend a feast given by Harpalus. There he saw on the table a gold cup, skillfully carved. "How much will this cup bring?" asked Demosthenes. The clever Harpalus replied, "To you it will bring twenty talents of gold." That night Harpalus filled the cup with gold coins and sent it as a bribe to the house of Demosthenes. He accepted this bribe and stopped speaking against Harpalus.

Figure 1.13 A gold cup from ancient times

The next day Demosthenes appeared with a wool cloth wrapped around his throat. The people asked him to speak. But he made signs as if he had lost his voice. Someone said that Demosthenes was not suffering from a common sore throat. Rather, his throat was sore from swallowing a gold cup full of gold coins! Then the people understood that Demosthenes loved money more than truth. A few days later he stood to defend himself. But the people refused to listen. They shouted and hissed at him. Because of the love of money, Demosthenes forever lost his influence over the citizens of Athens.

Q 23 *How many times can a pastor lose his influence in a church or city?*

Contrast Demosthenes with Abraham who would not compromise his integrity at any price (Gen. 14:23). No man can serve two masters. *"You cannot serve both God and Money"* (Matt. 6:24).

Consider the following parable. One pastor was doing well. Someone offered him part-time work selling eggs. The pastor agreed. At first, there was no problem. He sold a few eggs and earned a little extra money. But as time went on, he began to carry the eggs around with him. When he visited a home, he took his Bible and some eggs. But people began to notice a change in him. Little by little, he talked less about the Bible and more about the eggs. One day, he visited the house of a new family in town. They talked for a few minutes. The pastor did not mention the church, but he sold a dozen eggs. Finally, he became known as the "egg man," rather than the "man of God."

Q 24 *Have you known any pastors like the "egg man"?*

E. A pastor must be mature, not a recent convert.

Q 25 *Why is it dangerous for a new convert to be a pastor?*

"He must not be a recent convert, or he may become conceited and fall under the same judgment as the devil" (1 Tim. 3:6).

Satan was proud and arrogant about his position. Isaiah 14:12-14 may refer to Satan's fall. Jesus saw him fall from heaven like lightning (Luke 10:18). Truly, *"Pride goes before destruction, a haughty spirit before a fall"* (Prov. 16:18).

It is not wise for a new convert to be raised to the position of leadership. Too much attention will spoil a young child. It can also ruin a young convert. Give a man some years to put down roots of maturity. Then, public attention will not blow him over like a tree in the wind. Too much wood in the cart injures the young ox's back. Too much green wood causes the fire to go out. Never choose a boy to do a man's job. *"As is the man, so is his strength"* (Judg. 8:21).

Lesson 3 Characteristics That a Pastor Must Have

Goal: *Summarize 7 things a pastor must be. Illustrate each.*

A pastor gets a good reputation by avoiding bad characteristics and practicing good ones. We have looked at five bad traits to avoid. Now let us study seven good qualities of a pastor.

Q 26 *How can you recognize a pastor with a good reputation?*

A. A pastor must be the husband of one wife.

The Greek says literally, "be a one-woman man." People in Paul's day needed to hear this. Sexual sins were as common as the sunrise. Temples like the one in Corinth had a thousand harlots. Polygamy, easy divorce, and remarriage were ordinary.[15] Paul reminded the believers at Corinth of their past. Some of them had been very sinful. He insisted that the standard for the Church be higher than the standard for the world.

Figure 1.14   On top of a big hill in Corinth was a temple to Venus, goddess of love. Hundreds of female prostitutes had sex in the temple. On the back of their sandals were the words, "Follow me."

Q 27 *Can a young, unmarried man pastor a church in your culture? Explain.*

Q 28 *Do some people rub mud on themselves? Explain.*

Q 29 *Summarize Proverbs 6:32-33 in your own words.*

Q 30 *What are some steps that lead a man into sexual sin?*

The pastor is an example for the church. A pastor must be a one-wife man. Does this mean a young, unmarried man cannot pastor? There are many single people in fruitful ministry today. Many young men open new churches. They have fewer financial responsibilities than a married pastor. So young, single pastors can be a great blessing to God's kingdom. But, people will expect a young, unmarried pastor to marry as soon as he is able.

Derek was a young pastor. He attended Bible school for 3 years. While he was there, he preached on Sundays. As time went by, he led about 20 people to Christ. These were the first members of the new church he started. In time he graduated from the Bible school. He had no wife or house. His new converts were tithing. The National Church agreed to help him rent a house for 1 year. During that time, four new families of believers began to attend his little church. For a while, people accepted the fact that he had no wife. But he knew that he should marry soon. It was too hard to do the work of a pastor alone. Also, he knew that many mature people would respect him more after he married. Derek planned his sermons wisely. He did not preach about the family until after he married and had children. Each pastor must earn the right to counsel others.

A man named Gary was the favorite of many for president of his country. He was handsome, well educated, and popular. As a speaker, he was gifted and persuasive. It looked like he might be elected. Then someone discovered that he was unfaithful to his wife. Immediately, the people lost confidence in him, and he dropped out of the race. Even outside the church, people often expect a leader to be faithful to his wife. In the church, the Bible says that a pastor must be a man who is faithful to one woman.

Charles, a well-known author and radio preacher, was attending a meeting far away from his wife and children. Two women approached him, wanting to come to his hotel room. He said, "NO!" Today he remains a blameless, one-woman man. He is leading many to Christ and Christian maturity.

Pastor, Satan will offer you a woman that is not your wife. Before you bargain with him, ask yourself some serious questions. Do you want to betray the God who saved and called you? Do you want to rub dirt on your diploma or ordination that you worked so hard to get? Do you want to bring shame on your name and family? Do you want a brand on you that will last for a lifetime? Do you want to resign your church? A passing car may splash mud on someone walking. But some people put mud on themselves!

*Tattoo Proverbs 6:32-33 on your brain: ³²"A man who commits adultery lacks judgment; whoever does so destroys himself. ³³Blows and disgrace are his lot, and his shame will **never** be wiped away."*

Brands last for a lifetime. God put a mark on Cain for all to see. That mark lasted the rest of his life. People put a brand on animals like cattle, horses, and goats. The animals wear that brand throughout life. Deserters in some wars have been branded. One deserter was branded with a "D" on his face. From that day on he faced public reproach. A book called *The Scarlet Letter* tells of public reproach. A woman was involved in a sexual sin. Her punishment was to wear the red letter "A" that stood for adultery. She had to wear it for all to see. Likewise, a believer who commits sexual sins receives a brand and reproach. "*...his shame will never be wiped away*" (Prov. 6:33).

Though God will forgive him, people will continue to remember. Ask King David—he committed adultery with Bathsheba more than 3,000 years ago. People all over the world still talk about it today! A reputation of moral purity is like Esau's birthright. One who sells it can never regain it, though he seeks it with tears. Pastor, may it never be said of you as it was of Sisera that he was slain by a woman (Judg. 4). Marry a wife and be faithful for life (Mal. 2:14). Keep the promises you make on your wedding day. A pastor must be a man of one woman.

B. A pastor must be gentle.

We studied five characteristics a pastor must avoid. Among these, Paul said a blameless pastor is not quick-tempered, quarrelsome, or violent. Being gentle is the opposite of these bad qualities. A gentle pastor is meek, kind, humble, and forgiving. Paul reminded Timothy to be gentle with all, even enemies.

> [24]*And the Lord's servant must not quarrel; instead, he must be kind to everyone, able to teach, not resentful.* [25]*Those who oppose him he must gently instruct, in the hope that God will grant them repentance leading them to a knowledge of the truth* (2 Tim. 2:24-25).

 Q 31 How does Paul say a pastor should act toward those who oppose him?

A pastor frowned from behind his pulpit. He looked with angry eyes at the people in the pews. Then he spoke harsh words. "I do not mind feeding a believer milk with a bottle. But I get annoyed if I have to push the false teeth out of the way to get the bottle in!" This pastor was upset because elderly believers were still immature. He did not recognize that he himself was being childish. But the people recognized that he was not mature. In less than a year, they asked him to leave. Then, they chose a pastor who was gentler. Sheep do not like a shepherd who kicks them.

Q 32 Explain: Sheep do not like a shepherd who kicks them.

Jesus is our gentle Shepherd. Matthew emphasized his gentleness.

> [19]*"He will not quarrel or cry out; no one will hear his voice in the streets.* [20]*A bruised reed he will not break, and a smoldering wick he will not snuff out, till he leads justice to victory.* [21]*In his name the nations will put their hope"* (Matt. 12:19-21).

Q 33 Explain 3 ways Jesus is gentle (Matt. 12:19-21).

These poetic words contain at least three pictures. Jesus does not quarrel or shout at people in the street. He is so gentle that He will not break a weak reed that is bruised by the river. Finally, He is so gentle that He will not cause a smoking candlewick to go out. Jesus is as gentle as a dove.

Isaiah wrote about the gentleness of God. *"He tends his flock like a shepherd: He gathers the lambs in his arms and carries them close to his heart; he gently leads those that have young"* (Isa. 40:11).

A pastor must be gentle. And Jesus, the Good Shepherd, is our example. The apostle Paul was a rough man. But he was gentle with believers *"like a mother caring for her little children"* (1 Thess. 2:7).

Do you feel the need for more gentleness? Paul told Timothy that gentleness is something we must pursue. We must follow it, desiring to have more of it. God wants to help us all be gentler. Gentleness is a fruit of the Holy Spirit (Gal. 5:23). As we walk in the Spirit, others will see that we are gentle. Remember, the wisdom from above is peace-loving and gentle (James 3:17). Do not lose your temper and lash people with harsh words. Do not knock people down with your tongue. A wise person is a gentle person.

Figure 1.15
A pastor is like a gentle shepherd.

Sometimes people do not realize that they are not being gentle. Pastor, ask your wife and children to help you grow in gentleness. Invite them to tell you when you are being too harsh. Also, invite a friend to remind you to be gentle. Those humble enough to ask for help receive it. God opposes the proud, but gives grace to the humble (James 4:6).

Q 34 What are 2 ways a pastor can become gentler?

C. A pastor must be temperate, self-controlled, and orderly.

Be temperate and self-controlled. Limit the way you respond to your fleshly desires. Neither eat too much nor dress too fancy. Rule your desires as a rider controls a horse or a bicycle. If your lifestyle is excessive and not within accepted boundaries, you will get a bad name. Use the things of this world without abusing them (1 Cor. 7:31). As with

Q 35 What does it mean to be temperate?

Q 36 Do believers still have desires of the flesh? Explain.

Figure 1.16 A pastor should rule his desires as a rider controls a horse or a bicycle.

Q 37 *Explain: Many people enter the Kingdom through the pastor's front door.*

Q 38 *Explain: If there is room in the heart, there is room in the home.*

Q 39 *List some problems and solutions of hospitality.*

Q 40 *According to Hebrews 1:8-9, what is a key to being lifted up by God?*

Q 41 *Name 2 Scriptures that tell us to hate what is wrong.*

Q 42 *Give 2 examples of people who were exalted because they loved what was right and hated what was wrong.*

gentleness, depend on the Holy Spirit to produce the fruit of self-control in your life. Walk in the Spirit and you will not fulfill the lusts of the sinful nature (Gal. 5:16; See also Rom. 8:4-6).

Also, be orderly—that is, well behaved. Do not be known for rudeness, outbursts of anger, or neglect of duty.

The qualities of this lesson are the opposite of being drunken, or entangled with chains of the flesh and soul. Be a well-balanced, quiet citizen, respected and known for good deeds. A good name shines in the dark.[16]

D. A pastor must be hospitable.

A hospitable person opens his home to others. Be generous with your food and drink to the saved and the lost. You will open people's hearts as you open your home. Stingy people share words but not food. But many people enter the kingdom of heaven through the pastor's front door.

Barbara Tuttle served many years as a missionary in India. From her early years as a missionary, she tells about a great truth that a woman named Amani taught her. "I am so happy that I can barely stay on the ground," Amani announced. "Why is that?" Barbara asked. "Have you heard some good news?" "Yes," replied Amani. "Next week we have 14 people coming to stay in our house for 3 days!" Barbara was shocked. "In your little house with only two rooms? How will they fit? Where will they sit? Where will they sleep?" Amani was silent for a moment. Then she said, "You are a visitor here, so you do not know us very well yet. But one of our sayings is, 'If there is room in the heart, there is room in the home.'" Thus Amani taught Barbara a lesson that she never forgot. Let us be sure that we make room for people in our hearts. Then it will be easy for us to be hospitable.

E. A pastor must love what is good, and be holy and upright.

A pastor must hate what is evil and love what is good (Titus 1:8; Rom. 12:9). This is the key to being exalted by God. Jesus is the Chief Shepherd (1 Pet. 5:4). He is a great example of One who loved what is right.

[8]*But about the Son he says, "Your throne, O God, will last for ever and ever, and righteousness will be the scepter of your kingdom.* [9]*You have loved righteousness and hated wickedness;* **therefore** *God, your God, has set you above your companions by anointing you with the oil of joy"* (Heb. 1:8-9).

Joseph is another example of one who loved what was right. This caused him to live a holy, righteous life. So God exalted him to be a leader. Righteousness exalts people, but sin is a disgrace (Prov. 14:34).

Pastor, God has exalted you to be an example. *"Live a life worthy of the calling you have received"* (Eph. 4:1). Always obey Paul's advice to Timothy: *"Set an example for the believers in speech, in life, in love, in faith and in purity"* (1 Tim. 4:12). You will influence people more with your life than your sermons. Be known as a pastor who loves and lives what is right. Stand tall!

"A good name is more desirable than great riches; to be esteemed [respected] *is better than silver or gold"* (Prov. 22:1).

F. A pastor must be able to teach.

As we stated in the introduction, preaching and teaching are two expressions of one ministry. The preacher is also the teacher.

We can only teach what we learn. Therefore, the preacher must be a constant student of the Word. There is a sense in which preachers never graduate. (More will be said about this in chapter 2.)

Remember that teaching requires more than knowledge. To be a good teacher one must be a good person. Notice that in 2 Timothy 2:24, the phrase *"able to teach"* is surrounded by the virtues of a teacher:

> [24]*And the Lord's servant must not quarrel; instead, he must be kind to everyone, able to teach, not resentful.* [25]*Those who oppose him he must gently instruct, in the hope that God will grant them repentance, leading them to a knowledge of the truth* (2 Tim. 2:24-25).

A man able to teach has the humility of a servant, the gentleness of a mother, and the kindness of a grandmother. Take heart—good teachers get better!

G. A pastor must be a good manager of his own family.

We noted earlier that marriage causes many people to respect a pastor more. A pastor may begin as a young, single person. But his respect will grow as his family grows.

Q 43 *What are the qualities of a good teacher?*

Eli is an example of one who disqualified himself from spiritual leadership. His sons were immoral, and he did nothing about it (1 Sam. 2–3).

In contrast to Eli, some pastors try to command their wife and children like a man driving a donkey cart! This often causes rebellion rather than cooperation. A man must learn to love his wife as himself and as Christ loved the Church (Eph. 5:25). Then she will delight to live at peace with him. Also, a father is not to provoke his children to anger. Rather, he is to bring them up in the training and instruction of the Lord (Eph. 6:4). Children normally respond well to a father who treats them with love, tenderness, respect, and concern. If a man sows these good seeds in his family, he will reap a good harvest. And remember, a person has only as much influence as he has relationship. Healthy relationships are the result of spending time together talking, walking, working, playing, praying, and worshiping. So be sure to spend time with each member of your family. We discuss this important principle in our *Faith & Action Series* course on *Marriage & the Family.* Each pastor must learn to be a good husband and father.

Q 44 *Give 2 reasons why a man should not try to pastor if he cannot manage his own family.*

Q 45 *Explain how a pastor develops good relationships with his wife and children.*

Consider the following parable. It describes three ways parents taught a child.[11]

First Parent. "I took a little child's hand in mine. He and I were to walk together for a while. I was to lead him to the Father. It was a task that seemed so big to me. Such a responsibility! So I talked to the child only of the Father. I told the child that God becomes very angry when we displease Him. I told the child to be good so God would not be angry. We walked under tall trees, and I warned the child that the Father could send lightning and thunder to destroy the trees. We walked in the sunshine together. I emphasized that God makes the blazing, burning sun. Then, one evening, we met the Father. The child hid behind me. He was afraid to take the Father's hand. I was between the child and the Father. I wondered. Had I been too serious?"

Q 46 *Discuss the 3 methods in the parable. How is the third method different from the others?*

Second Parent. "I took a little child's hand in mine. I was to lead him to the Father. I felt the burden of so many things to teach him. So we did not waste any time. We hurried from place to place. We compared the leaves of different trees. Quickly we moved on to examine a bird's nest. The child began to ask questions about the nest. But I hurried him on to catch a butterfly. Sometimes the child became tired and fell asleep. But I woke him up so he would not miss a lesson. We spoke of the Father often and quickly. I told the child all the stories he ought to know. But so many times things interrupted us. Once the wind blew and I had to stop a story to explain the wind. In the middle of another story the child asked a question about a river. So I explained as much about the river as I could. Then one evening we met the Father. The child only glanced at Him, and his thoughts wandered in several other directions. The Father stretched out His hand toward the child. But the child was not interested enough to take it. Instead, the child lay down to rest. I wondered. Had I tried to teach him too many things?"

Third Parent. "I took a little child's hand in mine. I was to lead him to the Father. My heart rejoiced for this privilege. We walked slowly. I took short steps to match those of the child. We talked about the things the child noticed. Sometimes we picked the Father's flowers. We touched their soft petals and loved their bright colors. Sometimes we watched one of Father's birds build its nest. We saw the eggs that were laid. Later, we marveled at the way the bird cared for its young. Often we told stories of the Father. I told them to the child, and the child told them again to me. We told them, the child and I, over and over again. Sometimes we stopped to rest, leaning against one of Father's tall trees. We stood in silence, feeling His cool wind blow softly on our faces. Then one evening we met the Father. The child's eyes shone with joy. Eagerly, he looked with love and trust into the Father's face. He put his hand into the Father's hand. For the moment, I was forgotten, but content."

Perhaps the greatest test of a spiritual leader's maturity is his relationship with his own family. A man who fails to relate well to his family will probably make similar mistakes with the church. The man who learns to lead his wife and children well will probably learn the skills necessary to lead a larger group of people. Notice that Paul dealt with believers *"as a father deals with his own children"* (1 Thess 2:11). A man should be faithful with the least number of people before he is given responsibility for a greater number (Luke 16:10). To learn more about how to manage your family, study our *Faith & Action Series* course on *Marriage & the Family*.

Q 47 ✎ *Complete Figure 1.17.*

This is a review project. The following questions will help you examine yourself on the qualities we have studied. Circle the number that best represents your progress. The lowest grade is 1 and the highest is 5.

Question	1	2	3	4	5
1. How do you rate your reputation as a spiritual leader?					
2. How is your relationship with your spouse? If you are unmarried, how well are you handling sexual matters?					
3. To what degree are you temperate and self-controlled?					
4. How hospitable are you? Do you share well?					
5. Do you have the qualities of a good teacher, such as kindness, gentleness, tolerance, and patience?					
6. How much is your life free from things that control or make you a slave?					
7. How much are you known for being gentle?					
8. How well do you honor your principles above money? How willing are you to serve God on a low level of income?					
9. How much do your children respect you? If you don't have children, how much does your wife or a close friend respect you?					
10. What is your level of spiritual maturity in Christ-like character and Scriptural knowledge?					

Figure 1.17   A pastor should examine himself from time to time. Good pastors grow and become better!

If there is a particular area of your life that you feel the need to improve in, talk to your teacher or a friend about it. The first step in overcoming a problem is admitting it.

Test Yourself: Circle the letter by the *best* completion to each question or statement.

1. Homiletics is the study of
a) interpreting the Bible.
b) preparing and preaching biblical messages.
c) analyzing major doctrines of Scripture.
d) evaluating biblical sermons.

2. The most important part of a sermon is
a) preparing the Introduction.
b) preparing the Invitation.
c) preparing the people.
d) preparing the preacher.

3. A preacher must be blameless in his own eyes
a) because sin changes a brave man into a coward.
b) because others are watching our daily lives.
c) because our own family members know us best.
d) because only God knows who is blameless.

4. Preachers must be blameless to others because
a) the anointing is the key to every sermon.
b) God's Word is only as true as the preacher.
c) church members sin every day of the week.
d) each preacher is a sermon and example.

5. A person cannot be a pastor if he or she
a) is poor.
b) is a new convert.
c) has little education.
d) has little talent.

6. To qualify to be a pastor, a person must
a) be at least 30 years old.
b) know the Problem/Solution Method.
c) share his food and home with others.
d) have many sons and daughters.

7. The key to being exalted by God is:
a) love the right; hate the wrong.
b) read every book you can find.
c) pray 4 hours every day.
d) witness to everyone you meet.

8. What brand will last for a lifetime?
a) Getting drunk one time
b) Having a bad temper one time
c) Being selfish with food one time
d) Committing adultery one time

9. Every pastor must be able to
a) teach.
b) sing.
c) do miracles.
d) prophesy.

10. The Bible says every pastor must be
a) strong.
b) bold.
c) gentle.
d) Pentecostal.

 Essay Test Topics: Write 50-100 words on each of these goals that you studied in this chapter.

A Pastor Must Be Blameless and Have a Good Reputation

Goal: *Explain why a pastor must be blameless and have a good reputation.*

Characteristics That a Pastor Must NOT Have

Goal: *Analyze 5 things the Scriptures say a pastor must not be. Illustrate each. (Review Figure 1.2)*

Characteristics That a Pastor Must Have

Goal: *Summarize 7 things a pastor must be. Illustrate each. (Review Figure 1.2)*

Chapter 2:
The Preacher's Message

Introduction

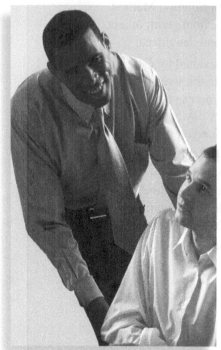

Figure 2.1 A troubled young preacher sought counsel from a man who had pastored for years.

Q 1 *What is a spiritual garden?*

A troubled young preacher sought counsel from a man who had pastored for many years. "How," asked the younger, "can I ever find enough sermons to preach? Even today I am desperate to get a message for tonight!"

The old man of God replied, "Each day you must spend time in God's presence and in His Word. In those times the Holy Spirit fills your heart and life. He leads you to study and apply biblical truths to your own life. These passages are seed thoughts that grow into sermons."

"But I am too busy to spend time each day praying, worshiping, and studying the Bible," the young man complained. "Oh!" said the elder, "If that is the case, then you must change your priorities. The hardest, most stressful thing you will ever do is try to get a sermon when you are under pressure. It is like waiting until the last minute to prepare for an exam, after not attending classes day by day!" Thus the elder counseled the younger.

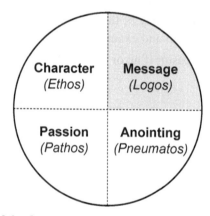

Figure 2.2 Second of four key parts of preaching

| Character (Ethos) | Message (Logos) |
| Passion (Pathos) | Anointing (Pneumatos) |

Lessons:

 Put Your Daily Devotions and Bible Study First
Goal: *Explain why devotions are essential, and give 6 guidelines for them.*

 Nine Keys for Preparing Biblical Messages
Goal: *Explain and give an example of each of the 9 keys for preparing biblical messages.*

 Key Words

devotions   pretext   historical context   literary context

Put Your Daily Devotions and Bible Study First

Goal: *Explain why devotions are essential, and give 6 guidelines for them.*

Setting

The pastor has many responsibilities. He organizes the church. He leads and guides members. He cares for all of the sheep, from the young to the old. He counsels those with problems. He disciples and mentors new believers. He marries and buries. He equips the saints to do God's work. He preaches and teaches the Bible.

All of the pastor's roles are important. But preaching and teaching the Word are key ways a pastor fulfills his ministry. God has called you to preach the Word! The apostles set the priority of preaching when they declared,

Q 2 *In what key way does a pastor fulfill his calling?*

> [2] *"It would not be right for us to neglect the ministry of the word of God in order to wait on tables.* [3] *Brothers, choose seven men from among you who are known to be full of the Spirit and wisdom. We will turn this responsibility over to them* [4] *and will give our attention to prayer and the ministry of the word."* . . . [7] *So the word of God spread. The number of disciples in Jerusalem increased rapidly, and a large number of priests became obedient to the faith* (Acts 6:2-4, 7).

What happened when the apostles gave themselves to prayer and preaching the Word? The church grew! Many people followed Jesus. Likewise, when a pastor puts prayer and preaching first, the church will grow. Believers will become strong. Unbelievers will repent and follow Christ. Many people in the church can help organize, guide, care for others, counsel, and disciple. But who will preach if the pastor neglects this ministry? That is why Paul emphasized one thing to Timothy:

Q 3 *Who will preach to and teach a church if the pastor neglects this duty? Explain.*

> [1] *In the presence of God and of Christ Jesus, who will judge the living and the dead, and in view of his appearing and his kingdom, I give you this charge:* [2] ***Preach the Word;*** *be prepared in season and out of season; correct, rebuke and encourage—with great patience and careful instruction* (2 Tim. 4:1-2).

Consider the importance of the hour when all of the church comes together. What if a pastor had 100 church members, but they never met together? Then, to spend an hour with each member would take him 100 hours, plus traveling time! But God's plan is for the 100 church members to gather for at least one hour. So let the pastor prepare well to preach and teach during that one hour. It is worth more than 100 hours!

Q 4 *Why is an hour in the pulpit worth many hours?*

Pastor, fulfill God's call on your life. Lead His sheep into the green pastures of His Word by preaching and teaching. And as Paul commanded Timothy, always be prepared to preach (2 Tim. 2:15).

A. A pastor prepares a message by first preparing his own heart.

As you prepare to preach, remember that you are not only preparing a message, but you are preparing yourself as well. The best-prepared message will lack the power to convict and transform unless it flows out of a life filled with God's Spirit. You bless others with what blesses you first. Talent and ability may entertain. But only the anointed Word of God can redeem and transform.

Q 5 *What is the first step in preparing a message?*

Two men made it into the finals of a speaking contest. Each of them chose to present Psalm 23. The first speaker had great talent. His voice was perfect. His pauses were effective. When he finished, the audience was so moved by his ability that they stood and clapped. The second speaker did not speak as well, but he was sincere. As he spoke, a holy hush fell over every listener. By the time he finished, some were crying, while the rest were in total silence. No one clapped or even moved. When asked to compare

Q 6 *Do you want people to clap after you finish your message? Explain.*

Q 7 *What are daily devotions? Why are they important?*

the two speakers, one man remarked, "The first speaker knew the Psalm, but the second knew the Shepherd." There is no substitute for knowing God through daily *devotions.

A pastor begins to prepare his heart through his daily devotions. By devotions, we mean the daily, quiet time a believer spends alone with God, praying and reading the Bible. In God's presence a pastor submits himself to the sanctifying work of the Holy Spirit. Alone with God, the pastor allows the Spirit to conquer pride, lust, ambition, jealousy, and greed. In these quiet hours, a pastor submits his carnal mind to the eternal truths of God's holy Word. God purifies him. The pastor's heart is aflame with passion for God and for His people. He has already prepared himself. Now he can turn his full attention to preparing the message.

Q 8 *What is the key to enjoying God's presence all day?*

Consider the following poem:

> *"I met God in the morning, when my day was at its best,*
> *And His presence came like sunrise, like a glory in my breast.*
> *All day long the presence stayed; as a friend, close to me;*
> *And we sailed in perfect calmness over a very troubled sea.*
> *Other ships were blown and beaten, by the storm that caused such stress,*
> *But the winds that seemed to drive them brought to us a peace and rest.*
> *Then I thought of other mornings, with a sadness in my mind,*
> *When I too began the voyage with His presence left behind.*
> *So I think I know the secret learned from many a troubled way:*
> *You must seek Him in the morning if you want Him through the day."*[1]

Figure 2.3   God's presence prepares a pastor to preach.

Messages for God's people grow out of the time we spend with Him. Let the preacher *begin* each day with a quiet hour or two. During this time, the preacher should seek not a sermon, but God Himself. The purpose of devotions is to meet with God and invite His presence for the day. This devotional time should be a balance of Bible study, prayer, and worship. For most, the best time for devotions is in the morning. As an old pastor once said, "You will always have time for what you do first!"

Prayer must be the first step in preparing a biblical message. Then, prayer must be a part of every step. We are to meet God through prayer in the morning, and then spend the day with Him. This is possible as we *"pray continually"* (1 Thess. 5:17). John Wesley liked to ask people if they were praying as he met them. Another wise preacher said we should not stop *to* pray, but rather not stop *from* prayer.[2]

- When we depend on organization, we get what organization can give, and that is something.
- When we depend on education, we get what education can give, and that is something.
- When we depend on money, we get what money can give, and that is something.
- When we depend on singing, we get what singing can give, and that is something.
- When we depend on preaching, we get what preaching can give, and that is something.
- When we depend on prayer, we get what prayer can give, and that is everything!

Each preacher needs what only God can do in his life and ministry.[3]

Prayer fills man's emptiness with God's fullness. It fills man's poverty with God's riches. It uses man's weaknesses as the channel for God's strength. It replaces man's smallness with God's greatness. The closest we are to God and living like Christ is the times we pray.[4]

We have emphasized prayer in this lesson. But it is so important that in the *Faith & Action Series,* we are creating one entire course on *Prayer & Fasting.* Remember that prayer is one of the best ways to study.[5]

B. Guidelines for daily devotions

The following points are suggested guidelines for a daily devotional plan.

1. Choose a time and a place to meet with God. Arise at an early morning hour. (Some believers prefer to have devotions at night.) Go to a private place to be alone with God. This should be a quiet place where you will not be interrupted. Pray that He will draw near to you as He has promised (James 4:8). Ask the Holy Spirit to teach you through the Scriptures. Remind yourself that God rewards those who earnestly seek Him (Heb. 11:6).

Q 9 *Comment on the time and place of devotions.*

2. Begin with a few minutes of praise and worship. [4]*"Enter his gates with thanksgiving and his courts with praise; give thanks to him and praise his name. [5]For the Lord is good and his love endures forever; his faithfulness continues through all generations"* (Ps. 100:4-5).

Sing some of your favorite worship choruses, songs, or hymns. Quote some of your favorite Bible verses. Bless God for some of His characteristics like His holiness, love, mercy, and grace. Praise the Lord for things He has done long ago and recently. Be specific, like David was in Psalm 103.

Q 10 *Why do many believers begin devotions with singing?*

Q 11 *How does praising God prepare you to be in His presence?*

3. Approach the Bible with a plan. For example, do not read a verse in Jeremiah on Monday, a passage in Deuteronomy on Tuesday, a chapter in Revelation on Wednesday. Have a plan. Choose a book of the Bible and read in it for several days or weeks. The Bible was written book by book and should often be studied that way. Many pastors read through the Bible every year. Also, it is good to study topics in the Bible. For example, study what the Bible says about topics like God, Jesus, the Holy Spirit, salvation, victorious living, and the Second Coming.

Q 12 *Why is it important to study the Bible with a plan?*

The Bible is the main book to read in devotions. It is the Word of God to us. His Word is a lamp for our feet and a light to our paths (Ps. 119:105). His Word helps us not to sin against Him. God's Word enables us to understand what He is like. It teaches us what He expects from us. Consider the words of John Wesley that follow.

Q 13 *How does reading the Bible prepare a person to commune with God?*

> To *candid, reasonable men, I am not afraid to lay open what have been the inmost thoughts of my heart. I have thought, I am a creature of a day, passing through life as an arrow through the air. I am a spirit come from God, and returning to God: just hovering over the great gulf; until, a few moments hence, I am no more seen; I drop into an unchangeable eternity! I want to know one thing—the way to heaven; how to land safe on that happy shore. God Himself has *condescended to teach the way; for this very end He came from heaven. He hath written it down in a book. O give me that book! At any price, give me the book of God! I have it: He is knowledge enough for me. Let me be *homo unius libri* [Latin for *a man of one book*]. Here then I am, far from the busy ways of men. I sit down alone: only God is here. In His presence I open, I read His book; for this end, to find the way to heaven. Is there a doubt concerning the meaning of what I read? Does anything appear dark or intricate? I lift up my heart to the Father of Lights: "Lord, is it not Thy word, 'If any man lack wisdom, let him ask of God'? ... Thou has said, 'If any be willing to do Thy will, he shall know.' I am willing to do, let me know, Thy will." I then search after and consider parallel passages of Scripture, "comparing spiritual things with spiritual." I meditate thereon with all the attention and earnestness of which my mind is capable. If any doubt still remains, I consult those who are experienced in the things of God; and then the writings whereby, being dead, they yet speak. And what I thus learn, that I teach.[6]

Q 14 *Summarize the illustration about John Wesley, a man of one book.*

Wesley was a man of one book. That is, the Bible was the main book he studied. No wonder he led more than 250,000 sinners to follow Christ!

There are many other spiritual books that are good to read with the Bible. We discuss this some in chapter 2 of our *Faith & Action Series* course on *Pastoral Ministry*. But the

Q 15 ✎ *Define the word context.*

Q 16 ✎ *What is the historical context?*

Figure 2.4   The Acrocorinth, or hill of Corinth, stood behind the city. A great temple to Venus stood on top of the mountain.

Bible is the Book of books! The time we spend reading the Bible should be more than the total time we spend reading all other books.

4. Identify the context of the verses you are studying.   The word *context* comes from two Latin words: *con* (together), and *texere* (to weave). Just like threads are woven together to make fabric, the words in a passage are "woven together" to communicate the whole meaning. They should not be separated from one another.

There are two types of contexts: the historical context and the literary (written) context. Let us look at each.

Historical context (setting). Knowing the *historical context helps us understand the meaning of a text.[7] To find the historical context we ask:

- **Questions about the speaker:** Who is writing or speaking? When did he write?
- **Questions about the readers:** Who are the readers or listeners? What was their city like? What do we know about their society? What relationship did they have with the author or speaker?
- **Questions about the problems and solutions:** What problems and solutions did the author write about? What principles for living are in this passage?

Let us look at an example by studying the historical context of 1 Corinthians 13.

An example of finding the historical context—1 Corinthians 13	
1.	**Questions about the speaker**—Who is writing or speaking? When did he write?	**Answer:** Paul wrote 1 Corinthians about A.D. 55-56. This was just after he stayed in Ephesus for 3 years (Acts 20:31; 1 Cor. 16:5-8).
2.	**Questions about the readers**—Who are the readers or listeners? What was their city like? What do we know about their society? What relationship did they have with the author or speaker?	**Answer:** The readers of 1 Corinthians lived in Corinth. Their city was located near the north shore of the Mediterranean Sea. It was a large pagan city known for immorality and idolatry. The Corinthians were mostly Gentiles with a few Jews (See 1 Cor. 6:9-11; 8:10; 12:13). They loved wisdom and knowledge (1 Cor. 1:18–2:5; 4:10; 8:1-13). And they were proud (1 Cor. 4:18; 5:2, 6). Paul started the church at Corinth on his second missionary trip (Acts 18:1-18).
3.	**Questions about the problems and solutions**—What problems and solutions did the author discuss? What principles for living are in this passage?	**Answer:** Paul wrote 1 Corinthians 13 to show that love is the path to walk on when we use spiritual gifts. When believers gather, love guides us to edify others, not just ourselves, with our spiritual gifts.

Figure 2.5   The historical context of 1 Corinthians 13

Problems and Needs	Solutions in 1 Corinthians
• Division	• 1:10–4:21
• Incest	• 5:1-13
• Lawsuits	• 6:1-11
• Fornication	• 6:12-20
• Misbehavior in marriage	• 7:1-24
• Counsel for the unmarried	• 7:25-40
• Food sacrificed to idols	• 8:1–11:1
• Women's head coverings	• 11:2-16
• Misusing the Lord's Table	• 11:17-34
• Misusing spiritual gifts	• 12:1–14:40
• Denying the Resurrection	• 15:1-58
• The poor in Jerusalem	• 16:1-11

Figure 2.6   Problems and needs Paul wrote about in 1 Corinthians

Literary context.   We are studying the two types of *contexts: historical* and *literary.* We have examined the meaning of the *historical context.* And we looked at an example by studying the historical context of 1 Corinthians 13. Now let us turn our attention to the **literary context.*

Q 17 ↗ *Define literary context.*

The word *literary* may be new to you. But you are probably familiar with such words as *literate* and *literature.* A literate person is one who can read written or printed material, which we call literature. The *literary context* is the written words, paragraphs, and pages that surround a text.

The *literary context* of a text is made up of the ideas that come before and after it. A biblical author did not write just one verse for his readers. He wrote a full Gospel like Matthew, or a complete account like Acts, or an entire letter like 1 Corinthians. Words are part of a verse or text. A text is a part of a paragraph. A paragraph is part of a chapter. A chapter is part of a book. And a book is part of the Bible. In studying the literary context of 1 Corinthians 13, we must pay careful attention to the chapter before it and the chapter after it. Why? Because 1 Corinthians 12–14 are all on the same topic of spiritual gifts.

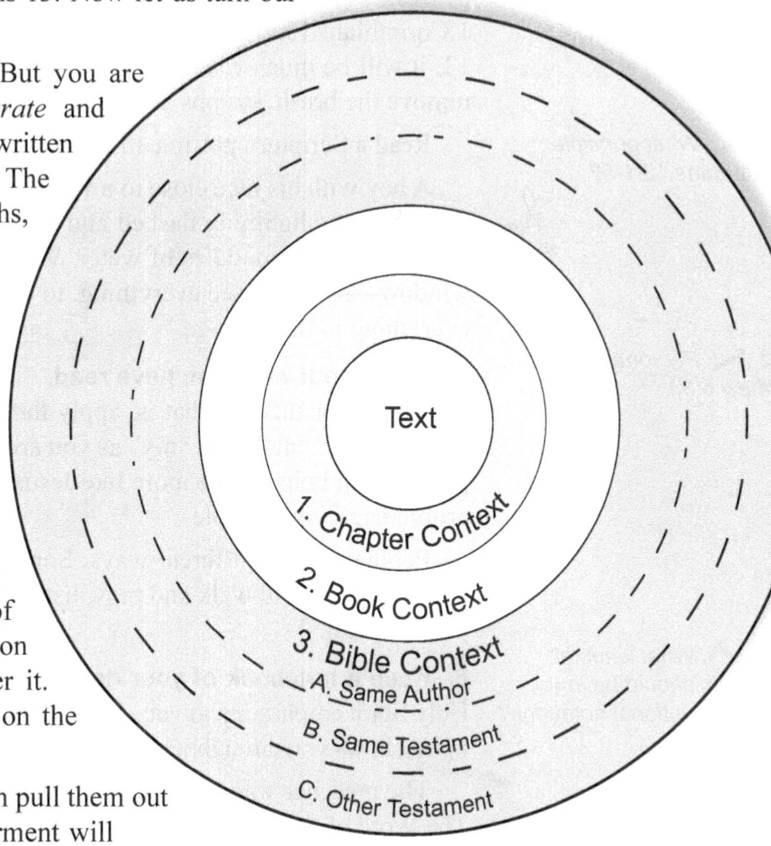

Threads are woven into a garment. You can pull them out of the garment—but both the threads and garment will be damaged. Likewise, you can pull a text out of its context. But if you do this, you will spoil both the text and the context.[9] The Bible is like a garment. We need all of it, not just a few threads or a sleeve!

Text

1. Chapter Context

2. Book Context

3. Bible Context
   A. Same Author
   B. Same Testament
   C. Other Testament

Figure 2.7   The literary context of a verse includes the written things around it: the paragraph it is in; the chapter and book it is in; and the rest of the Bible.[8]

A verse taken out of its literary context is a dangerous weapon of Satan. He has twisted Scripture verses to deceive many Christians. In fact, Satan tried this weapon on the Son of God. Matthew 4:5-6 records:

> [5]*Then the devil took him to the holy city and had him stand on the highest point of the temple.* [6]*"If you are the Son of God," he said, "throw yourself down. For it is written: 'He will command his angels concerning you, and they will lift you up in their hands, so that you will not strike your foot against a stone.'"*

Satan quoted part of Psalm 91:11-12: *"For he will command his angels concerning you to guard you **in all your ways**; they will lift you up in their hands, so that you will not strike your foot against a stone."* But notice that the devil left out the key words: **"in all your ways."** Thus, Satan used the verse out of the literary context. Jumping off of the temple is not in all your ways—it is out of the way! Also notice the way Jesus rebuked Satan. Jesus answered him, ***"It is also written: 'Do not put the Lord your God to the test'"*** (Matt. 4:7). Notice that Jesus referred to the larger literary context of the Bible. We must always interpret each verse within the literary context of the whole Word of God.

The Word of God is the sharp, two-edged sword of the Spirit (Eph. 6:17; Heb. 4:12). However, a text can become the sword of Satan if it is removed from its context. Satan misused the context of Psalm 91. Peter warned of those who (like Satan) twist and distort the Scriptures to their own destruction (2 Pet. 3:16).

Q 18 ↗ *Can the sword of the Spirit become the sword of Satan? Explain.*

Q 19 ✎ *What problem is in Romans 13:1-5?*

Q 20 ✎ *What solution is in Romans 13:1-5?*

Q 21 ✎ *What principle is in Romans 13:1-5?*

Q 22 ✎ *Personalize Matthew 6:33.*

Q 23 ↗ *What kinds of comments should be in a pastor's devotional notebook?*

Q 24 ↗ *Explain the "new and old" principle of Matthew 13:51-52.*

Q 25 ↗ *What is the least amount of time a pastor should spend on devotions each day?*

When you study the Scriptures, always find the historical and literary contexts. Since we only have one Bible, it becomes easier to understand its context as you study year by year. For example, the first time you examine the historical and literary context of 1 Corinthians 13, it requires much work. But the second time you come to 1 Corinthians 13, it will be much easier. A new field is hardest to plant the first year. A farmer must remove the brush, stumps and stones! But the second year requires much less work.

Read a Scripture portion all the way through without stopping.

A boy with his face close to a window looked out into the darkness. It was storming. Suddenly, the lightning flashed and in a moment he saw everything: the rain, the trees being blown, the puddles of water. When you first read a passage, be as a child in the window—read it to see everything, to see the whole. You want to become familiar with everything in the passage.

5. Pray about what you have read.   Try to retell the passage to God using your own words. Personalize it. That is, apply the passage to yourself. Insert your name and the pronouns "I," "me," and "my" as you are able. Ask the Holy Spirit to show you how the passage can help you be more like Jesus. Then, ask Him how the passage applies to the problems of your people.

People pray in different ways. Some like to kneel and pray. One of the authors of this course likes to walk and pray, listening to spiritual music. Use a form of prayer that you like best.

6. Keep a notebook of your devotions.   Write notes on truths and principles that the Holy Spirit emphasizes to you. Also, write down biblical examples and illustrations that the Spirit shows you throughout the day. These will help you later, when you plan sermons.

The preacher who practices this habit of daily devotions will be filled with Scripture. The Word of Christ will dwell in him richly (Col. 3:16). He will find more exciting texts than there are opportunities to preach. Because he meets with God in the morning, he will recognize illustrations of his devotions throughout the day. He will be bubbling over, filled with truths from the Bible, and sharing them with his family and those close to him.

In Matthew 13 Jesus told His disciples seven **new** parables. Then he asked them, *"'Have you understood all these things?'... 'Yes,' they replied."* Jesus then said that a person *"instructed about the kingdom of heaven is like the owner of a house who brings out of his storeroom **new** treasures as well as **old**"* (Matt. 13:51-52). We fill the spiritual storeroom through devotions and Bible study. The spiritual shepherd must first search out the green pastures and still waters of God's Word for himself. *Then* he must lead others into those places of blessing.[10] We comfort others with the comfort that we ourselves first find from God (2 Cor. 1:3-4).

In 1980 I met a man named Don Stamps, author of the study notes in the *Full Life Study Bible*. Don and I became missionaries that same year. One day he asked me, "How much time do you spend in your devotions each day, praying and reading the Bible?" I said it was a personal matter between God and me. But that answer did not satisfy Don. So he asked, "Is the time you spend in devotions closer to 5 minutes or 30 minutes?" I told him that I try to pray throughout the day. Still, Don was not satisfied. He said that having an attitude of prayer does not replace the time we set aside to be alone with God. Then came a great challenge. Don asked me to commit to spending 1 hour a day to pray and study the Bible. Because he insisted, I agreed to try it. Amazing! That was more than 20 years ago. Today, I can testify that this hour alone with God has been the secret of my spiritual power and ministry. I have not always kept the hour. But the hours I have spent with God are the reason I am able to minister to others. And so I challenge you, dear reader. Make the commitment to spend at least 1 hour a day praying and studying your Bible. In this daily hour God will fill your life with His Word and His Spirit. This is the hour that changes the world. Sometimes it will be so precious to you, and pass so quickly, that it will grow into 2 hours!

Lesson 5

Nine Keys to Preparing Biblical Messages

Goal: *Explain and give an example of each of the 9 keys for preparing biblical messages.*

This whole course is about preparing biblical messages. So we are not trying to cover everything in this chapter! But there are nine things we want to emphasize here.

A. Study your Bible.

Devotions are not enough by themselves. A full heart is no excuse for an empty brain![11] Two types of study will lead you to sermons. The *first* is studying the Bible. During devotions, the Lord may quicken certain verses to you. To preach these verses, you must do more study. Learn to identify the author, the listeners, the context, the meaning, the problem and the solution. Then begin to shape your message according to the Five-Step Method. We will teach you how to create each of these steps in this course.

A common question is, How much time should a pastor use to prepare a sermon? One famous preacher said, "An hour in the study for a minute in the pulpit."[12] This standard is not realistic for pastors who preach sermons three or more times each week! But many pastors spend 8-15 hours on each sermon. The time each pastor needs to prepare will vary.

For now we are underlining an important truth: God often speaks to a pastor about a message as he studies the Bible.

Q 26 *Is the time in devotions enough time to prepare for preaching? Explain.*

B. Study your people.

The *second* kind of study that leads to a sermon is studying people. Pastors should study their people as carefully as they do their Bible. We err if we know much about biblical times, but little about today. No one can be true to the biblical text unless he is true to his local church members.[13] Why? Because the Word was given for man, not man for the Word.

It is not enough for a pastor to explain what a passage of Scripture says. All good preaching connects man's problems with God's solutions.[14] Study the lives of your people and you will see many issues about which you must preach. All messages must be based on the Scripture. However, the Spirit will guide you to preach some biblical messages as you study your people.

Pastor, *you* must preach the biblical solutions to your people's problems. If they face the problem of fear, you must preach faith and trust in God. Since they face the problem of temptations, you must preach the biblical solution how to overcome temptations. Whatever problems people face, you, the pastor, must preach the biblical solutions.

Q 27 *How can studying his people lead a pastor to preach a message?*

When God spoke from heaven, some said it thundered (John 12:29). But a preacher does not need to hear a voice thundering from heaven in order to know what to preach. Learn to discern that it is the Holy Spirit who shows you the needs of the people. You, the pastor, are the one God has called to help people with their problems. If you see that your people have an obvious need, do not keep praying about what to preach. Do not waste time looking for a problem to preach about when God has already shown you a problem. Spend more hours preparing one sermon than you spend trying to choose between two. There are many problems and needs about which every good pastor must preach. These include topics like redemption, forgiveness, temptation, loving one another, God's faithfulness, and major doctrinal truths. You will need several hours to prepare a sermon, so get started. Choose an obvious need that the Holy Spirit brings to your attention while studying your people or your Bible. Another sermon will cover another need.

Q 28 *Suppose 10 Spirit-filled preachers were told to prepare 10 sermons for the same church. Let us say that all 10 men prayed and studied the people and the Bible equally. Should we expect that all would choose the same text for the first sermon? Would the texts, the topics, and the timing differ for each man's list? Explain. Make some conclusions.*

C. Avoid odd topics.

It is possible to preach odd or strange topics, even when speaking from the Bible. One preacher had not been to Bible school. He tried to preach on the difference between the Holy Spirit and the Holy Ghost. This was a very strange topic, since *Holy Spirit* and *Holy Ghost* are different names for the same Spirit!

Let us look at two kinds of odd topics to avoid.

Q 29 *Give an example of a topic that is not clear enough to preach on.*

1. Unclear topics.   Some topics are not explained much in Scripture. Examples of unclear topics include:

- baptism for the dead (1 Cor. 15:29),
- the angels who sinned (2 Pet. 2:4),
- Michael's dispute with the devil about the body of Moses (Jude 9),
- Jesus preaching to the spirits in prison (1 Pet. 3:19),
- the third toe of the beast (Dan. 2:42).

A preacher may mention a passage of Scripture that is not clear. He may even weave it into a sermon or comment on it briefly. But an unclear passage should never be the main topic of a sermon.

Q 30 *Can a topic be unbiblical if it is related to a verse of Scripture? Explain.*

2. Unbiblical topics.   Some sermons are based on texts that a preacher is twisting. We call these *pretexts.* "Negative confession" is an example of an odd topic based on a pretext. Some preach that we should never say we are sick, weak, or poor. They call such statements "negative confessions." Some preach on this topic by misusing Proverbs 6:2, *"...you have been trapped by what you said, ensnared by the words of your mouth."*

Preaching about negative confession from the text above is not good. Why? This text is not talking about negative confession. It is talking about someone who agreed to pay the debts of a stranger. In fact, Proverbs 6:2 is about a *positive* confession!

The Bible encourages us to confess many "negative" things. These include our weaknesses (2 Cor. 12:9-10), our lack of wisdom (James 1:5), our sickness (James 5:14), and our sins (1 John 1:9). All of these *negative* confessions are New Testament commands. Therefore, a sermon that warns against making a negative confession is an odd topic. It is odd because it is based on a misused text (pretext).

A second example of an unbiblical topic is eternal life without physical death. Some have preached on the topic of endless life on earth. They misuse the words of Jesus found in John 11:26: *"Whoever lives and believes in me will never die."* Jesus was talking about spiritual eternal life. He never taught that Christians could avoid physical death. The Lord warned His own disciples that they would die for Him (John 21:19). Thus, "no physical death" is an odd topic based on a twisted interpretation of a biblical text.

Preachers should avoid odd topics. These include topics that the Scriptures do not clearly explain and topics based on misused texts. Most people come to church to worship God and to receive spiritual food. The pastor is responsible to God for leading and feeding these hungry sheep. So he must avoid odd texts. He should never serve people a "dry bone." He has plenty of spiritual meat available.

Q 31 *What are some of the major themes of the Bible?*

D. Choose major themes and topics.

It can be a good practice to preach several sermons on one theme. But the theme must be a big one. For example, Spurgeon preached 12 sermons on the great theme that God invites us to find rest in Him.

[28] *"Come to me, all you who are weary and burdened, and I will give you rest.* [29] *Take my yoke upon you and learn from me, for I am gentle and humble in heart, and you will find rest for your souls.* [30] *For my yoke is easy and my burden is light"* (Matt. 11:28-30).

Avoid odd texts by preaching the major themes in Scripture. Do not be like the pastor who preached 12 sermons on words beginning with the letter *O*. Instead, preach on subjects like the major doctrines of the faith. Each of these doctrines emphasize a major theme in Scripture.

Pastor, keep busy preaching the Scripture's big themes. You will not be tempted to preach odd little topics. Preach on major topics such as temptation, forgiveness, stewardship, prayer, and walking by faith. Preach on evangelism and discipleship for all nations. Preach on overcoming discouragement, greed, and love for the world. Emphasize watchfulness, good deeds, and principles for a Christian home. Leave the odd topics. The main things are the plain things, and the plain things are the main things.[15] One proverb says that a lion should not hunt for a mouse. Preach the major themes!

E. Include Old Testament topics.

Pastors make two errors in relation to the Old Testament.

1. Some do not apply the Old Testament correctly.   Some pastors do not correctly handle the Old Testament. They preach from the Old Testament as if Christians were still under the Law. They emphasize such things as circumcision, ritual cleansing, and avoiding pork. Also, they confuse the promises God made to Israel with the promises we enjoy under the new covenant.

Some preachers confuse Christians by telling them to claim Old Testament promises. An example of such a promise is found in Deuteronomy 28:7, *"The Lord will grant that the enemies who rise up against you will be defeated before you. They will come at you from one direction but flee from you in seven."*

Q 32 *Should we expect all of our enemies to flee from us (Deut. 28:7)? Explain.*

Preachers *must* correctly handle the Word of Truth! Deuteronomy 28:7 was a promise to the nation of Israel under the old covenant. It does *not* apply to Christians under the new covenant. Jesus never promised that our enemies would flee from us. Instead, He told His followers this: *"When you are persecuted in one place, flee to another"* (Matt. 10:23). Most of the early church fled from Jerusalem. Stephen's enemies stoned him. James was beheaded. Paul once escaped by night in a basket. Hebrews, James, and 1 Peter are addressed to Christians who fled from their houses and lands to save their lives. These believers lost nearly all of their possessions to follow Christ. They were scattered all over the earth, and thousands were killed because of their faith.

2. Some do not preach at all from the Old Testament.   Some pastors ignore the Old Testament. But the New Testament quotes from the Old Testament more than 1,100 times. Believers need to be taught about many Old Testament topics. Some of these important Old Testament topics are:

Q 33 *What are some great themes to preach from the Old Testament?*

- the story of Creation,
- types (examples) of Christ in the Old Testament,
- lessons from the lives of Old Testament men and women,
- great themes in the Psalms,
- wisdom from Proverbs,
- themes of the Prophets, and
- Old Testament principles, such as the Ten Commandments.

These are only a few of the many topics a pastor should preach about from the Old Testament. We must not misuse the Old Testament by teaching that we are under the Law. Neither should we ignore it. The Old Testament has many excellent sermon topics containing great truths.

F. Offer a balanced spiritual diet.

Let me tell you a mystery. Some pastors claim to be led by the Spirit in their preaching. Yet they oppose planning sermons. They think the Holy Spirit will not help them plan

Q 34 *Is it possible for a pastor to be led by the Spirit, but not offer a balanced spiritual diet? Explain.*

Q 35 *How can a pastor know whether he is preaching a balanced spiritual diet?*

their messages. They wrongly believe that spiritual preachers get a sermon topic a day or two before they must preach it. Such preachers avoid entire books of the Old and New Testaments. Thus, they ignore major biblical themes. These misguided men repeat the same topics week after week in their sermons. They are like a wife who serves the same food at every meal. This is indeed a mystery! How can a man who is truly led by the Spirit *not* preach a balanced spiritual diet? Let us believe that planning is a spiritual thing.

People must plan ahead when they want to travel from one city to another. They must also plan ahead to build houses to live in. How much more should men of God plan ahead to build the "house" of God—the body of Christ! Pastors must plan in order to lead people to spiritual maturity. If you preach regularly, ask yourself the following questions:

- "What topics have I preached during the past 3 months?"
- "Have I neglected any great topics and themes?"

Many preachers need to improve their skills of planning a balanced spiritual diet.

G. Plan sermons for special days.

Q 36 *How should holidays guide a pastor's message?*

A preacher knows what to preach in one of several ways. We noted above that the Spirit leads pastors as they study their Bible and their people. Holidays, such as Christmas, Easter, and Independence Day should also influence a message. On holidays, it is usually wise to preach about the big theme people are already thinking about. At Christmas, the Spirit will not normally lead a pastor to preach about Jonah and the whale! All preachers will preach the Christmas story sometime. Preach it at Christmas, and it will be easy to get the attention of people. If you preach an Easter message on Christmas day, you are walking the opposite direction from your people. Should a father teach his son about fishing when they are kicking a ball? For everything there is a time (Eccl. 3:1)!

H. Plan groups of sermons.

Q 37 *Describe the closed-eyes method of choosing a sermon text.*

One pastor claimed to have a spiritual method for knowing what to preach each service. We may refer to his method as the *closed-eyes* method. He stood before the people with his eyes closed, holding his Bible in both hands before him. Then, he let the Bible open and put his finger on one of the pages. When he opened his eyes, he preached on the text his finger was on! What a terrible method! Note that this pastor did not obey 2 Timothy 4:1-2. He was never prepared to preach! If the closed-eyes method is bad, what is a good method for planning a message?

Q 38 *Is it unspiritual to plan a group of messages? Explain.*

Let the Spirit lead you to plan a series or group of messages. For example, every pastor should preach at least one message on each of the basic truths of our faith. We will study 16 truths in the *Faith & Action Series* course on *Bible Doctrines*. Likewise, every pastor should preach a group of messages on God's plan for husbands, wives, and children. (See our *Faith & Action Series* course *Marriage & the Family*.) Also, preaching through biblical books, like John or Acts, is good. This method gives the pastor the advantage of knowing what he will speak about next (unless, of course, the Holy Spirit guides him to change his plan for a time).

Q 39 *What are the 2 most important things about a pastor's message?*

God can use many messages to meet the spiritual needs of your people. Does it matter if a cook fixes chicken on Wednesday instead of Sunday? Is it important to serve greens only on Tuesdays and corn only on Thursdays? Isn't a hot, fresh meal the important thing? What really counts when people are hungry is that they eat good food. Likewise, the two most important things about your message are that it is fresh from the Bible and fresh from the Holy Spirit.

Q 40 *How many messages do you think you will preach in 20 years?*

You cannot preach about all people's problems in one message. So let the Spirit guide you to help them with one problem. Next week, help them with a different problem. If you preach three times a week, you will preach more than 150 messages in 1 year! And in 10 years you will preach 1,500 messages. In 40 years you will preach 6,000 messages. Plan so that you will preach through most of the Bible. If you do not plan, you will preach the same messages over and over. Then you will be like the pastor who fed his people only beans and rice every meal. If you do not plan, there will be big topics and whole books of the Bible that you never preach about. Are you glad that in this *Faith & Action Series* we have planned 40 different courses for you to study? Likewise, your people will be glad if you plan messages on many different topics.

Pray and plan a group of messages on a theme or book of the Bible. For example, Pastor Robert Njamba was a District Superintendent over about 100 churches in Kenya. He was a mature, spiritual pastor. His church had started about 30 other churches. He attended an extension Bible school class on the Gospel of John. About 50 pastors gathered in Nairobi and studied John for 40 hours together. Pastor Njamba was filled with the truth of John's Gospel. As a result, the Spirit led him to preach 13 sermons from John. He did this on Sunday mornings over a period of 3 months. What was the result? Many sinners were saved, and believers were filled with the Spirit. His people were so blessed that they gave a special offering to send him to the next Bible school class on Acts.

Pastor, be open to the leading of the Spirit. He may guide you to preach a group of messages. If He leads you this way, you must work hard. Spend many hours preparing each message. Be like Elijah on Mount Carmel. Do your part as God leads you to build the altar and prepare the sacrifice. Then depend on God to send down the fire of His presence. Pray and fast as you plan your sermons. Then the Holy Spirit can easily guide you. But remember this: the Spirit can guide you to plan *ten* sermons as easily as *one* sermon.

I. Pray and follow the leading of the Holy Spirit.

It is good to plan sermons ahead. But our plans should be like soft clay, not like hard iron. We *must* allow the Holy Spirit to guide us as we plan. Paul once planned to enter Bithynia, but the Spirit would not allow him to go there. Instead, the Spirit guided Paul toward Macedonia. Planning is good *if* we allow the Spirit to guide us at all times.

Should a pastor be willing to preach a different sermon than the one he has planned? Yes, always! Suppose a pastor is in the middle of a series when a problem develops in the church. The Holy Spirit might lead him to leave the series for a short time. The pastor could preach about an urgent need or problem. Later, he could return to the preaching series.

Bernard Johnson preached evangelistic meetings throughout Brazil, of which many were held in soccer stadiums. One night in a crusade, he did not know what message the Lord wanted him to bring. This was unusual because he had spent the day in Bible study, prayer, and fasting to receive it, as was his custom. Yet he felt no clear direction that day. The time came in the crusade service for him to preach to the crowd of thousands that had filled up the sports arena. At that moment, the Holy Spirit impressed him to begin preaching by telling the story of two miracles that Jesus performed on earth, starting with blind Bartimaeus at the entrance to Jericho. While he was preaching, a blind woman up in the stands was healed. She immediately gave her testimony, which led to hundreds of people receiving Jesus Christ as Savior and many others receiving miracles, deliverance, and healing that night.[16]

Most of the time, the Spirit will enable you to plan your messages ahead of time. But always be willing for Him to guide you in the direction He chooses.

Q 41 Explain 2 bad results of not planning groups of messages.

Q 42 Summarize the illustration about Robert Njamba.

Q 43 A pastor's sermon plans should be like _____, not like _____.

Test Yourself: Circle the letter by the *best* completion to each question or statement.

1. A pastor's most important work is
a) marrying.
b) burying.
c) visiting.
d) preaching.

2. A key factor in having devotions is
a) choosing the right biblical book.
b) finding a time and a place.
c) studying 3 hours each day.
d) memorizing a verse a day.

3. The first step of preparing a message is
a) preparing the title.
b) preparing the Introduction.
c) preparing your own heart.
d) preparing the outline.

4. The main purpose of devotions is to
a) secure the presence of God for the day.
b) discover topics for biblical messages.
c) praise God for all of His blessings.
d) present needs to God in prayer.

5. In devotions, Bible study should be
a) planned, through a book of the Bible.
b) varied, depending on the need of the hour.
c) from a different book each day.
d) based upon books other than the Bible.

6. A pastor should
a) ignore national holidays.
b) preach some from the Old Testament.
c) teach that we are under the Old Testament.
d) avoid writing notes on devotions.

7. Every pastor should preach on the topic of
a) forgiveness.
b) the widow's offering.
c) baldness.
d) spiritual drought.

8. Those who refuse to plan groups of messages
a) ignore entire books of the Bible.
b) depend on the leading of the Spirit.
c) offer their listeners a balanced spiritual diet.
d) refuse to plan most things in life.

9. Those who plan a group of biblical messages
a) are like the rich fool.
b) are like Jannes and Jambres.
c) are like Demetrius.
d) are like our heavenly Father.

10. A plan for a group of sermons should be like
a) clay.
b) wood.
c) gold.
d) iron.

Essay Test Topics Write 50-100 words on each of these goals that you studied in this chapter.

Put Your Daily Devotions and Bible Study First

Goal: *Explain why devotions are essential, and give 6 guidelines for them.*

Nine Keys for Preparing Biblical Messages

Goal: *Explain Sand give an example of each of the 9 keys for preparing biblical messages.*

Chapter 3:
The Preacher's Passion and Delivery

Introduction

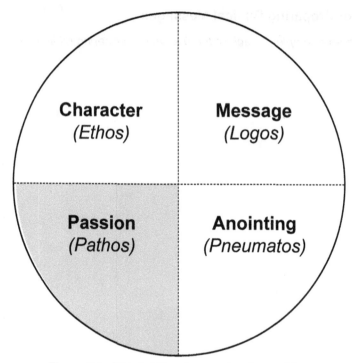

Figure 3.1 Third of four key parts of preaching

A preacher must preach with strong feelings. In this chapter, we will discuss ten basic areas of concern. Observe these ten commandments of *delivery so that people will feel what you feel. All of the teachings that follow are serious, but it is best to shoot at some targets with the light arrows of humor.[1]

Lessons:

 ## Commandments 1–5 of Delivery
Goal: *Summarize the commandments on passion, neatness, posture, manners, and voice.*

 ## Commandments 6–10 of Delivery
Goal: *Explain the commandments for speech, gestures, the hands, face, and eyes.*

🔑	Key Words		🔑
delivery	conviction	manners	gestures
passion	posture	filler words	

Commandments 1–5 of Delivery

Goal: *Summarize the commandments on passion, neatness, posture, manners, and voice.*

Q 1 ↗ *Why do people like preachers with strong feelings?*

A. Preach from a heart that is full of your message.

One leader said, "I like a preacher who looks like he's swatting bees." It was not so much the motion that appealed to the leader. Rather, he liked the emotion and *passion of a preacher with *conviction, that is, strong feelings and values. People will judge your message by how much they think you care about it.

One church member told a preacher after the sermon, "Pastor, I could feel your spirit this morning!" The world follows passionate people. A pastor's message must be one that has touched his heart. Only then will it be a blessing to others.

Q 2 ↖ *Evaluate the method of the country preacher.*

A country preacher known for his heart-felt messages was once asked about his method. He explained, "First I read myself full. Then I sing myself happy. Next I pray myself hot. Then I preach myself empty!"

This is a good plan to follow. A preacher must preach with passion and conviction.

Some preachers wrestle with the fear of standing before people. Saul was once like this. Before he became king, he was so scared that he hid among some baggage (1 Sam. 10:22). Perhaps Timothy was timid. That is probably why Paul encouraged him, saying, *"God did not give us a spirit of timidity, but a spirit of power, of love and of self-discipline"* (2 Tim. 1:7).

The best way for a preacher to overcome fear or feeling nervous is to have a fresh message people need to hear. *"Brothers, if you have a message of encouragement for the people, please speak"* (Acts 13:15). Go to the pulpit with a message from God Almighty for people who need help. The cook who has prepared a good meal is not nervous when hungry people come to the table.

B. Be neat.

It is not enough for you to have a message from God. People will judge your message by your appearance. If you dress like John the Baptist, you must preach in the wilderness! If you want people to listen, appear as though you deserve to be heard. Your clothes can look nice without being too costly. Use the iron. Sew your buttons. Shine your shoes. Dress for success.

C. Have good *posture.

Do not sit on a platform as relaxed as a man who is fishing beside a river. Thou shalt not slump or slouch! Do not lean on the pulpit like you are tired. Stand up and sit up straight. This shows that you have come to church on an important mission. Keep your head up and your shoulders back. When you stand, your weight should be on both feet, not just one!

D. Observe pulpit *manners.

Q 6 ↖ *What are some poor pulpit manners you have seen?*

Do not cough, sneeze, sniff, or blow your nose while facing people. These actions are crude and vulgar. Be polite. One person's advice was, "Scratch where it itches and not where it looks the best." This is good advice to follow privately, but NOT publicly!

Also, when you sit, be gracious. Keep your knees together, rather than spread apart. Remember that people are watching you.

Figure 3.2
"I have just come from the presence of God, and have an important message for you!"

Q 3 ↗ *What is the key to being bold?*

Q 4 ↗ *Why is neatness important?*

Q 5 ↗ *What does good posture communicate?*

Figure 3.3
Do not preach standing on one leg like a man leaning against a tree in the shade!

One pastor had a habit of pulling up his pants about once a minute. He did not realize why some people, especially the youth, smiled at him from time to time. Many were watching him closely. He thought they were listening to his message. Rather, they were counting the number of times he pulled up his pants!

Q 7 *Explain 4 ways to use your voice wisely.*

E. Use your voice wisely.

First, match the loudness of your voice to the number of your listeners. Your voice is like a radio. It can be soft or loud. When 20,000 are before you, speak like thunder. But do not speak so loudly for a crowd of only 20! Speak slightly louder than you would in normal conversation. If the person at the back of the church can hear you, you are preaching loudly enough.

Q 8 *If you shout "God loves you," will your listeners believe you? Explain.*

Second, match your voice to your topic. Do not shout about the gentleness of God! Do not use your lowest voice to talk about the highest heavens! Do not use only one tone in your voice, or you will sound like a child who has memorized a poem. Your voice should sound natural. Then your listeners will feel the personal concern you have for them. Above all, use your normal voice. Do not use one voice for talking and a *more holy* voice for preaching and praying.

Third, do not preach so loudly that people cannot think. Some preachers mistake perspiration for inspiration. They run into their messages with fast and loud words like a horse running because a bee is in his ear! As Spurgeon says, "This kind of speaking can never be powerful...for it turns an army of words into a mob, and drowns the sense in floods of sound."[3] People may be excited if you preach loudly. But they will not learn much. Too much noise prevents people from thinking clearly. An empty cart makes the most noise!

Use a loud voice when you need it. Sometimes words on a page are underlined for emphasis. But if every word in a chapter is underlined, then nothing is emphasized. Likewise, save the loud voice until you want to emphasize something. There are times when God is not in the wind, the earthquake, or the fire, but in the gentle whisper (1 Kings 19:11-13). Even pauses, when there is only silence, can help a preacher make his point (Luke 4:20-21; John 8:6-7). Get your authority from your text, not the loudness of your voice.

Fourth, take care of your voice. Beat the same spot over and over on a drum and you will soon wear a hole in it. Likewise, you will wear your voice out more quickly if you do not vary the loudness and tone. Some preachers have abused their voice in one way or another and can no longer proclaim the good news. Take care of your voice; it is the only one you have. *"Don't harm yourself!"* (Acts 16:28).

Lesson 7

Commandments 6–10 of Delivery
Goal: *Summarize the commandments for speech, gestures, the face, hands, and eyes.*

Q 9 *Explain 3 helpful rules for saying words correctly.*

A. Pronounce your words clearly.

Open your mouth! Avoid speaking like a person who does not want people to see his lips move. Those who use puppets may want to hide the fact that they are talking. But preachers must speak clearly. Do not be like a *ventriloquist. There is an obvious truth in the words, *"And **opening his mouth** he began to teach them"* (Matt 5:2 NASB).

Use your lips, tongue, and teeth. Vowels have their own sounds, but you must give special attention to the consonants like r, s, t, and p. Use your lips for more than kissing! Some preachers sound like bees. Others sound like they are still chewing food from the previous meal. Be humble, but do not mumble! Do not talk through your nose. The best authorities agree that it is for smelling, not speaking.[4] Pronounce your words clearly; let there be space between them like the words on this page.

Avoid useless *filler words,* like "Praise the Lord." Don't say, "And Judas went out, (Praise the Lord), and hanged himself, (Hallelujah)." Filler words are a bad habit. Like trash scattered on a path, they clutter a message.

Q 10 ↗ *Why do some preachers use filler words?*

B. Use the right gestures.

It is better to stand perfectly still and use no *gestures than to use bad ones. Some speaker's hands are always moving, but do not match the message. Others shake their heads or bounce up and down like a ball. A few walk rapidly back and forth from one side of the room to the other. Prune your preaching (John 15:2)—get rid of habits that distract or subtract from what you are saying. People are just people, and they stumble at things they should not. It is important to have good gestures. But it is even more important to get rid of distracting ones.[5]

Q 11 ↗ *What are gestures? Which ones are best?*

We want to use the whole body to communicate. The best gestures are the natural ones—those that are not planned. Natural motions cause listeners to see you as a friend rather than a professor.[6] A pastor will gain confidence as he stands week after week before the same group of people. Then, he will gain freedom with his actions. Be encouraged—a warm audience helps a preacher's cold emotions. As a preacher's message burns within him he may feel the freedom to move about, instead of hiding behind the pulpit. Then the listeners can see more than just his head and shoulders! Those who stand in only one place look like a living statue that is set on the pulpit. A preacher should be as free with his gestures as a lawyer or advocate in a courtroom.[7]

Q 12 ↗ *Explain: A warm audience helps a preacher's cold emotions.*

C. Talk with your hands.

Do not "wring your hands" as someone might squeeze water out of clothes. Do not fumble with a ring on your finger. Do not tug at your ear lobe, scratch your nose, or smooth your hair. These actions only show that you are nervous.

Q 13 ↗ *What mistakes do some make with their hands?*

Think of how many things you can say with your hands. By using your hands alone, you may ask, count, promise, honor, bless, praise, dismiss, welcome, or threaten. Also, you can use the hands to show fear, joy, grief, doubt, agreement, disagreement, and repentance. Other parts of the body help the speaker, but the hands speak themselves. Take your hands out of your pockets and use them!

Q 14 ↗ *List 5 things you can say with your hands.*

D. Remember that people must look at your face!

Look pleasant. It is a fact that people will receive your message better if your face looks kind rather than hard. Listeners do not open up well to stone-faced preachers. A face with few expressions is as boring as a voice with only one tone, or a song with only one note. Too stern of a face creates a negative, resisting attitude in the hearers. There are many things that people will receive if you are smiling. Be cheerful, but not silly.

Q 15 ↗ *How can your face match your message?*

Figure 3.4   This person says that the joy of the Lord is our strength. But what does his face say?

E. Look at the people you preach to!

Q 16 *Explain how some pastors look like Paul, Belshazzar, or Peter.*

Some pastors gaze at the rafters while preaching. They seem, like Paul, to be having a heavenly vision, or talking to those who have gone on before us (Acts 9:1-9; 26:19). *"Men of Galilee, ...why do you stand here looking into the sky?"* (Acts 1:11). Others, like King Belshazzar, stare at the back wall as though a hand were writing on it (Dan. 5). Then there are those, like Peter, who seem to fall into a trance (Acts 10:10). They fix their eyes on the Bible and rarely look up!

Figure 3.5
Look at the people you preach to!

Q 17 *Prepare a brief skit to illustrate some mistakes preachers make in their deliveries. If you are in a class, ask your teacher to divide the class into two parts, and to tell each group which mistakes to illustrate.*

Most people expect you to look at them if you have something to tell them. This does not mean that you should try to stare a hole through them. Neither should you try to strike terror into their hearts through a lengthy, wide-eyed look. The sermon may call for a glance toward heaven. But in general, you must look people in the eyes to be personal and to keep their attention.

Do your best to keep the ten commandments of delivery. Above all, be full of your subject. Have fire and passion in your spirit. Be excited about your message. Then, people will care little about your delivery and rejoice instead over a word from heaven. Let them, if they please, say that your bodily presence is weak but that your message is weighty and powerful (2 Cor. 10:10).

Test Yourself: Circle the letter by the ***best*** completion to each question or statement.

1. A preacher overcomes the fear of speaking by
a) thinking about the needs of people.
b) being full of the message he preaches.
c) thinking about the cross of Christ.
d) being too busy to have time to fear.

2. If you dress like John the Baptist,
a) people will think you are a prophet.
b) you must eat locusts and wild honey.
c) you must preach in the wilderness.
d) you must preach on the coming of Christ.

3. Show you have an important message by
a) looking very serious at all times.
b) standing up straight as you preach.
c) using at least 1 hour to preach.
d) announcing that your message is from God.

4. A pastor shows good manners in the pulpit by
a) referring often to his family or friends.
b) placing his hands behind his back.
c) sitting with his knees spread far apart.
d) covering his mouth if he coughs.

5. A preacher uses his voice wisely by
a) matching his voice to his topic.
b) speaking like the sound of many waters.
c) preaching quickly most of the time.
d) whispering softly when possible.

6. Filler words are like
a) a wind from heaven.
b) a trip to the dentist.
c) trash on a path.
d) water in a well.

7. The best gestures in preaching are those that
a) are planned.
b) are natural.
c) all can see.
d) all understand.

8. Which parts of the body speak for themselves?
a) Eyes
b) Ears
c) Hands
d) Feet

9. Why should a preacher smile at times?
a) To help people receive his message
b) To hide the fact that he is nervous
c) To cheer up those who are sad
d) To keep the attention of children

10. A mistake some make with their eyes is to
a) stare at the back wall.
b) read a text from the Bible.
c) glance briefly toward heaven.
d) look directly at each person.

 Essay Test Topics Write 50-100 words on each of these goals that you studied in this chapter.

Commandments 1–5 of Delivery

Goal: *Summarize the commandments on passion, neatness, posture, manners, and voice.*

Commandments 6–10 of Delivery

Goal: *Explain the commandments for speech, gestures, the hands, face, and eyes.*

Figure 4.1 Everyone knew that Moses had been in the presence of God.

Chapter 4:
The Preacher's Anointing

Introduction

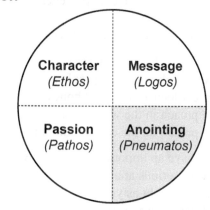

Figure 4.2 Fourth of four key parts of preaching

 Q 1 ✏ *Summarize 2 biblical pictures of God's anointing.*

Samuel poured oil over the head of a young shepherd boy. This *anointing on David was a sign that God approved of his life. Through this anointing, God enabled a shepherd to serve as the leader of the people.

So Samuel took the horn of oil and anointed him in the presence of his brothers, and from that day on the Spirit of the Lord came upon David in power (1 Sam. 16:13).

29When Moses came down from Mount Sinai with the two tablets of the Testimony in his hands, he was not aware that his face was radiant because he had spoken with the LORD. 30When Aaron and all the Israelites saw Moses, his face was radiant, and they were afraid to come near him (Exod. 34:29-30).

The Israelites could see that Moses had been in the presence of the Lord. Likewise pastor, your people will know whether you have spent time in God's presence. There may not be a glow of light around your head. But you cannot hide either the absence or the presence of God's anointing. If a person spends time in a flower garden, he will smell like the flowers.

Lessons:

 ### What the Anointing Is Not
Goal: *Explain 5 things the anointing is not.*

 ### What the Anointing Is
Goal: *Summarize 5 things the anointing is.*

 ### The Anointing Related to a Preacher's Character, Message, and Passion
Goal: *Describe how the anointing affects a preacher's character, message, and passion.*

 Key Word

anointing

What the Anointing Is Not

Goal: *Explain 5 things the anointing is not.*

Setting

The ancient Greeks were famous for their great speakers. But they did not refer to the anointing. They ignored it. Likewise, modern secular speech teachers say nothing about the anointing. They teach speakers to depend upon themselves alone. But the anointing of the Holy Spirit is what makes God's man different from a common man.

¹⁵Then Moses said to him, "If your Presence does not go with us, do not send us up from here. ¹⁶How will anyone know that you are pleased with me and with your people unless you go with us? What else will distinguish me and your people from all the other people on the face of the earth?" (Exod. 33:15-16).

Lose the anointing and you become like Samson without his strength. We must, above all concerns of homiletics, covet God's Spirit—His presence in and upon our lives. Let us now take off our shoes as we walk on holy ground.

In this first lesson, let us consider five things the anointing is not.

A. The anointing is not the ability of man.

Paul enlightens us:

¹When I came to you, brothers, I did not come with eloquence or superior wisdom as I proclaimed to you the testimony about God. ²For I resolved to know nothing while I was with you except Jesus Christ and him crucified. ³I came to you in weakness and fear, and with much trembling. ⁴My message and my preaching were not with wise and persuasive words, but with a demonstration of the Spirit's power, ⁵so that your faith might not rest on men's wisdom, but on God's power (1 Cor. 2:1-5).

The best that man has to offer is inferior to the anointing.

Again, contrasting Holy Spirit anointing with mere human talent, Paul says,

¹⁹I will come to you very soon, if the Lord is willing, and then I will find out not only how these arrogant people are talking, but what power they have. ²⁰For the kingdom of God is not a matter of talk but of power (1 Cor. 4:19-20).

NO! The anointing is not the ability of man. *"We have this treasure in jars of clay to show that this all-surpassing power is from God and not from us* (2 Cor. 4:7).

B. The anointing is not an escape from hard work.

The anointing is not a license to be lazy. It is not a substitute for hard work. Yes, the Spirit did supernaturally guide Philip to the Ethiopian's chariot (Acts 8:26-30). But Philip had to *walk* and perhaps *run* to get there! Yes, the Holy Spirit gave Paul a vision of a man saying, *"Come over to Macedonia and help us"* (Acts 16:6-10). But, Paul was already busy doing the Lord's work. Yes, Moses got water by merely speaking to the rock. But remember how many miles he walked to reach the rock! And father Abraham had to dig wells. Yes, God feeds the birds, but watch how hard they work to get the free food! Don't be like the farmer who sat under a shade tree and prayed for God to prevent weeds. Pray and hoe at the same time! Only vehicles that are *moving* need to be steered. The fire falls *after* the altar is built, *after* the wood is cut, and *after* the animal is slain! Those with the anointing, like Timothy, are still rightly called *workmen* (2 Tim. 2:15). Paul told the anointed Timothy, *"Do your best..."* (2 Tim. 4:9). Do your part and God will do His.

Q 2 *What major thing makes God's preachers different from all other speakers?*

Q 3 *A preacher without the anointing is like _____.*

Figure 4.3   A marble statue of Demosthenes, a famous Greek speaker

Q 4 *What big contrast do you see in 1 Corinthians 2:4?*

Q 5 *Comment on the contrast between a clay pot and the treasure in it.*

Q 6 *Explain: "The anointing is not a license to be lazy."*

**Figure 4.4
The treasure is *in* the clay but not *of* it.**

C. The anointing is not a substitute for Bible school.

Q 7 *If Paul studied in the desert, why shouldn't we?*

Do not think that the most spiritual men choose to learn in the desert from the Spirit, while more fleshly men go to Bible school. This is contrary to Scripture. Even a man given to visions, such as Daniel, was a man of books (Dan. 9:2). Yes, Paul learned in the desert from the Spirit. But, the Spirit inspired Paul to teach Timothy and write to him: *"And the things you have heard me say in the presence of many witnesses entrust to reliable men who will also be qualified to teach others"* (2 Tim. 2:2).

Paul did not send anyone to a desert seminar. He himself taught in a Bible school for more than 2 years (Acts 19:9-10) in Ephesus. The Holy Spirit anointing leads preachers to Bible school, not away from it.

D. The anointing is not a substitute teacher.

Q 8 *Does 1 John 2:27 mean that we do not need teachers? Explain.*

God does not say that we may either learn from Him *or* from teachers. Yes, the Scripture does say, *"As for you, the anointing you received from him remains in you, and you do not need anyone to teach you"* (1 John 2:27). But remember the lesson we studied earlier about context. John wrote because of the problem of Gnostic teachers. The Gnostics were men who claimed to have special revelation contrary to Scripture. John was not saying we do not need godly teachers. He is saying we do not need false teachers like the Gnostics. After all, if these believers John wrote to did not need any teachers, then they did not need John to write and tell them that!

Figure 4.5   Don't be like the farmer who sat under a shade tree and prayed for God to prevent weeds.

The Bible does not say, "He gave apostles, prophets, evangelists, pastors and the Holy Spirit anointing..." (See Eph. 4:11). God gave teachers! Teachers are not in opposition to the Spirit. They are a part of God's gifts to the Church, to prepare God's people for works of service, and bring them to unity and maturity (Eph. 4:12-13). It is funny that the men who say we do not need teachers, want to teach!

E. The anointing is not an invitation to independence.

The anointing is not a path away from cooperation with the rest of the body of Christ. Yes, Paul was probably the chief of the apostles. But he was led by divine revelation to relate to other church leaders, lest his work be in vain (Gal. 2:1-2). When a man does not relate properly to others, the work he does will not last.

Q 9 *Why did the anointing lead Paul to Jerusalem?*

Q 10 *Why have confusion and division been the lasting fruit of William Branham?*

The Church is a body, not a collection of *superstars. We need each other. When especially anointed men of God begin to feel superior to their brothers in Christ, the results are tragic. For example, those who baptize only in the name of Jesus look down on others. This is a result of William Branham. He was anointed by God as a healing evangelist. Unfortunately, he lost his sense of depending on the rest of the body. He came to believe that he was the only leader with the light. He began to reject the doctrine of the Trinity that the whole Church had believed for more than 1900 years. He said that anyone who disagreed with him was wrong. Confusion and division have been his lasting fruit. All this happened because he misunderstood the anointing. He falsely believed that because he was anointed to preach and heal, he was wiser than all other anointed servants were. Some of the greatest hindrances to sound doctrine and unity result when men anointed in one area take themselves too seriously. *"Do not think of yourself more highly than you ought..."* (Rom. 12:3).

Q 11 *Relate the anointing to James 3:17.*

God is not the author of confusion or division, but of peace (1 Cor. 14:33). Even when prophets speak, others should weigh and evaluate their words (1 Cor. 14:29). If anybody thinks he is a prophet or spiritually gifted, he is to acknowledge the writings of Scripture (1 Cor. 14:37). Those who ignore their relationship to the Word and the body of Christ should themselves be ignored (1 Cor. 14:38). The anointing, if followed completely, will cause us to build bridges, not burn them.

Lesson 9 — What the Anointing Is

Goal: *Summarize 5 things the anointing is.*

Having considered five things the anointing is not, let us now turn our attention to five things the anointing is.

A. In the Old Testament, the anointing is a sign that people or things are holy—separated unto God for a special purpose.[1]

²²Then the Lord said to Moses, ²³"Take the following fine spices: 500 shekels of liquid myrrh, half as much (that is, 250 shekels) of fragrant cinnamon, 250 shekels of fragrant cane, ²⁴500 shekels of cassia—all according to the sanctuary shekel—and a hin of olive oil. ²⁵Make these into a sacred anointing oil, a fragrant blend, the work of a perfumer. It will be the sacred anointing oil. ²⁶Then use it to anoint the Tent of Meeting, the ark of the Testimony, ²⁷the table and all its articles, the lampstand and its accessories, the altar of incense, ²⁸the altar of burnt offering and all its utensils, and the basin with its stand. ²⁹You shall consecrate them so they will be most holy, and whatever touches them will be holy. ³⁰Anoint Aaron and his sons and consecrate them so they may serve me as priests. ³¹Say to the Israelites, 'This is to be my sacred anointing oil for the generations to come. ³²Do not pour it on men's bodies and do not make any oil with the same formula. It is sacred, and you are to consider it sacred. ³³Whoever makes perfume like it and whoever puts it on anyone other than a priest must be cut off from his people'" (Exod. 30:22-33).

> **Q 12** ⟋ *What types of things and people did God tell Moses to anoint? Why?*

Figure 4.6 The anointing oil was made from five ingredients. Clockwise from top: olives (olive oil), fragrant cane, cinnamon, cassia, myrrh [center] (liquid myrrh)

Preacher, do you want the anointing of God upon your life? Then you must live a holy life. We emphasized the preacher's life and character in chapter 1 of this course.

The Lord detests the way of the wicked but he loves those who pursue righteousness (Prov. 15:9).

¹Surely the arm of the Lord is not too short to save, nor his ear too dull to hear. ²But your iniquities have separated you from your God; your sins have hidden his face from you, so that he will not hear (Isa. 59:1-2).

Live a holy life so that the Lord will anoint you.

B. In the New Testament, the anointing is related to Jesus in a unique way.

The word *Messiah is a Hebrew word that means "Anointed" or "the Anointed One." The Greek word for anointed is *Christos,* from where we get *Christ.* Today, the word *Christ* has lost much of its meaning to believers. Since most of us do not speak Greek or Hebrew, the words *Messiah* and *Christ* have become synonyms or titles for Jesus. But we should remind ourselves that the words *Messiah* and *Christ* mean "the Anointed One." Many New Testament passages refer to Jesus as the One anointed by God (Matt. 1:18; 16:16, 20; 26:63; 27:22; Mark 8:29; 14:61; Luke 2:11, 26; 9:20; 22:67; John 4:29; 7:26, 31, 41; 9:22; 10:24; Acts 2:36; 3:20; 4:26; 5:42; 9:22; 17:3; 18:28; 26:23).[2]

> **Q 13** ⟋ *What does the word Christ mean?*

Jesus is our example of being anointed by the Spirit of God.

C. In the New Testament, the anointing is the Holy Spirit.

In the Old Testament, oil was used for anointing. Moses poured the anointing oil upon Aaron. Samuel poured the anointing oil upon David. Likewise, in the New Testament,

> **Q 14** ⟋ *Is the anointing a thing or a person? Explain.*

elders anoint sick believers with oil (James 5:14). In both the Old and New Testaments, oil is a symbol of the Holy Spirit. In other words, the Holy Spirit is the anointing. So it is correct for us to speak of the anointing as a person, not a thing. The anointing is the presence of the Holy Spirit upon a believer.

As Jesus was baptized, the Holy Spirit came down on Him in the form of a dove. From that day on He was ready to minister. Because of God's special presence Jesus said,

Q 15 How does Luke 4:18 relate the Holy Spirit to the anointing?

[18] *"The Spirit of the Lord is on me, because He has **anointed** me to preach good news to the poor. He has sent me to proclaim freedom for the prisoners and recovery of sight for the blind, to release the oppressed, [19]to proclaim the year of the Lord's favor"* (Luke 4:18-19). (Note that Luke 4:18-19 is a quote from Isaiah 61:1-2.)

Q 16 How does Acts 10:38 describe the anointing?

*"But you will receive **power** when the Holy Spirit comes on you; and you will be my witnesses…"* (Acts 1:8).[3]

Q 17 Explain: "God has not called us to work for him, but with Him."

*"God **anointed** Jesus of Nazareth with the **Holy Spirit** and power, and … he went around doing good and healing all who were under the power of the devil, because God was with him"* (Acts 10:38).

The anointing is not the fruit or the gifts. Rather, the anointing is the Holy Spirit who produces fruit and gifts. All spiritual fruit and spiritual gifts are evidences, signs, and manifestations of the Spirit (1 Cor. 12:7-11). So the anointing we are seeking is not the result of an event. Rather, the anointing is the result of our relationship with God. God has not called us to work *for* Him, but *with* Him.[4] And without Him we can do nothing (John 15:5). This is why it is so important for a pastor to have daily devotions and Bible study, and to pray throughout the day. As we spend time in God's Word and His presence, our relationship with Him grows stronger. And the stronger our relationship is with Him, the more His presence and anointing will show in our lives. As we emphasized in chapter 2, continuous prayer is the key to the Spirit's anointing in and on our lives.

Figure 4.7   The Holy Spirit descended on Jesus at His baptism.

D. The anointing of the Spirit is a gift of grace that results in power to fulfill God's call.

Q 18 Name 2 or more words often linked to the anointing.

Consider the following Scriptures. They emphasize that the ministry we receive from God is by grace. We do not deserve to be called to preach God's Word. And we do not deserve His presence upon our lives. We are called and anointed by grace.

Likewise, any gifts and power in our ministry are from God. They are not things that we created or designed. We cannot take credit for any good things in our ministry. All grace, gifts, and power come to us from God. The anointing of the Holy Spirit is an act of God alone. As David said, *"**You** anoint my head with oil"* (Ps. 23:5).

Q 19 Summarize the theme of 1 Corinthians 1:26-29.

For who makes you different from anyone else? What do you have that you did not receive? And if you did receive it, why do you boast as though you did not? (1 Cor. 4:7).

*With great **power** the apostles continued to testify to the resurrection of the Lord Jesus, and much **grace** was upon them all* (Acts 4:33).

*Now Stephen, a man full of God's **grace** and **power**, did great wonders and miraculous signs among the people* (Acts 6:8).

*I became a servant of this gospel by the **gift** of God's **grace** given me through the working of his **power*** (Eph. 3:7).

God's anointing gives us supernatural ability *to do* the work of the Lord and *to live* a Christ-like life.

Pastor, take heed that you do not become puffed up (1 Cor. 8:1). As air causes a tire to expand, a title, like *pastor*, can cause a person to be puffed up and proud. If God's anointing on you brings success, remember the words of Jesus:

> *"So you also, when you have done everything you were told to do, should say, 'We are unworthy servants* [called and anointed by grace]; *we have only done our duty'"* (Luke 17:10).

Q 20 *Have you seen pastors become proud and stumble over what God did in their lives? Explain.*

E. The anointing is for different purposes on each believer.

⁴There are different kinds of gifts, but the same Spirit. ⁵There are different kinds of service, but the same Lord. ⁶There are different kinds of working, but the same God works all of them in all men. ⁷Now to each one the manifestation of the Spirit is given for the common good. ⁸To one there is given through the Spirit the message of wisdom, to another the message of knowledge by means of the same Spirit, ⁹to another faith by the same Spirit, to another gifts of healing by that one Spirit, ¹⁰to another miraculous powers, to another prophecy, to another distinguishing between spirits, to another speaking in different kinds of tongues, and to still another the interpretation of tongues. ¹¹All these are the work of one and the same Spirit, and he gives them to each one, just as he determines (1 Cor. 12:4-11).

Q 21 *How does 1 Corinthians 12:7-11 say the anointing differs on believers?*

³For by the grace given me I say to every one of you: Do not think of yourself more highly than you ought, but rather think of yourself with sober judgment, in accordance with the measure of faith God has given you. ⁴Just as each of us has one body with many members, and these members do not all have the same function, ⁵so in Christ we who are many form one body, and each member belongs to all the others. ⁶We have different gifts, according to the grace given us. If a man's gift is prophesying, let him use it in proportion to his faith. ⁷If it is serving, let him serve; if it is teaching, let him teach; ⁸if it is encouraging, let him encourage; if it is contributing to the needs of others, let him give generously; if it is leadership, let him govern diligently; if it is showing mercy, let him do it cheerfully (Rom. 12:3-8).

Q 22 *What does Romans 12:3-8 say about the various expressions of God's anointing?*

Q 23 *How might an evangelist's anointing differ at times from a pastor's anointing?*

The passages above make one thing clear. The anointing of the Spirit differs according to the person and the need. There are times when the anointing of the Spirit results in signs and wonders. This is especially true in front-line evangelism. There are other times, as for a teacher, that the anointing of the Holy Spirit does not bring a miracle, but a helpful Scripture, illustration, or question to mind (John 14:26). When preaching under the anointing, a preacher may feel led to say things he had not planned. Also, he may find other gifts of the Spirit working through him. Let us not envy the anointing of an apostle if we are doing the work of a pastor. Paul's anointing varied from Timothy's. The anointing will always match the work God calls a person to do. This is the Holy Spirit's will. Our part is to walk with God and earnestly desire spiritual gifts (1 Cor. 12:31). Then, the Head of the Church will anoint us as He purposes.

Figure 4.8 As we yield to the Spirit of Christ, He produces the good fruit of character in us.

Much has been said about *doing* in this lesson. In the following lesson, we will explore the way the Holy Spirit enables us to *be* like Jesus.

Lesson 10 The Anointing Related to a Preacher's Character, Message, and Passion
Goal: *Describe how the anointing affects a preacher's character, message, and passion.*

A. The anointing and a preacher's character (*ethos*)

In chapter 1 we studied about the *ethos* or character of a man of God. A pastor must be blameless. We studied five bad things he must not be. In contrast, a pastor must be respected for seven good characteristics.

Too often, preachers try to live up to these 12 qualifications by their own strength. They see the 12 requirements as 12 steps on a ladder. But Christian maturity is not the result of

Q 24 *How does the Spirit help a pastor be blameless and respected?*

Q 25 *Which of the 7 good characteristics is the hardest for you? Explain.*

Q 26 ⤷ *Explain: The ladder of the Law kills.*

climbing a ladder. Never! The *letter* and the *ladder* of the Law kill. We do not climb a ladder to please God. Rather, we abide in the vine (John 15:4). As we yield to the Spirit of Christ, He produces the good fruit of character in us.

1 Tim. 3:2	Titus 1:6-7	(-) Negative 5 Bad Characteristics to Avoid (Blameless: Not guilty of 5 accusations)	(+) Positive 7 Good Qualities to Have (Respected for 7 good reasons)	1 Tim. 3:2, 7	Titus 1:7
3:3	1:7	1. Not given to drunkenness	1. The husband of one wife	3:2,12	1:6
3:3	1:7	2. Not overbearing or quarrelsome	2. Gentle	3:3	—
3:3	1:7	3. Not quick-tempered; not violent	3. Temperate; self controlled; disciplined	3:2	1:8
3:3	1:7	4. Not a lover of money; not pursuing dishonest gain	4. Hospitable	3:2	1:8
3:6	—	5. Not a recent convert	5. One who loves what is good; upright and holy	—	1:8
			6. Able to teach; holding firmly to sound doctrine	3:2	1:9
			7. A good manager of his own family	3:12	1:6

Figure 4.9 Twelve requirements for a pastor to be blameless and have a good reputation

[22]But the fruit of the Spirit is love, joy, peace, patience, kindness, goodness, faithfulness, [23]gentleness and self-control. Against such things there is no law. [24]Those who belong to Christ Jesus have crucified the sinful nature with its passions and desires. [25]Since we live by the Spirit, let us keep in step with the Spirit (Gal. 5:22-25).

What would be lacking in the *ethos*, or character, of a man abounding in the fruit of the Spirit? Character includes more than the fruit of the Spirit. For example, character includes such things as faithfulness, righteousness, honesty, integrity, loyalty, and holiness. But we depend on the Holy Spirit for these qualities too! We need the Spirit to produce all kinds of good fruit in us.

Fruit is the natural product of a fruit tree. The tree does not struggle to produce fruit. Its roots go down into the soil. Its branches and leaves reach up to the sunlight and rain. Thus, as the tree is fed, it produces good fruit.

Cooperate with God's Spirit in you. Depend on Him. Learn to respond to His leading with no resistance. Blow on your hand softly. Sometimes the Spirit's voice is that soft. Yield to Him.

Read Galatians 5:24 above. Crucifying the sinful nature is a hard, daily task. But we do not conquer fleshly desires by mental effort or willpower. Rather, the key to overcoming the flesh is to *"keep in step with the Spirit"* (Gal. 5:25). This *internal anointing* of the Spirit is the key to being like Jesus. Let us depend as much on the Spirit's anointing for daily living as we depend on the Spirit in the pulpit.

Imagine a man who has his first car. The car is new. He shows it to his friends. He brags on the color, the seats, the radio—all of it. But the man does not realize there is a motor in the car. So he pushes the car everywhere he goes. He enjoys going down the hills. But he dreads going up the hills. The blessing of the car has become a burden to him. This man is very foolish! Could anyone be so foolish? There are many believers trying to push themselves to serve God, rather than depending on the power of the Holy Spirit. They are like the man trying to push the car everywhere he goes. Following Jesus should be a blessing, not a burden! Depend on the Spirit, not your own strength![5]

B. The anointing and a preacher's message (*logos*)

Q 27 ⤷ *Explain: Spend time each day with God and you will never lack a message.*

In chapter 2 we stressed that sermons grow out of a preacher's devotions and worship. We emphasized that the purpose of devotions is not to find sermons, but to find God. The anointing of the Holy Spirit we desire in the pulpit comes from the same Holy Spirit we fellowship with morning by morning.

Would you make a habit of asking a favor of a stranger? Would you dare seek the Holy Spirit in public when you have not sought Him in private? Would an athlete expect to run well in a race without training some hours each day in preparation?

Oswald J. Smith was a pastor with *fire in his bones*. His church, The People's Church of Toronto, Canada, sent out more than 400 missionaries. The fire he had in the pulpit was lit in his private devotions. His method was to go to his place of prayer each morning after breakfast. He would read a chapter or two in the Scriptures, following a plan. To him, this was like going to the upper room and preparing for Pentecost. After reading, he would arise from his chair for prayer. He said that the purpose of morning devotions is to secure the presence of God for the day.[6]

Pastor Smith's goal was not only to know the Bible, but its author. His reading was not a substitute for God. He did not bow to the printed page, but unto his Maker. He, like Watchman Nee (an author and Christian leader in China, 1903-1972), practiced the daily presence of God.

God's presence is the anointing we are talking about. Let the preacher seek a relationship with the Holy Spirit that he renews day by day. Spurgeon said that when he was awake, he did not spend one quarter of an hour in which he was not aware of the presence of God. His public anointing was like his private anointing. John Wesley began each day with 2 hours of prayer. Luther started each morning with 4 hours of prayer and Bible study. David Yonggi Cho pastors a church of about one million people. He does not meet people until he has met with God for at least 3 hours.

> [40]*Martha was distracted by all the preparations that had to be made. She came to him and asked, "Lord, don't you care that my sister has left me to do the work by myself? Tell her to help me!"* [41]*"Martha, Martha," the Lord answered, "you are worried and upset about many things,* [42]*but only one thing is needed. Mary has chosen what is better, and it will not be taken away from her"* (Luke 10:40-42).

Choose the habit of sitting at the feet of Jesus to learn and worship. The Spirit will lead you into all truth (John 16:13). The presence of the Holy Spirit in your devotions will be seen and felt by all when you preach.

C. The anointing and a preacher's passion (*pathos*)

In chapter 3 we considered the importance of passion in the pulpit. We discussed the importance of people feeling what the preacher feels. People are persuaded when a pastor preaches truth straight from his heart. They will follow a leader with convictions. Our emotions are touched by someone with deep feelings about his subject.

It is at this point that the anointed preacher has a double advantage over a mere public speaker. On the one hand, the Holy Spirit births in the preacher a message from God to man. This enables even a young preacher to rise above his own personal fears. His soul is aflame. His passion cannot be missed in his delivery.

Yet, on the other hand, there is a factor that goes beyond the preacher's sincerity. The man of God is not limited by his ability to persuade. The Holy Spirit convinces and convicts the listeners. The secular speaker does not have this power, but the preacher depends on it!

> *"When he [the Spirit] comes, **he will convict** the world of guilt in regard to sin and righteousness and judgment"* (John 16:8).
>
> *When the people heard this, they were **cut to the heart** and said to Peter and the other apostles, "Brothers, what shall we do?"* (Acts 2:37).
>
> *As Paul discoursed [preached] on righteousness, self-control and the judgment to come, Felix **was afraid*** (Acts 24:25). The convicting power of the Holy Spirit was upon him.

The anointing is the key to a preacher's success in character, in the message, and in a passionate, powerful delivery. May we always live by the principle: *"'Not by might, nor by power, but by my Spirit' says the LORD Almighty"* (Zech. 4:6).

Q 28 *Name a great spiritual leader you know who meets with God each morning.*

Q 29 *What did Jesus say was the one thing we need?*

Q 30 *What double advantage does the anointing give a preacher over a secular speaker?*

Q 31 *Give a biblical example of how the Spirit helps a preacher.*

Q 32 *What should the preacher's motto be?*

Test Yourself: Circle the letter by the *best* completion to each question or statement.

1. A biblical example of God's anointing is
a) laughter.
b) oil.
c) falling.
d) shouting.

2. Paul contrasts the anointing with
a) the ability of man.
b) the fruit of the Spirit.
c) the gifts of the Spirit.
d) speaking in tongues.

3. The anointing enables us to
a) preach without studying.
b) work by ourselves.
c) minister with power.
d) have a large church.

4. When you lose the anointing, you become like
a) Samson without his strength.
b) David without his sling.
c) Moses without his staff.
d) Elisha without his cloak.

5. Paul taught in a Bible school for
a) 0 years.
b) 2 years.
c) 7 years.
d) 9 years.

6. The anointing is
a) a skill.
b) a person.
c) a revelation.
d) an event.

7. The anointing is the result of
a) our relationship with Christ.
b) our knowledge of the Bible.
c) our spiritual maturity.
d) our position as a pastor.

8. The anointing of the Spirit
a) is the same on each minister.
b) is greater on the old than the young.
c) matches the work of the minister.
d) is greatest in evangelism.

9. The main key to having godly character is
a) saying No to worldly temptations.
b) depending on the Spirit within.
c) reading the Bible every morning.
d) choosing the right kind of friends.

10. Why is passion important?
a) It makes us seem spiritual.
b) It shows that we have studied.
c) It causes the Holy Spirit to move.
d) It touches people's hearts.

 Essay Test Topics Write 50-100 words on each of these goals that you studied in this chapter.

What the Anointing Is Not

Goal: *Explain 5 things the anointing is not.*

What the Anointing Is

Goal: *Summarize 5 things* **the anointing is.**

The Anointing Related to a Preacher's Character, Message, and Passion

Goal: *Describe how the anointing affects a preacher's character, message, and passion.*

Unit 2: Illustrations

In Unit 1, we laid the foundation for our study. We took a close look at four parts of preaching: character, the message, the delivery, and the anointing. Now it is time to focus on illustrations. As skin covers a skeleton, illustrations cover the structure of a preacher's message.

In Chapter 5 we consider the question, What are illustrations? We will guide you to:
- *Use each of the following to illustrate a biblical truth: a story, testimony, quote, and statistic.*
- *Illustrate a biblical truth with each of the following: a comparison, event, parable, proverb, riddle, and contrast.*
- *Illustrate a biblical truth with each of the following: a drama, visual aid, poem, and song.*

Chapter 6 focuses on the question, Why use illustrations? You will discover how to:
- *Explain how illustrations clarify, persuade, inspire, add variety, shorten, and make preaching easier.*
- *Describe how illustrations repeat, apply, transition, are appreciated, feed, and connect.*
- *Summarize how illustrations are indirect, relax the listeners, help memory, touch the heart, and convert people.*
- *Analyze the use of illustrations in the Bible and the ministry of Jesus.*

Chapter 7 emphasizes guidelines for managing and using illustrations. We will teach you to:
- *Identify five sources of illustrations.*
- *Explain five steps to make illustration files, and five details for writing illustrations.*
- *Explain five guidelines for a preacher's attitude toward illustrations.*
- *Describe five guidelines for preparing illustrations.*
- *Summarize five guidelines for presenting illustrations.*

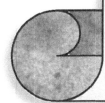

Chapter 5:

What Are Illustrations?

Introduction

Figure 5.1 Illustrations are like windows; they let in light.

Q 1 *What is the first and most important type of sermon illustration?*

In Unit 1, we talked about the preacher. He is both the illustrator and an illustration. As one church member said, "It takes 20 years to evaluate a sermon. In each local community, the message is evaluated together with the man who preached it." That is why we must be able to say with Paul, *"Follow my example, as I follow the example of Christ"* (1 Cor. 11:1). The pastor is the most important type of sermon illustration.

*Illustrations are windows that let light come into the mind and the soul. As windows come in various shapes, sizes, and styles, so do illustrations. We have studied the pastor. In this chapter we will study 14 other types of illustrations. Also, we will help you learn to illustrate topics and principles in the Bible.

Lessons:

 Types of Illustrations: Stories, Testimonies, Quotes, and Statistics

Goal: *Use each of the following to illustrate a biblical truth: a story, testimony, quote, and statistic.*

 Types of Illustrations: Comparisons, Events, Parables, Proverbs, Riddles, and Contrasts

Goal: *Illustrate a biblical truth with each of the following: a comparison, event, parable, proverb, riddle, and contrast.*

 Types of Illustrations: Drama, Visual Aids, Poems, and Songs

Goal: *Illustrate a biblical truth with each of the following: a drama, visual aid, poem, and song.*

	Key Words		
illustrations	parable	riddle	visual aid
testimony	proverb	drama	poem
statistic			

Types of Illustrations: Stories, Testimonies, Quotes, and Statistics

Goal: *Use each of the following to illustrate a biblical truth: a story, testimony, quote, and statistic.*

We have divided the 14 types of illustrations into three groups because we wanted three lessons in this chapter. There are 35 lessons in the book because many Bible schools meet about 40 class periods. So we plan one lesson for each class period. The illustrations in group 1 are quite varied. Those in groups 2 and 3 are more similar to one another.

Q 2 *Do all stories for sermons come from the Bible? Explain.*

A. Stories

A story is probably the most familiar way of illustrating. Stories may be personal, cultural, or historical.

Let us use a story to illustrate greed, a topic in Scripture.

Isaiah 56:11 states that some people are like greedy dogs. An old story illustrates this point well. A dog with a bone in his mouth went to a river. The river was still and shiny like a mirror. As the dog looked into the water, he saw his own image. But he thought he saw another dog with a bone better than his own.

This dog was greedy. He wanted his bone and the other dog's bone. The dog jumped into the water to get the other bone. As he jumped, he opened his mouth and lost the bone he had. We should learn to enjoy and be content with what God has given us. We should not be like greedy dogs. Hebrews 13:5 says, *"Be content with what you have."*

Figure 5.2   Don't be like a greedy dog.

People never tire of hearing stories, because stories underline the tale of life itself.

God likes stories. We know this because God's book is full of stories! Take a moment to look at Appendix A, near the back of this book. It lists 150 stories that are in the Bible. Also, Appendix B lists the miracles of Jesus. These are true stories about people that Jesus helped. Learn to use biblical stories to illustrate the principles and truths you preach. One preacher practiced illustrating each principle two times: once from the Old Testament and once from the New. Practice this as you preach. Using stories from the Bible has three benefits. *First,* Bible stories are easy to find. They are right there in your Bible! *Second,* Bible stories, like all illustrations, help your people in many areas, like memory. In the next chapter we will study 15 ways illustrations help people. *Third,* when you use stories from the Bible, it helps your people learn the Bible better.

Q 3 *What page number is on Appendix A?*

Q 4 *What are 3 reasons why a pastor should use some Bible stories to illustrate each message?*

Q 5 *Select stories from Appendix A or B to complete the chart in Figure 5.3.*

Now it is time for you to practice.

Biblical Truth	Bible Story to Illustrate the Truth
A. Faith is the hand that reaches out to God.	A.
B. Obedience is a key to receiving God's blessings.	B.

Figure 5.3   Practice using biblical stories to illustrate biblical truths.

B. Testimonies

*Testimonies are personal stories. To put it another way, testimonies are the stories of what happened to people in life. Testimonies are powerful ways of showing that God's Word is true. They *convince* people that what is being preached is correct. Support your main points with proofs. Share testimonies from people who have experienced your message.

Suppose you decide to preach on tithing. Give testimonies of people who tithed and found that it brought God's blessing. Or let one or two of your members testify about the blessing of tithing.

Q 6 *How could you use a testimony to illustrate a message on prayer?*

Q 7 Summarize an encouraging testimony on the topic of giving.

If you preach on prayer, share some answers to prayer. For example, missionary Adoniram Judson prayed sincerely and earnestly. If he did not receive the first time, he prayed again and again. Judson testified that he *never* failed to receive anything he asked for in this way. Some answers took a long time, but they did come! That is an encouraging testimony!

Q 8 Name 3 places a pastor can find quotes for his message.

C. Quotes

Quotations can make your message sparkle like a diamond in the sunlight. Do not just repeat your own experiences. Tell what someone else has said or written about the subject. Quote Jesus, or an apostle, a prophet, an evangelist, a pastor, or a teacher. Quote a famous person, a family member, or a friend. Give people a breath of fresh air. How? Let them hear someone's words besides yours! Add some salt to the food!

Q 9 Explain the method and purpose of quoting a verse wrongly.

One preacher uses quotes by planning to quote wrongly from Scripture. He does this to emphasize the true meaning. <u>Of course, he quotes the passage correctly after emphasizing his point!</u> Two examples follow. The wrong (misquoted) words are in parentheses.

> *For the grace of God that brings salvation has appeared to all men. It teaches us to* [do whatever we please and still expect to reach heaven] (Titus 2:11-12).

> *The apostles left the Sanhedrin,* [complaining because they were treated badly] (Acts 5:41).

Q 10 Quote John 3:16 wrongly, to draw attention to the truth.

Q 11 Does the Bible teach that to whom much is given, 10% will be required (Luke 12:48)?

Some might not feel free to quote a Scripture wrongly. Or they might fear that their listeners would misunderstand. If this applies to you, ask a question about the verse you are quoting. For example, ask, "Does grace teach us to do whatever we please and still expect to reach heaven?" This will cause people to think about what Titus 2:12 says.

Oliver Wendell Holmes Jr. once said, "The saddest words of tongue or pen are these four words – 'It might have been!'"[1] Use quotations such as this one by Holmes. Do not neglect this important tool, or one day you will realize what "might have been."

Q 12 Give 2 quotes on the topic of truth. Feel free to quote Scriptures.

A pastor once heard a great statement. He turned to his friend and said, "Wow, I wish *I* had said that." "Don't worry, you will!" his friend replied.[2] He knew that it was wise to use quotations when preaching.

D. Statistics

Q 13 What are 2 ways to get statistics for a sermon?

*Statistics involve the use of numbers and research. You can find statistics in sources like books, newspapers, magazines, and the Internet. Some pastors have church members help them get statistics on certain topics. Statistics add authority and help prove your point. Consider the following statistics as illustrations:

- Three out of every four words of Jesus in the Gospel of Luke are part of an illustration.[3]
- Half of the people in the world have never heard the gospel.
- 50 percent of the people in Africa are under the age of sixteen.
- 44 percent of all professional people in Zambia are HIV positive; they will soon die of AIDS.
- Big cities, like Nairobi, are growing by more than 1,000 people per day!
- In some countries like Pakistan, 85 percent of the women cannot read.
- Half of Africa's children will never attend school.

Q 14 State a statistic related to the topic of evangelism.

- 160,000 believers will be martyred for Christ this year.[4]

Statistics are a powerful way of illustrating the truth.

Lesson 12 — Types of Illustrations: Comparisons, Events, Parables, Proverbs, Riddles, and Contrasts

Goal: *Illustrate a biblical truth with each of the following: a comparison, event, parable, proverb, riddle, and contrast.*

A. Comparisons

Comparisons have been used by preachers for centuries. To use a comparison, you first decide what truth you want to preach. Then ask yourself, "To what can I compare this truth?"

Jesus often preached about the unique qualities of Christians. He *compared* believers to:

- the salt of the earth,
- a candle giving light,
- a city set on a hill (Matt. 5:13-14).

Q 15 *Name 3 things to which Jesus compared believers.*

Train yourself to think like Jesus thought. Ask yourself, *"To what can I compare this...?"* (Matt. 11:16). Bless your church members by using comparisons with *every* principle or truth in your message.

Topic	Comparison
A. Sin	Sin is like leprosy—it is a disease that will eventually kill you.
B. Righteousness	Righteousness is like
C. Love	Love is like
D. The Bible	The Bible is like
E. Tithing	Tithing is like

Figure 5.4 Practice using comparisons to illustrate biblical truths.

Q 16 *Complete Figure 5.4. The first comparison has been done for you as an example.*

B. Events

Events make good comparisons. Past or current events make excellent illustrations. Both history books and today's newspapers are filled with events. You can speak of either amusing or serious events. Use events as illustrations in your sermons.

One day, Jesus preached on repentance. He mentioned a well-known event: a tower fell and killed 18 people (Luke 13:4). He used that event to make a comparison. One group of people was killed by a tower. Likewise, all who do not repent will perish. He used the event to emphasize His point: repent or perish!

Q 17 *Relate a recent, deadly accident to the theme of repentance.*

Another time the Lord preached on the Second Coming. In that one message, He referred to three events. He referred to the event of the Flood (Luke 17:27), the event of Sodom and Gomorrah's destruction (Luke 17:28-29), and the event of Lot's wife turning to a pillar of salt (Luke 17:32). Thus Jesus compared the former times to the future times by using events.

Q 18 *Which 3 events did Jesus use to illustrate the day of the Second Coming?*

Do not be blind and deaf to the events around you. Use them to illustrate your messages. Look for opportunities to hold people's attention by referring to the important talk of the day. Is a war being fought? Is there a famine? A sports match? An election? Relate such events to your messages.

Q 19 *Relate a robbery at night to a message on the Second Coming.*

C. Parables

*Parables are another form of comparisons. Jesus used 15 different parables to show what the kingdom of God was like.

Parables help people enjoy a message. Share one in your sermons to illustrate your content. Use the everyday parables around you, or create one of your own. The parables

Q 20 *Which 2 parables did Jesus use in Matthew 13 to illustrate the final judgment?*

of Jesus are listed in Appendix C. *"He did not say anything to them without using a parable"* (Mark 4:34).

Ezekiel often used parables to illustrate his messages. This great prophet told parables in Ezekiel 15, 16, 17, 19, and 23.

Q 21 *What parable did Jotham create or use to illustrate his message (Judges 9)?*

Q 22 *What parable did Ezekiel use to show that God does not want holy people to unite with sinners (Ezek. 23)?*

Q 23 *Which 2 parables did Jesus use to illustrate that we should persevere in prayer (Luke 11; 18)?*

Q 24 *Create a parable about a garden to show that perseverance pays.*

D. Proverbs

Q 25 *Explain the Swahili proverb "The thank-you of a donkey is a kick!"*

*Proverbs are often comparisons, using words like *better*, *like*, or *as*. The Bible is a great source of proverbs.

> *All at once he followed her **like** an ox going to the slaughter, **like** a deer stepping into a noose (Prov. 7:22).*

> ***Like** cold water to a weary soul is good news from a distant land (Prov. 25:25).*

> ***Like** a gold ring in a pig's snout is a beautiful woman who shows no discretion (Prov. 11:22).*

> ***As** a door turns on its hinges, so a sluggard turns on his bed (Prov. 26:14).*

> ***Better** to live in a desert **than** with a quarrelsome and ill-tempered wife (Prov. 21:19).*

> ***Better** a little with the fear of the LORD **than** great wealth with turmoil (Prov. 15:16).*

> ***Better** a meal of vegetables where there is love **than** a fattened calf with hatred (Prov. 15:17).*

> ***Better** a dry crust with peace and quiet **than** a house full of feasting, with strife (Prov. 17:1).*

Q 26 *What proverb did Jesus state about his hometown (Matt. 13:57)?*

> *It is **better** for him to say to you, "Come up here," **than** for him to humiliate you before a nobleman (Prov. 25:7; Luke 14:7-11).*

Proverbs are short paths to truth. You can choose proverbs from the Bible, from the local culture, or from history. A proverb displays a truth as a ring displays a precious stone. A wise preacher, like Jesus, will use proverbs often.

Q 27 *How can a pastor find local proverbs?*

Sometimes a pastor can buy a book of local proverbs at a bookstore. This is a wise way to spend a small amount of money. You will use a book of proverbs many times if you can find one. Also, those who are old and wise know many proverbs. Ask the elderly people in your church to write down some of the proverbs they know. Give them a small gift for helping you. Look at the 360 topics in Appendix D. Choose some of the topics and ask your elders to write proverbs related to these topics. Many elders have time to help you, and they will appreciate being asked. When you preach a message and use a proverb from an elder, be sure to mention the name of the elder who helped you. This will honor the elder and it will cause your people to listen well. Elderly believers are also a great source of stories!

We have taught you a valuable way to find proverbs and stories. Those who are *wise* will do it! As the proverb says, "A word to the wise is sufficient." Matthew 11:19 says: *"Wisdom is proved right by her actions."*

Biblical Truth	Proverb to Illustrate the Truth
A. Patience leads to success.	**A.**
B. Laziness is a path to poverty.	**B.**
C. Unity brings strength.	**C.**

Figure 5.5   Practice using proverbs to illustrate biblical truth.

E. Riddles

*Riddles, like proverbs, are delightful ways to present truth. A schoolteacher once told the following riddle: "He walked on earth; he talked on earth; he reproved man of sin; but he can never enter in."

A number of people visited the teacher to ask about the answer. The teacher even received two phone calls from pastors who wanted the solution! Their members were asking them for the answer!

Use an occasional riddle in your preaching. It will create an atmosphere of enthusiasm and excitement for the Bible. Riddles make good introductions to sermons.

F. Contrasts

Contrasts are the opposite of comparisons. If you are preaching about the north, a contrast is about the south. People see truth clearly when they see the opposite of truth. For example, the Good Samaritan is clearly a good neighbor in contrast to the priests and Levites (Luke 10).

Jesus was the master of using contrasts! Six times in the Sermon on the Mount, He contrasted His teachings with the teachings of the Pharisees. *"It has been said ... but I tell you"* (Matt. 5–7)!

Matthew	Contrast
5:13	
5:14-15	
5:17-18	
5:19	
5:20	
5:33	
5:38	
5:43	
5:47-48	
6:2-4	
6:19-20	
7:24-27	

Figure 5.6   A few of the contrasts in Matthew 5–7

Using contrasts is easy and effective. Develop the habit of illustrating truths by contrasting them with their opposites.

In this book, we will teach you to create sermons that contrast the problem with the solution. Then in the final chapter, we will teach you to use contrasts near the end of each message. Jesus used contrasts often.

Q 28 ✎ *Complete Figure 5.5.*

Q 29 ✎ *Who is it that can never enter in (Num. 22:21-30)?*

Q 30 ✐ *What riddle did Samson tell in Judges 14:14?*

Q 31 ✎ *State a riddle you know, and relate it to a sermon topic.*

Q 32 ✎ *Complete Figure 5.6 by identifying the contrasts.*

Q 33 ✐ *What contrast did Jesus make in Matthew 8:20?*

Q 34 ✐ *With which 2 things did Jesus contrast John the Baptist (Matt. 11:7-8)?*

Q 35 ✐ *What contrast did Jesus state between the evil of his day and future evil (Luke 23:31)?*

Q 36 ✐ *What contrasts did Jesus make in the 3 parables of Matthew 25?*

Q 37 ✐ *Contrast the difference in Peter before and after Pentecost (Acts 2).*

Lesson 13 Types of Illustrations: Drama, Visual Aids, Poems, and Songs

Goal: *Illustrate a biblical truth with each of the following: a drama, visual aid, poem, and song.*

A. Drama

Q 38 *Why do you think people become very excited about a short drama?*

*Drama can illustrate your messages well. Short skits can have lasting results because they involve the listeners. Asking one or more listeners to assist you increases everyone's attention. A drama causes as much excitement as a bird flying into a church! Every eye in the building will be looking at the drama, and every ear will listen. The interest a drama creates is amazing! The same people who fall asleep during a sermon will pay careful attention to a drama. Almost unbelievable!

Q 39 *Summarize the drama in John 3:3.*

A pastor once preached on John 3:3: *"I tell you the truth, no one can see the kingdom of God unless he is born again."* He was preaching outside in a crusade. The meeting was in a field. Church members had helped build a small platform for the preacher and singers. The pastor prepared a skit to illustrate John 3:3. It is a good example of the power of drama to support a sermon. There were only two characters in the drama: the king and a foreigner. The pastor played the role of the foreigner. He had chosen a friend to be the king.

This "king" sat on a chair, wrapped in a beautiful robe. He wore a crown and held a short rod. The king announced that he was the ruler of a great kingdom called Pururi. (*Pururi* means "forever" in Romanian.) The people in his kingdom received many blessings. However, the kingdom of Pururi had an important rule. The only way to enter that kingdom was to be born into it.

The pastor played the role of a foreigner who wanted to enter this kingdom. He told the listeners that he would try to enter the kingdom by another way—without obeying the rule. He would change his name to a name of the Pururi kingdom. So he went to the king and tried this.

The king refused this attempt to enter. He explained again that the only way to enter his kingdom was through birth.

Then the pastor applied the lesson. He turned to the listeners and preached for a few minutes. "God has said that a person must be born again to enter His kingdom. Yet many people try to enter His kingdom by changing their names at water baptism. They think taking a Christian name makes a person a Christian. The King of kings will not accept this."

Then the drama continued:

Pastor: "The king has said that I can enter his kingdom only by being born into it. But I will try another way. I will put on a beautiful robe like his. Perhaps the king will not recognize me." The preacher went to the king, but the king recognized him at once!

King: "You have returned! Why are you trying to enter by another way? I told you that the only way someone can enter my kingdom is to be born into it."

The pastor then turned and spoke again to the listeners. "Some people believe that they will enter heaven because they dress like Christians. Certainly it is good to dress in a way that pleases God. But we cannot enter the kingdom of heaven without being born again."

The drama continued. Next, the foreigner tried to enter Pururi by changing his language. The king refused this trick also.

The preacher turned and spoke to the congregation: "Many think that God will accept them because they use 'Christian' language." They pray over their food in the name of Jesus. They lead their children in family prayers. They say the Lord's Prayer and the grace of 2 Corinthians 13:14. They can even quote the Ten Commandments and Psalm 23. But they have not been born again. Learning religious language will not open the doors of God's kingdom."

Finally, the foreigner tried to bribe his way into Pururi. He came to the king with money in his hand. He said that he would do good deeds and attend kingdom meetings faithfully. All of this the king refused.

The preacher continued his message. "Likewise, God will refuse to receive those who try to bribe their way in through money and good works. To enter the kingdom of heaven, you must be born again."

The pastor then explained how to be born again. As a result, many people came forward to receive Jesus and be born from above, by the Holy Spirit.

Q 40 *Could the men, women, or youth of your church create a short drama on Colossians 3:5-14? Explain.*

Another pastor once asked some ladies to prepare a drama on Colossians 3:5-14. The theme of the drama was taking off the old clothes of sin, and putting on the new clothes of holiness. One of the women wore an old, dirty, ragged coat. She took it off, and another lady gave her a clean, white coat. As the clean coat was put on, everyone there understood the meaning.

Q 41 *Is a pastor who refuses to use dramas as dumb as a stump? Explain.*

B. Visual aids

*Visual aids are pictures, drawings, videos, or objects that people can see. A wise pastor will learn to use visual aids to make the truth clear.

Over and over, God used visual aids to teach the prophets. He showed Amos a basket of summer fruit (Amos 8:2). He showed Jeremiah a clay pot (Jer. 18:1-11). He told Ezekiel to use an iron pan (Ezek. 4:3). He also showed the apostle Peter a sheet with animals in it (Acts 10). In fact, all of the visions and dreams that God showed to people were visual aids! Why did God use so many visual aids? Because people understand better what they SEE!

The Son is like the Father. Jesus loved to use visual aids. All of his healings and miracles were visual aids for His messages. He knew that people needed more than words to see the truth clearly. He used things like water and bread to make the truth plain (John 4; 6). Jesus used a child as a visual help to teach His disciples. He placed the child among the disciples. The Lord used the child to illustrate the truth of humility (Matt. 18:1-4). This would be a good visual aid or drama to have some youth or adults act out before you preach on humility.

Q 42 *Why did God use so many visual aids to teach those he called?*

Another time Jesus used a fig tree as an object to make truth clear (Matt. 21:18-22). Again, He used a coin to teach (Matt. 22:18-22). And cleansing the temple made a truth very clear.

Q 43 *Name 3 visual aids that Jesus used.*

Teachers have found that after several days students only remember 10 percent of what they *hear*. They remember up to 30 percent of what they *see*. But students remember 50 percent of what they both *hear* and *see*. This is important for preachers to know. Adding visual aids to your sermons helps the listeners remember.[+]

Pastor, we have seen that in the past, the Father and the Son used visual aids to communicate truth. Do you think that God has changed His mind about using visual aids? He has not changed! He gave the prophets many ideas for visual aids. Likewise,

Q 44 *A pastor must pray for eyes to see illustrations for his message. Explain.*

+ Studies have shown that students remember up to 70 percent of what they *see, hear,* and *say.* You might at times have your listeners say aloud a main truth from your sermon.

He will show you things to help your people *see* the truth. But how well are you seeing the things that God is trying to show you?

Near the beginning of Jeremiah's ministry, God showed the young prophet an almond branch (Jer. 1:11). Then, the Lord asked, *"What do you see, Jeremiah?"* The prophet replied, *"I see the branch of an almond tree."* The Lord said to him, *"You have seen correctly"* (Jer. 1:11-12). Prophets were sometimes called *seers* because a big part of their calling was seeing what God put in front of them. Pastor, an important part of your ministry is learning to see correctly the illustrations that God puts in front of you.

Pray about the visual aids you can use in your sermons. Spend time in God's presence asking Him to help you with illustrations. God answers prayer! But you must have *eyes to see!* The things you can use to help people see the truth are all around you. You walk past visual aids every step of every day. Walk more slowly. Pray as you walk. Pray always. Ask the Spirit to give you *eyes to see*. And do not refuse to use simple things. The *Son of God* used a coin as a visual aid to teach adults. So nothing *you* can choose is too simple to use. Remember, your task is not to impress people with big words and long sentences. God has called you to change people's lives by making the truth clear! A key to being an effective preacher is learning to *see* correctly.

A pastor once preached on peace from Philippians 4:8. During his message, he held up a large picture for the people to see. It showed a mountain. Beside the mountain was a beautiful, clear lake. The water was calm and smooth. The lake was like a mirror laid below the mountain. The image of the mountain was seen in the calm waters of the lake.

Suppose the surface of the lake had turned rough and stormy. No one could have seen the reflection of the mountain on a stormy lake. The preacher then made his point. Only when we are calm and peaceful can we reflect the image of our heavenly Father. Truly, *one picture is worth a thousand words.*

Q 45 *What visual aid did God plan for us in James 5:14?*

Q 46 *What visual aids did God plan for us in 1 Corinthians 11:23-26?*

Q 47 *How is water baptism a visual aid to us (Rom. 6:4)?*

Q 48 *How did a pastor use a visual aid on Philippians 4:8? Explain.*

Figure 5.7   Still, peaceful waters reflect the beauty above them.

C. Poems

*Poems, whether well known or unknown, may help move a thought from the head to the heart. One of my favorite poems is on John 12:24-26. I do not know who wrote it.

"A grain of wheat to multiply,
Must fall into the ground and die;
Wherever golden fields you behold,
Waving to God their sheaves of gold;
Someone has suffered, bled and died,
Some soul has there been crucified."

Some pastors are able to buy a book of poems. Some write poems for their sermons. Others ask a member of their church to write a poem that will illustrate a truth in their sermon. For example, one pastor asked people to write poems about their mother. He enabled them to help him by planning ahead. He felt the Spirit leading him to preach about mothers on May 15. So on May 1, he asked the people to give him poems or stories about mothers by May 8. This gave them time to write the poems, and it gave him time to become familiar with them. He read some of the poems to the people. And some of the people read their own poems for all to hear. Thus the pastor illustrated his sermon. This method was good for two reasons. *First,* it helped him get good illustrations. *Second,* his church members were very excited about his sermon because they had a part in it. The people were so moved by the sermon that many cried. Several visitors accepted Jesus as Savior.

Q 49 *What biblical truth does the following poem illustrate?*

Q 50 *How did one pastor get poems to illustrate his sermon on mothers?*

Q 51 *Write a short poem praising a good mother or father.*

D. Songs

Songs are musical illustrations. We sing about the great truths and doctrines of our faith. What better way is there to illustrate a sermon on grace than to sing the hymn, *Amazing Grace?*

Write the title of a song that could be used to illustrate **each** of the following topics:

Q 52 *Complete Figure 5.8 by writing the title of a song that illustrates each biblical truth.*

Biblical Truth	Song to Illustrate a Truth
A. The blood of Jesus cleanses us from sin.	**A.**
B. God calls us to submit and surrender our lives to Him.	**B.**
C. We love God because He first loved us.	**C.**

Figure 5.8   Practice using songs to illustrate biblical truths.

Conclusion

We have surveyed 14 different kinds of illustrations. As you read your Bible daily, learn to recognize the various ways God's Word has been illuminated. Illustrations are as plentiful as flowers and birds. However, you see more of them when you are searching.

Figure 5.9   A preacher's outline is like an animal's skeleton: both should be covered!

A well-known preacher once said that he always smiles inside when he hears someone say, "Here's an outline that will really preach." Outlines themselves will not preach, and people are not interested in hearing outlines. People enjoy looking at animals, but are not interested in their skeletons. Likewise, the average listener is not interested in the skeleton or outline of a sermon. But most listeners are very interested in illustrations. Church members will remember the illustrations of a good sermon much longer than its skeleton or outline. It is true that a good preacher will organize his thoughts into an outline, but the outline should remain in the background. When illustrations are properly used with a good sermon outline, people are interested in the message and helped by it. So a preacher's outline should be covered with good illustrations, just as an animal's skeleton is covered with flesh and skin.

Look at all the examples we have given you in this chapter. Did you appreciate them? Or would you have liked it better if we omitted all the illustrations and just listed 14 types of illustrations? Likewise, your people will appreciate you more and tithe better if you use illustrations in your messages!

Q 53 *Do you think illustrations in a message affect tithing? Explain.*

Test Yourself: Circle the letter by the ***best*** completion to each question or statement.

1. The most important illustration is
a) history.
b) nature.
c) the pastor.
d) the church.

2. Why should a pastor use biblical stories?
a) Many people already know them.
b) They fill up a sermon.
c) They help people learn the Bible.
d) Charles H. Spurgeon used them often.

3. Should a preacher use statistics?
a) Yes, they make truth come alive.
b) Yes, everyone expects them.
c) No, they are not dependable.
d) No, they may upset people.

4. Parables and proverbs are types of
a) comparisons.
b) riddles.
c) psalms.
d) dramas.

5. How should a pastor relate to current events?
a) Ignore them and study the Bible.
b) Use them to emphasize a truth.
c) Relate each one to Revelation.
d) Write his outline around them.

6. Jesus told 15 parables about
a) the lost sheep.
b) the Resurrection.
c) the Pharisees.
d) the kingdom of God.

7. "Wisdom is proved right by her actions" is a
a) riddle.
b) proverb.
c) parable.
d) contrast.

8. Examples of visual aids include
a) stories.
b) pictures.
c) statistics.
d) songs.

9. A way to involve people is to use a
a) drama.
b) quote.
c) statistic.
d) poem.

10. Illustrations are like
a) a tail on a monkey.
b) skin on an animalg.
c) claws on an eagle.
d) ears on a rabbit.

Essay Test Topics Write 50-100 words on each of these goals that you studied in this chapter.

Types of Illustrations: Stories, Testimonies, Quotes, and Statistics

Goal: *Use each of the following to illustrate a biblical truth: a story, testimony, quote, and statistic.*

Types of Illustrations: Comparisons, Events, Parables, Proverbs, Riddles, and Contrasts

Goal: *Illustrate a biblical truth with each of the following: a comparison, event, parable, proverb, riddle, and contrast.*

Types of Illustrations: Drama, Visual Aids, Poems, and Songs

Goal: *Illustrate a biblical truth with each of the following: a drama, visual aid, poem, and song.*

Chapter 6:
Why Use Illustrations?

Introduction

Why is a sermon better compared to a meal than a house?

Some say that illustrations should be few. They allow illustrations, but object to using many of them. We stated earlier that illustrations are like windows. They allow light to enter. Some argue that as a house has few windows, a sermon should have few illustrations! Thus, they compare a sermon to a house.

Pressing the comparison beyond all limits, they say that too many windows weaken a house. They add that thieves come in the windows. Others say that no one wants to live in a glass house. What shall we say to those who compare a sermon to a house?

Although an illustration is like a window, a sermon is not like a house! People do not come to church to watch the pastor build a house. Nor do they expect a new house each church service. Illustrations are like windows, but sermons are not like houses.

Scripture compares preaching and teaching to a meal, not a house. People come to church with spiritual appetites. They hunger and thirst for righteousness (Matt. 5:6). They want to

Figure 6.1   A sermon is like a meal.

be fed with the pure spiritual *milk* of the Word (1 Pet. 2:2). They want solid food—spiritual *meat* (Heb. 5:14). So Jesus emphasized, *"Feed my sheep"* (John 21:15-17).

After a sermon, when members have eaten the *bread* of life, they feel satisfied. The spiritual food they get from the sermon gives them strength to face life's problems. Truly, a good sermon is like a meal, not a house!

Good illustrations are an important part of the spiritual meal that we call a sermon. In this chapter, we will give you 19 reasons for using illustrations. One of these reasons is that illustrations feed people spiritually.

Lessons:

Reasons 1–6 for Using Illustrations
Goal: *Explain how illustrations clarify, persuade, inspire, add variety, shorten, and make preaching easier.*

Reasons 7–12 for Using Illustrations
Goal: *Describe how illustrations repeat, apply, transition, are appreciated, feed, and connect.*

Reasons 13–17 for Using Illustrations
Goal: *Summarize how illustrations are indirect, relax the listeners, help memory, touch the heart, and convert people.*

Reasons 18–19 for Using Illustrations
Goal: *Analyze the use of illustrations in the Bible and the ministry of Jesus.*

Reasons 1–6 for Using Illustrations

Goal: *Explain how illustrations clarify, persuade, inspire, add variety, shorten, and make preaching easier.*

In this chapter, we will examine 19 reasons why every pastor should use illustrations.

A. Illustrations *clarify.

Illustrations help us explain clearly what we mean. We have nothing to hide as we preach! So we have no desire to be unclear.

A man once wrote a poem that was difficult and confusing. Later, he promised that he would hang himself on a tree if anyone could interpret the poem. We are thankful that no one tried. But some pastors might make the same offer about their sermons! Some pastors are like the man known as the Dark Doctor. His sermons were beyond understanding. Why? Because of the hard words he used. "Lord, may any education that we get help us to speak more plainly."

Sometimes a pastor cannot give an example of what he is trying to say. This is because the point is not clear enough in his own mind. Most listeners are not trained in theology. But you can take steps to be sure that people understand what you are preaching. How? Give them an illustration or two. If you cannot illustrate a point you want to make, put it back in the garden! A truth is not ripe enough to preach until it is easy for you to illustrate!

Q 1 ⟋ *Explain this statement: If a pastor cannot illustrate a truth, he is not ready to preach it.*

One church member had lived a very sinful life. He was having trouble believing that God could completely forgive his sins. The pastor wrote a list of many sins on a blackboard. Then he erased all of them. Not even a trace of one word remained. This illustration helped the sinner understand that God can forgive our sins and take them away forever.

Q 2 ⟋ *How did one pastor make his point about forgiveness clear?*

Several church members were confused about the Trinity. They could not understand why we say the Father, Son, and Holy Spirit are three separate persons, but only one God. Then the pastor gave two illustrations to help them. *First,* he held a mango in his hand. He explained that this fruit had three parts: the outer peel, the part we eat, and the seed. One mango with three parts. Likewise, there is one God with three persons. *Second,* the pastor referred to marriage as an example of the Trinity. As a husband and wife become one flesh, God is one, completely united. Use illustrations because they clarify.

B. Illustrations persuade.

Illustrations increase the pastor's ability to persuade people. A good example can do more than just make a point clear. Some people are, at first, unwilling to accept the truth. Yet a powerful illustration can cause them to accept it. Through illustrations, we present truth in real-life situations. This is hard for listeners to resist.

One pastor argued that illustrations should be few. He said the listener gets the thought after only one illustration. Some make this mistake because they do not realize that the heart is harder to reach than the head. The question is not, "Did the listener get the thought?" The question is, "Did the thought get the listener?" That is, did it get into him deep enough to touch his heart? A single illustration may not be enough to move a listener to action. If you use few illustrations, you will influence few people.

Some pastors gathered for their yearly meeting in East Africa. They needed money to build a new national office. The pastors agreed that all of the members of their churches should each give five shillings on Easter Sunday. But the pastors began arguing about

Q 3 *What did the illustration about the wild pigs persuade a group of pastors to do?*

how the building should look. One elderly pastor advised them that it would be better to collect the money first. He said they could decide the exact style of the building later. To persuade pastors, he told the following story:

Figure 6.2   Wild pigs

Some farmers discovered that wild pigs were eating their maize at night. Each farmer agreed to bring a spear to the field on a certain night. They would surround the pigs, kill them, and have a great feast. That night, the plan was going well. Slowly and silently the farmers closed in on the pigs. They would taste so good. Then the farmers foolishly began to argue about who would get the best ones. While the men were arguing, the pigs ran away. No one got anything!

All of the pastors at the meeting clapped when the story was finished. They agreed to stop arguing about the design of the building. Instead, they would first collect the money. That wise elder pastor used an example that convinced others. In the same way, pastors who illustrate their messages will persuade many people to follow God's ways.

C. Illustrations inspire.

Q 4 *Why do pastors need fresh illustrations?*

Q 5 *Explain this proverb: "That knife is as dull as a sermon!"*

Pastors should use illustrations because they make sermons come alive with emotions. The Word of God is alive (Heb. 4:12). But too often, pastors kill the Word of Life by preaching dead sermons. One proverb says, "That knife is as dull as a sermon!" How can pastors prevent a sermon from being dull and dead? We need fresh new examples because the gospel is an old story.

Imagine preaching about Christ's victory over death on Easter. An illustration, like the one that follows, can make this old truth come alive.

A woman stands in a busy shop. Patiently she waits her turn to buy bread and sugar. On the wall behind the counter, she sees a picture of the president. He lives in that same city. As she waits, her eyes look up at the picture from time to time. She thinks of the wonderful way her president has led her nation in freedom and progress. What a blessing it is to have a leader like this, she thinks. Suddenly, she hears people behind her talking with excitement. She turns to see a line of cars coming down the street. The president was passing by. As the cars pass, she sees him for just a moment—face to face! What a difference between the picture and the person!

Q 6 *Give an inspiring illustration of this truth, Jesus saves.*

Something more wonderful than this woman's experience happens in church. People go there to listen to the reading of a Book. They sing songs about a Savior who has led people into greater freedom than any president can offer. They suddenly become aware of the presence of Jesus Himself. He is risen and alive among His people. Mary met Jesus beside the empty tomb. And in church, we do more than think about Jesus. We experience His living presence! Illustrations like this one can inspire people to rejoice in old truths.

D. Illustrations add variety.

A sermon without variety is as tiring as a road without a bend. Variety happens as you change your posture, voice pitch, or volume. You may also use gestures to add variety. But you should never forget that illustrations also add variety.

People do not like to eat just one kind of food at a meal. They like some meat, some vegetables, and coffee or tea. Likewise, they do not like a spiritual meal that lacks variety.

Q 7 *To what can we compare a road without a bend?*

People do not like to sing only one song when they go to church. They like a variety of songs. Likewise, they do not just want to hear what you think. Mix in some illustrations. People like variety.

People enjoy looking at color photos more than at black and white ones. Use some color in your sermons. Add illustrations, and you will add variety.

E. Illustrations shorten.

Illustrations should also be used because they can shorten sermons. Some sermons fail to create change because they are too long. Long sermons lose their force, grip, or impact on the listeners. People may be ready to make a decision while listening to a message. But, if the sermon is too long, their hearts begin to cool off again. Then, their eagerness to decide for Christ is lost.

Q 8 *Which sermons seem the longest?*

Some say that a sermon with illustrations is too long. It is true that some sermons are too long. But the sermons that seem the longest are the ones with the fewest illustrations! A sermon without illustrations is neither worth preaching nor worth listening to. Read the 19 reasons for illustrations given in this chapter. Note that a sermon without illustrations will be lacking in these 19 areas! All sermons without illustrations are too long. What makes a sermon too long is leaving out the illustrations!

An illustration is like lightning. It can light up an area in only a few seconds. In contrast, an explanation might require several minutes. Illustrations shorten. If you use several illustrations, you will not need to preach all night. And the Eutychus in your church will not fall asleep (See Acts 20:9)! Unskilled preachers state the same truths over and over. Good preachers state a truth and then illustrate it.

Consider how quickly each of the following illustrations reveals a truth:
- Remember Lot's wife (Luke 17:32).
- As it was in the days of Noah, it will be when Christ returns (Matt. 24:37).
- Sinners go back to their old ways like a dog returns to its vomit, or a pig to the mud (2 Pet. 2:22).
- Babylon will fall as quickly as a stone sinks into the sea (Rev. 18:21).
- Be as shrewd as snakes and as innocent as doves (Matt. 10:16).

F. Illustrations make preaching easier.

The hardest message you will ever preach is the one without illustrations. But the easiest message you will ever preach is the one with several illustrations. Illustrations allow a pastor to look away from his notes and into the eyes of his people. As he tells an illustration, he speaks from his heart. This enables him to depend more on the Holy Spirit.

Consider Luke 15. In this chapter, Jesus emphasized one truth: **There is rejoicing in heaven when one sinner repents.** This would make a great theme for any pastor to preach. And the message would be easy because Jesus gave us three illustrations on one truth!

Pastor, you do not need more than a few principles or truths in a sermon. Then, you need two or three good illustrations for each truth. This will make your message easy for you to remember and easy to preach. If you like this idea, you are studying the right book. In this course we will teach you how to plan messages like this. In fact, you may have already learned more than you realize.

Reasons 7–12 for Using Illustrations

Lesson 15

Goal: *Describe how illustrations repeat, apply, transition, are appreciated, feed, and connect.*

A. Illustrations repeat a truth.

Q 9 *Repeating a truth is like _____.*

Repeating a truth is like re-drawing a line in the sand with a stick. Each time you go back over the line, the stick goes in deeper. Repeating a truth is like hitting a nail with a hammer. The nail goes in deeper each time the hammer hits it.

Pastors want truth to go deep into the hearts of their listeners. Each time a pastor repeats a truth, it goes in deeper. Illustrations are a good way to repeat and reinforce what you have just said. The following story illustrates this principle.

A politician was traveling around making speeches. His young son was with him. In every speech, the politician kept repeating the same things. Finally, the son asked him whether he had run out of new ideas to talk about.

Q 10 *Why did the politician repeat statements?*

"No, my son," said the father. "Repetition is necessary. The first time I make a statement, only 1/5 of the listeners get the meaning. The next time I say it, 1/4 understand. The third time, 1/2. The fourth time, 3/4. By the time I have made a statement five times, everyone understands and remembers it!"

Q 11 *How can a pastor repeat his main thoughts without tiring his listeners?*

Listeners will profit if pastors repeat their main truths. But, pastors must do this without tiring the listeners. Illustrations repeat a truth in a new way. This repetition strengthens the truth and causes it to go deeper into the listeners.

A pastor was preaching about Jesus being a High Priest who feels what we feel. He gave several illustrations of this important truth. This pastor said that Jesus was a carpenter who worked hard. Jesus walked long distances and got tired during His ministry. He worked long hours and needed sleep. Our Lord was rejected by His own people. He was tempted by the devil. And Jesus felt great pain and suffering on the cross. The pastor thus helped his listeners fully understand that Jesus feels what we feel.

Q 12 *Why did Jesus repeat the same truth over and over?*

Jesus shows us the value of repeating a truth. In the Gospels, notice how many times He repeated the truth about His suffering and death.

From that time on Jesus began to explain to his disciples that he must go to Jerusalem and suffer many things at the hands of the elders, chief priests and teachers of the law, and that he must be killed and on the third day be raised to life (Matt. 16:21).

9As they were coming down the mountain, Jesus instructed them, "Don't tell anyone what you have seen, until the Son of Man has been raised from the dead." 10The disciples asked him, "Why then do the teachers of the law say that Elijah must come first?" 11Jesus replied, "To be sure, Elijah comes and will restore all things. 12But I tell you, Elijah has already come, and they did not recognize him, but have done to him everything they wished. In the same way the Son of Man is going to suffer at their hands" (Matt. 17:9-12).

At the bottom of the mountain, Jesus cast a demon out of a boy. Then He repeated the big truth.

43And they were all amazed at the greatness of God. While everyone was marveling at all that Jesus did, he said to his disciples, 44"Listen carefully to what I am about to tell you: The Son of Man is going to be betrayed into the hands of men" (Luke 9:43-44).

Q 13 *Give 3 illustrations to show that heaven rejoices when one sinner repents.*

After Jesus and the disciples moved on, He repeated the truth again.

Q 14 *Give 2 illustrations to show that gaining the kingdom is worth all we have (Matt. 13:44-45).*

When they came together in Galilee, he said to them, "The Son of Man is going to be betrayed into the hands of men" (Matt. 17:22).

Do you get the point? The more important a truth is, the more times a pastor must repeat it.

B. Illustrations apply a truth.

Illustrations bring heavenly truths down to earth. Sermons can contain too much theory or heavy doctrine. Sermons can talk too much about ideas and not enough about real life. Illustrations are the bridge between the Bible and people today. Illustrations bring the truth from the past to the present.

Pastors must spend time studying the Word. But too much studying can be dangerous. Many hours of study can lead pastors to enjoy reasoning and logic more than common people enjoy it. The danger is that the pastor will forget that many people are not used to much reading. Their minds are not used to the discipline of much study. So they will become mentally tired of one truth after another. "Too many cooks spoil a meal." And too many ideas spoil a sermon. So pastors should use only two or three big truths in a sermon. Then, they should use several illustrations to apply truth to the paths we walk on. Common people will not become weary of illustrations about real life.

Consider how Jesus illustrated a truth three ways. Truth: Christians should live a life different than sinners (Matt 5:13-16).

Illustration 1:

We are the salt of the earth.

Illustration 2:

A city set on a hill cannot be hidden.

Illustration 3:

We are the light of the world.

There is a wonderful difference between *illustrating* a truth and merely *stating* it. Illustrations bring truth down from the heavens to the places where our feet touch the earth.

C. Illustrations serve as transitions.

A transition is a change from one place to another, or from one truth to another. Illustrations make good transitions from one main truth to another. Some pastors move roughly from point to point like a car racing over railroad tracks or speed bumps! Illustrations provide a smooth way to pass from one thought to the next. Also, illustrations are like signs. They warn listeners that the "road" of the sermon is going to make a turn. As an illustration ends, the listeners will respond. They may laugh, smile, nod their heads, say "amen" or "praise the Lord." This becomes a natural time to change from one truth to another.

Later in this course we will give you practice in using illustrations to move from point to point.

D. Illustrations are appreciated.

People enjoy illustrations! Those who are young, old, rich, poor, educated, or uneducated *all* enjoy hearing truth illustrated. All of your listeners will pay attention when you use illustrations.

Q 15 *Give 3 illustrations to show that the Jews rejected Jesus, but the Gentiles accepted Him (Matt. 21–22).*

Q 16 *Give 3 biblical stories that show that disobedience brings loss.*

Q 17 *What mental danger must a pastor guard against?*

Q 18 *One pastor spoke only 20 minutes before his listeners began to sleep. Another pastor spoke an hour and the people wanted him to continue. What do you think might have made the difference?*

Q 19 *State 3 illustrations of this truth: "Christians should bear fruit."*

Q 20 *What are transitions?*

Q 21 *How did Jesus transition from teaching to closing the Sermon on the Mount (Matt. 5–7)?*

Q 22 ✎ *Which did you appreciate more: a) the statement: "Some students are very committed to studying," or b) the illustration that followed this statement? Explain.*

See whether you appreciate the illustration that follows on the topic: **Study to present yourself to God as one approved** (2 Tim. 2:15).

Some students are very committed to studying. A young missionary in Nigeria started a Bible school. He used a room in his house as a library for students to study in. The house had no electricity, so the missionary used a diesel generator to provide power for lights. Each evening he turned on the generator so the students could study. He usually turned the generator off at 9:30 p.m. Students were to be in bed by 10:00 p.m. according to the school's rule.

One night the missionary forgot about the generator. He did not go to turn it off until 10:30 p.m. He found that the students were still studying! The missionary became angry because they had broken the rule. They should have been in their beds. Then one student explained, "As long as there is light, we will study." The missionary was thankful for their desire to learn, and felt ashamed of his anger.

E. Illustrations feed.

The 11th reason you should use illustrations is that they feed people spiritually. In the Introduction of this chapter, we stated that a sermon is like a meal. Preparing a good sermon is a lot like preparing a good meal.

To have a meal, a cook must plan it, prepare it, and serve it. Cooks may enjoy what they do, but they work hard. They select raw food and cook it. Preparing the raw food to eat requires pots, pans, plates, bowls, cups, and utensils.

Likewise, a pastor enjoys his work, but he must work hard. The Spirit guides him to the raw truths of Scripture. Then, he must prepare these truths for his people to eat spiritually. As a cook needs dishes, a pastor needs an outline. An outline has three parts. It has Roman numbers or numerals (I, II, III, IV, and V); capital letters (A, B, and C); and small numbers (1, 2, 3, and 4). As a cook uses dishes over and over, a pastor uses the parts of an outline over and over. A cook organizes and serves his food using dishes. A pastor organizes and serves his food using an outline.

Q 23 ✎ *Explain the author's proverb: "A potato is a potato whether it is raw or cooked."*

This brings us to an important question. How does a pastor *cook* spiritual food? Many have misunderstood the food relationship between statements of truth and illustrations. A statement of truth, without an illustration, is like raw food—hard to eat. A potato is a potato, whether it is raw or cooked. A potato is a potato whether it is sliced, mashed, boiled, baked, roasted, or fried. But hungry people seldom eat a potato until after it has been cooked in one way or another. Few eaters like raw potatoes!

Figure 6.3   Few people like to eat raw potatoes.

Likewise, truth is truth whether it is in the form of a plain sentence, a story, a proverb, a parable, or any other illustration. Do not think of truth and illustrations as opposed to each other. They are of the same essence and nature.

It is normal to cook raw food before you serve it. Likewise, it is normal to cook raw truth into illustrations if you want people to eat! Too many pastors present many raw truths, but few illustrations. After 10 minutes of serving raw truth, they offer the starved listeners something they can eat!

Q 24 ✎ *Tell a Bible story to a child and notice how it brings the two of you together.*

Q 25 ✎ *Have people in a class each tell the story of their conversion. Note how the stories draw the group together.*

Do not be deceived, my beloved brothers and sisters. The common person chokes on dry truth as much as he would choke on dry flour. Would you prefer eating a live chicken or a baked one? Cook something! If you can't spread a banquet, at least offer a basic meal. Serve truth in the form of good illustrations. People will like your spiritual cooking. And you will have healthy, well-fed Christians. Illustrations feed people spiritually!

Topic	Comparison
A. Cook	A. Pastor
B. Dishes	B.
C. Raw food	C.
D. Cooked food	D.

Figure 6.4   A sermon is like a spiritual meal.

Q 26 ✎ *Complete Figure 6.4*

Figure 6.5   Chicken is easier to eat after it is cooked!

F. Illustrations connect.

An illustration brings the pastor and the listener closer together. They connect while sharing the illustration. We speak of this connection as a "bridge."

You cannot talk to someone on the telephone until he or she picks up the receiver. Likewise, an illustration allows you to "get through" to your listeners. They will connect with you while listening to a story, a comparison, a testimony, and such. An illustration brings the speaker and the listeners together, as they share a common story or event of life. They think less about each other and more about the illustration. In the process they move toward each other.

Lesson 16

Reasons 13–17 for Using Illustrations

Goal: *Summarize how illustrations are indirect, relax, help memory, touch the heart, and convert people.*

A. Illustrations are *indirect.

Illustrations are windows to the mind and soul. They are so useful because they make their points indirectly. People defend and justify themselves mentally if they think a pastor is preaching at them personally. But illustrations can carry truth to a person's heart without creating resistance.

**Figure 6.6
Nathan told David a story about a man with a little lamb.**

Nathan told King David a story about a man with a little lamb. The story went straight into David's heart (2 Sam. 12:1-6). The king was affected by Nathan's message before he realized that the prophet was on a mission! Illustrations often hide the truth until it is too late for listeners to guard themselves against it.

B. Illustrations relax and refresh.

Another reason to use illustrations is that they allow your people to rest mentally. A person taking a walk enjoys stopping to rest in the shade to have a drink of cool water. Likewise, those listening to a sermon like to rest briefly at times. Good illustrations relieve the strain of hard thinking and careful listening. Present a serious truth, then let your listeners relax into "easy understanding" by sharing an illustration.

Q 27 ✎ *What is the value of making a point indirectly?*

Q 28 ⤢ *What story of Nathan got past the gate of David's heart?*

Q 29 ⤢ *What story did Jesus tell to Simon the Pharisee to make an indirect point (Luke 7:36-48)?*

Q 30 ✎ *How is listening to an illustration like drinking a glass of cool water in the shade?*

Telling an illustration is like opening a window on a hot day and letting a fresh, cool breeze blow in. Notice the change that comes over your people as you tell an illustration. Some of them will look so happy that you might think they had just won a prize! Illustrations relax and refresh people's minds and emotions.

Suppose you are preaching against criticism. You want to convince people to use love, not criticism, to change someone. This truth is easy to apply with the illustration that follows:

The wind and the sun once had a contest. They saw a man walking down the road wearing a coat. They wanted to see which of them could make the man take off his coat. The wind tried first. It blew and blew, trying to blow the coat off of the man. But the harder the wind blew, the more tightly the man held onto his coat. Finally, the wind gave up. Then the sun tried. It shined its warm light on the man for a few minutes. The man removed his coat with no resistance. In the same way, people hold more tightly to their faults if we "blow" our criticism against them. But let them feel the warmth of our love, and they will be more willing to change. Learn a lesson from the wind and the sun.

Listening to a pastor tell you what he thinks is like standing on a rock in the sun. But listening to a pastor tell you an illustration is like drinking a cool soda in the shade!

C. Illustrations help memory.

Nails in a wall keep pictures from falling. In the same way, illustrations keep the truth from being lost. They hold thoughts firmly in the mind. Illustrations will shorten your sermons, but they will also help your people remember them longer.

D. Illustrations touch the heart.

One of the big reasons for using illustrations is that they touch the heart and emotions. Tell people that God loves them even though they do not deserve that love. They may nod their heads in agreement. But a more powerful way to communicate this truth is to illustrate it with Hosea and Gomer.

Hosea and his wife Gomer are illustrations of God's undeserved love (Hos. 1–3). Gomer was a prostitute. Hosea loved her and gave her food and clothing. Yet she was not faithful to him. She left him and later became a slave. But her husband *bought* her back! Hosea pleaded with her to stop running to other men. He loved her when she did not deserve it. This is the way God loved Israel, and the way He loves us. We have sinned, but He still loves us. The illustration of Gomer touches our hearts. This is one of the reasons God used the illustration.

E. Illustrations help convert sinners.

Pastors should use illustrations because they convert sinners. Many can testify that the Holy Spirit used an anointed illustration to turn them from hell toward heaven. The following story is one man's testimony.

"Sixty years ago, I was enjoying a holiday in a small village. I attended a service at the local church to hear the children sing. The pastor's text was the cry of Christ on the cross: *'My God, my God, why have you forsaken me?'* (Mark 15:34). The first part of his sermon did not touch me. But then the pastor gave an illustration that changed my life.

"He described a little girl whose mother had died. She was left in her father's care. The father and daughter meant everything to each other. Then the little girl became sick from a poisoned foot. A very good doctor examined her. The poison in her foot was spreading. For her to live, he must cut off part of her leg.

Q 31 *What truth does the story of the wind and sun illustrate?*

Q 32 *Illustrate the truth: "The Lord disciplines those he loves" (Heb. 12:6).*

Q 33 *How is an illustration like a nail in the wall?*

Q 34 *What do you remember from the last 2 sermons you heard, the explanations or the illustrations? Explain.*

Q 35 *True or False: Statements of truth touch the mind, but illustrations touch the heart. Explain.*

Q 36 *Illustrate this truth: A bribe destroys justice.*

Q 37 *Summarize the illustration about Mark 15:34.*

"The doctor decided that the father should tell the child. In his sorrow, the father accepted this painful task. When he told his daughter, she made a strange request. 'Daddy, they may cut off my leg if you will make me one promise.' 'And what is that?' asked the father. 'Promise to put your arms around me during the surgery and look straight into my eyes,' she replied. 'Then I will agree.'

"Who can know the sadness in this father's heart as he considered his daughter's hard request? Yet he knew he must do as she asked. Otherwise, he would lose his beloved child to the poison attacking her. 'My darling, I promise,' he whispered.

"The day came for the surgery. The father kept his promise. The doctor's task was hard, because it was before the days of painless operations. The father saw the suffering that grew in his child's face. Finally, he could bear it no more. He was forced to turn his face away. Immediately his daughter cried out, 'Father, Father, you promised to look at me!' With that cry on her lips, she died.

"I do not need to describe how the pastor applied the story to the cry of Christ on the cross. That simple story revealed to me the love of God the Father toward sinners. My life changed completely. I later became a preacher of the redeeming love of God in Christ. I have never been sorry for that decision. Sixty years have passed since that day. I am so thankful that the pastor used that illustration."[1]

Good illustrations often live longer than the pastors who tell them! A two-minute illustration can make an eternal difference!

Q 38 *Give an example of how a short illustration made an eternal difference.*

Lesson 17

Reasons 18 and 19 for Using Illustrations
Goal: *Analyze the use of illustrations in the Bible and the ministry of Jesus.*

A. God used many illustrations in the Bible.

God is the author of the Bible. He put hundreds of illustrations in His book. The Holy Spirit inspired those who wrote for God to use such illustrations as stories, comparisons, contrasts, songs, psalms, proverbs, parables, miracles, healings, visions, events, and others. In the Appendices of this book are several lists of illustrations.[2] These lists include: A) 150 Famous Bible Stories, B) The Miracles of Jesus, C) The Parables of Jesus, and D) 360 Topics. The point is clear. No one is wiser than our heavenly Father. And He, in sharing the truth with us, chose to use many illustrations. So consider one question as you decide whether or not you will use many illustrations. That question is, "Will you follow God's example, and use many illustrations?" Let us preach the gospel, which is itself a story, using sermons filled with good illustrations. And let our illustrations be like arrows that go straight to the center of our targets.

Q 39 *Why do you think God used so many illustrations in His book?*

Q 40 *Will you follow God's example and use many illustrations if we teach you how? Explain.*

B. Jesus always used many illustrations to preach.

Jesus never preached or taught without using illustrations. Look at the Gospel of Luke. More than half of it is made up of stories! And if we study the words of Jesus Himself in Luke, we find that 75 percent of His words are part of illustrations. Consider that! Three out of every four words of Christ in Luke's Gospel are part of an illustration![3]

Jesus could have communicated through any method. But He chose the best method: using illustrations. He used the common things of life to explain great truths and principles. He spoke of:

Wolves, foxes, dogs, and pigs;
Sheep, goats, oxen, and camels;
Eagles, sparrows, doves, and chickens;
The sun, moon, stars, and sky;
The earth, mountains, sea, and wind;

Q 41 *In Luke's Gospel, what percent (%) of Christ's words are part of illustrations?*

Q 42 *How many common things are in the list of illustrations that Jesus used?*

Q 43 ⤸ *Can you think of any common thing Jesus used as an illustration that is not in the list?*

Soil, seed, trees, and flowers;
Rocks, grass, thorns, and vines;
Candles, beds, rooms, and roofs,
Yeast, wheat, money, and pearls;
Fish, eggs, wine, and bread;
Cups, saucers, salt, and flour;
Barns, houses, foundations, and doors;
Nets, plows, mills, and yokes;
Weddings, banquets, markets, and tombs;
Winter, rain, lightning, and clouds;
Morning, evening, daylight, and dark;
Managers, beggars, rich men, and tax collectors;
Fathers, mothers, children, and widows;
Kings, judges, masters, and servants;
Shepherds, thieves, builders, and brides;
Eyes, ears, mouths, and hearts.

This list could go on for many pages!

In other words, Jesus talked about the events and things common to life. He loved to dress truth in plain clothes. His teaching and preaching were filled with illustrations from life. Let us, His disciples, follow in His footsteps. Let the Holy Spirit fill your mind with illustrations from life about God's truth![4]

C. Jesus liked to state a truth and then illustrate it.

We have given you 18 reasons to use illustrations! Hopefully, the Holy Spirit will use these reasons to convince you that wise pastors use many illustrations in their messages.

Before leaving this unit on illustrations, let us note one great truth. This truth will serve as a transition from this unit to the next one. The great truth is: Jesus was fond of stating a truth, then illustrating it. Here are four examples of times when Jesus mixed illustrations with raw truth.

Q 44 ⤴ *In which 5 ways did Jesus illustrate that we should guard against the wrong attitude about things that we own?*

First example: A man asked Jesus to help settle a quarrel over the family inheritance (Luke 12:13). The Great Teacher refused, but stated a raw truth: *"Watch out! Be on your guard against all kinds of greed; a man's life does not consist in the abundance of his possessions"* (Luke 12:15).

Jesus stated a truth in only one sentence. Then He illustrated the truth with the parable of the rich fool. Note that the parable was at least seven times longer than the truth he was illustrating!

Immediately after the parable of the rich fool, Jesus illustrated the same truth FIVE MORE TIMES! We may outline the truth and its six illustrations as follows:

Truth: **Guard against greed, because life is not measured by possessions** (Luke 12:15).

- Illustration 1: Parable of the rich fool (Luke 12:16-21)
- Illustration 2: Comparison to the ravens (Luke 12:22-26)
- Illustration 3: Comparison to the lilies (Luke 12:27-28)
- Illustration 4: Contrast to the pagans (Luke 12:29-31)
- Illustration 5: Comparison to a flock of sheep (Luke 12:32)
- Illustration 6: Proverb of the treasure and the heart (Luke 12:33-34)

Notice that the word *therefore* in Luke 12:22 connects the illustrations that follow to the truth stated before in Luke 12:15. As the 6th illustration, Jesus summarized the truth as a proverb: *"For where your treasure is, there will your heart be also"* (Luke 12:34). Notice how the *six* illustrations make the *one* truth come alive. Amazing!

Second example: Jesus stated a truth and then illustrating it in Luke 13:1-9. People reported to the Master that Pilate had slaughtered some Galileans, mixing their blood with their sacrifices. Jesus took their illustration and linked it to a principle or truth: *"Unless you repent, you too will all perish"* (Luke 13:3).

Next, He illustrated the truth again with the story of the tower that killed 18 people when it fell. After the story He stated the truth again: *"Unless you repent, you too will all perish"* (Luke 13:5).

To illustrate the truth a third time, He told the parable of the fruitless fig tree (Luke 13:6-9). Notice the final line of the illustration of the fig tree. If it did not change, it would perish!

The best preachers spend much more time telling illustrations than they do stating and restating raw truths.

Q 45 ⚒ *How do the best pastors spend most of their time in the pulpit?*

Q 46 ⚒ *How many examples did Jesus use to illustrate the cost of following Him?*

Third example: We are doing our best to teach you to state a truth or principle, and then illustrate it. Sometimes, as in Luke 14:26, Jesus started with an illustration and stated the principle *after* it. Then He told another illustration of the principle. In this third example, the principle is: **You cannot be my disciple without putting Me first, above everything**. This principle is stated three times (Luke 14:26, 27, 33). Notice that the principle is mixed with five illustrations.

- Illustration 1: A disciple's love for Christ must be greater than his love for father, mother, wife, children, brothers, and sisters (Luke 14:26).
- Illustration 2: A disciple must be willing to die on a cross for Christ (Luke 14:27).
- Illustration 3: As in building a tower, a person should count the cost before choosing to be a disciple of Christ (Luke 14:28-30).
- Illustration 4: As a lesser king and army submit to a greater king, a disciple must submit all to Jesus (Luke 14:31-32).
- Illustration 5: A disciple who does not put Jesus above all is as useless as salt without taste (Luke 14:34-35).

Note that Jesus used five illustrations on the theme of being a disciple! When Jesus finished hammering a nail, it stayed in the wall!

Fourth example: This also shows that Jesus loved to state a truth—and then illustrate it several times. The truth or principle is that **heaven rejoices when one sinner repents** (Luke 15:7, 10, 32). Jesus used three parables to illustrate this one truth.

Q 47 ⚒ *Which entire chapter in Luke is made up of 3 illustrations on 1 truth?*

- The lost sheep (Luke 15:3-7)
- The lost coin (Luke 15:8-10)
- The lost son (Luke 15:11-32)

Jesus clothed statements of truth with illustrations that touch the heart! Are you thankful for the way Jesus did this?

The main point of these four examples is to show that Jesus used principles and illustrations together. Notice that Jesus did NOT make a statement of truth for 15 minutes, and then give an example! His method was to state a truth and then illustrate it several times. Do not imagine that you can present truth by a better method than your Lord can. A servant is not above his Master (Matt. 10:24)!

Enough about what illustrations are and why you should use them. It is time to move on. In the next chapter you will learn how to manage and share your illustrations.

Test Yourself: Circle the letter by the *best* completion to each question or statement.

1. Illustrations are like spiritual
a) food.
b) gifts.
c) hills.
d) roads.

2. What problem might illustrations help with?
a) People do not pay attention.
b) People do not accept truth.
c) People do not understand.
d) All of the above

3. Which is FALSE?
a) Illustrations lengthen.
b) Illustrations clarify.
c) Illustrations persuade.
d) Illustrations inspire.

4. Illustrations prevent a sermon from
a) touching people's hearts.
b) explaining the Bible.
c) becoming dull and dead.
d) sounding too spiritual.

5. Repeating a truth
a) wears it out.
b) helps it go deeper.
c) confuses people.
d) makes people listen.

6. Using illustrations as transitions
a) causes people to forget the outline.
b) confuses people who are taking notes.
c) helps guide people through your sermon.
d) helps people connect with one another.

7. More than principles, stories
a) teach truth.
b) result in miracles.
c) touch emotions.
d) explain the Bible.

8. Nathan's message to David shows the value of
a) psalms.
b) testimonies.
c) cultural fables.
d) indirect stories.

9. Jesus liked to state a truth and then
a) divide people into small groups.
b) let the disciples teach.
c) give a test.
d) illustrate it.

10. In Luke's Gospel,
a) 25% of Jesus' words are in illustrations.
b) 50% of Jesus' words are in illustrations.
c) 75% of Jesus' words are in illustrations.
d) 90% of Jesus' words are in illustrations.

Essay Test Topics Write 50-100 words on each of these goals that you studied in this chapter.

Reasons 1–6 for Using Illustrations

Goal: *Explain how illustrations clarify, persuade, inspire, add variety, shorten, and make preaching easier.*

Reasons 7–12 for Using Illustrations

Goal: *Describe how illustrations repeat, apply, transition, are appreciated, feed, and connect.*

Reasons 13–17 for Using Illustrations

Goal: *Summarize how illustrations are indirect, relax the listeners, help memory, touch the heart, and convert people.*

Reasons 18–19 for Using Illustrations

Goal: *Analyze the use of illustrations in the Bible and the ministry of Jesus.*

Chapter 7:
Guidelines for Managing and Using Illustrations

Introduction

Q 1 ➤ *If the Spirit reminds you of a new illustration while you are preaching, what should you do?*

Depend on the Holy Spirit as you preach. When you are preaching, the Holy Spirit may bring a new illustration to your mind. Listen to God and obey Him as you preach. Learn to recognize Him when He whispers. Once in a while, He may even urge you to preach a different message than the one you had planned. The Spirit might lead you to spend more time than you had planned telling an illustration. What should you do if this happens? You can skip some points of your outline if you see that your sermon is taking too long.

Figure 7.1 Not all mechanics have a tool box.
Not all pastors have an illustration file.

Q 2 ➤ *Is it better to have too many illustrations or too few? Explain.*

We all enjoy inviting hungry people for dinner. But it would be terrible not to have enough food. The same applies to preaching. It is terrible to face your church members without having enough to feed them spiritually. However, satisfying spiritually hungry people with a full message from God is a wonderful feeling. We are wiser to have too much prepared than too little!

Lessons:

Guidelines for Finding and Managing Illustrations
Goal A: *Identify 5 sources of illustrations.*
Goal B: *Explain 5 steps to make illustration files, and 5 details for writing illustrations.*

Guidelines for Your Attitude Toward Illustrations
Goal: *Explain 5 guidelines for a pastor's attitude toward illustrations.*

Guidelines for Preparing Illustrations
Goal: *Describe 5 guidelines for preparing illustrations.*

Guidelines for Presenting Illustrations
Goal: *Summarize 5 guidelines for presenting illustrations.*

 Key Word

cross-reference

Guidelines for Finding and Managing Illustrations

Goal A: *Identify 5 sources of illustrations.*
Goal B: *Explain 5 steps to make illustration files, and 5 details for writing illustrations.*

A. Finding illustrations

Finding illustrations depends on having *eyes to see* them, and knowing where to look. Let us consider five sources of illustrations.

Q 3 *Explain 5 sources of illustrations.*

The *first* place to find illustrations is in the Bible. Whenever you have a principle to preach, try to illustrate it at least once from the Old Testament and once from the New Testament. God's Word contains hundreds of illustrations. Remember that *Appendix A* lists 150 Bible stories. The better you know the Bible, the easier it will be to find illustrations in it. One wise pastor, a lady, practiced illustrating each of her points at least twice—once from the Old Testament and once from the New.[1] In chapter 11, we will practice using a biblical concordance to find principles and illustrations.

A *second* source of illustrations is books. In many languages, there are books of local proverbs, stories, riddles, songs, and quotations. For those who read English, a famous book is the *Encyclopedia of 15,000 Illustrations* (Bible Communications, Inc., P. O. Box 797803, Dallas, Texas, 75379 USA, 1998). This book of 15,000 illustrations lists them by topics. Also, *Faith & Action Series* books like the one you are studying contain many illustrations. For those who have access to the Internet, you will find more sources there as well.

A *third* place to get illustrations is in newspapers. These contain many things like events, quotes, and stories. Likewise, magazines may have some good illustrations. Some pastors cut events and stories from used newspapers and put them in their illustration files.

A *fourth* source of illustrations is people. We mentioned earlier that one pastor asked his people to write a short poem about their mother or father. Likewise, a pastor may ask people for stories on any topic. The older people are, the more illustrations they will have to tell. Learn to get illustrations from the members of your church or community. This is a source that is available to every pastor. Write these illustrations down on paper, and file them in the way we will teach you later in this lesson.

A *fifth* source of illustrations is your own life. Wise, spiritual pastors seek the Spirit *before* it is time to preach. They learn to let the Spirit guide them on what they will preach several days or weeks before the message. Then, they go through each day praying and watching for illustrations for a certain message. As we mentioned earlier, they learn to have *eyes to see.* These pastors train themselves to walk slowly through life, watching and praying step-by-step. They learn to see illustrations in nature, in others, and in their own families. Also, the Spirit helps them recall illustrations from their past. And when they see or recall an illustration for any message, they write it down and put it in a file. The problem is not that illustrations are hard to find. Those who train themselves to be alert, and write down what they see, have more illustrations than they can preach!

We have considered five sources for illustrations. Now let us study how to make a file for illustrations. Many experienced pastors have hundreds of illustrations in their files.

B. Managing illustrations with a file

The need for a file. Everyone who works with tools has a certain place for them. Cooks keep their pots, pans, and dishes in a special place. Mechanics, carpenters, doctors, artists, and farmers all keep their tools in certain places too. They do this so that the tools will not get lost. When they need a tool, they will know where to find it.

Q 4 *A pastor with an illustration file is like* _____.

Likewise, a pastor needs a special place to keep his illustrations. He will spend much of his time preparing biblical messages. And a big part of preparing these sermons is finding the right illustrations. So a pastor must learn to manage his illustrations well.

A few pastors have a computer and can easily save their illustrations in the computer's files. But most of the pastors in the world do not have a computer. Still, they will find it easy to make a file to manage their illustrations. A pastor may have only a few illustrations when he begins his ministry. But as the years go by, he will use hundreds of illustrations. There must be a good plan for filing and managing them. Having many illustrations in a file will improve sermons and save hundreds of hours. It only takes a short time to write an illustration down. But every minute spent writing down an illustration can save an hour of searching for one.

You should file your sermons in a similar manner, either using topical files, or making a file for each book of the Bible. For example, make a file for Matthew and keep all of your sermons on Matthew in it.

Making illustration files.   You can make an illustration file in five easy steps. We will teach you these steps now. But we want you to do more than just read about it here. **Do each step after you have read the instructions.**

First, get as many sheets of paper as there are letters in your alphabet (e.g., 26 sheets for English). These sheets will become your files. Each sheet of paper should be letter size (like this page). You will use each sheet for one letter of the alphabet. Some pastors prefer to use manila folders or large envelopes as files. Thicker paper lasts longer than plain paper. You can also use boxes or cartons to make files. If you are at a Bible school, perhaps there is a teacher who can help all of the students find materials for making their files. Students should have many illustrations in their files by the time they graduate.

Q 5 *Suppose you attend Bible school for 2 years, and you file one illustration each day. How many illustrations will be in your files when you graduate?*

Second, fold a sheet of paper in half. Write the first letter of the alphabet on it (*A* in English), centered at the top (Figure 7.2). This is your file for illustrations on topics that begin with *A*.

Third, turn to *Appendix D* in this book. Use it as a guide to write some topics on your *A* file. As the years go by, whenever you add an illustration to a file, write down the topic on the front of the file. Your *A* file should look like the file in Figure 7.2. But the topics beginning with *A* in your language may vary.

Q 6 *Name three topics that start with the letter A.*

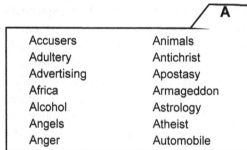

Accusers	Animals
Adultery	Antichrist
Advertising	Apostasy
Africa	Armageddon
Alcohol	Astrology
Angels	Atheist
Anger	Automobile

Figure 7.2   A sample file for illustrations beginning with the letter A

Fourth, fold the other 25 sheets of paper in half. Write a different letter of the alphabet on each paper, as you did for step 2 above.

Fifth, put all 26 files together in a box, a carton, a bag, or a briefcase. Your files will become more valuable to you as the years pass. After 1 or 2 years, you may need a bigger box for your files. Do not be afraid to spend time and money on your illustration file. It is like a bank that you are putting money into for your own ministry.

Q 7 *Summarize the 5 steps for creating an illustration file.*

Q 8 *Show the new files you have made to another pastor or friend.*

Using illustration files   An illustration file will not help you unless you use it! Some pastors find great illustrations, but they never file them. Some try to keep illustrations in their Bibles. Others take notes when they hear or see a good illustration, but they often lose the notes. Three steps will help you use your illustration files.

First, write the details. You can write an illustration on a small sheet of paper or a note card. Whatever you do, it must fit in your file. When you write an illustration, you should include five things:

- the topic
- other related topics (*cross-references)
- a biblical text
- the illustration itself
- the source

> **Topic:** Prayer
> **Related Topic:** Fruitfulness
> **Text:** Mark 1:35
> **Illustration:** John Wesley helped bring 250,000 sinners to Christ. He made it a habit to start each day with two hours of prayer.
> **Source:** Paul Lee Tan, *Encyclopedia of 7,700 Illustrations,* #4534.

Figure 7.3   Example of a written illustration about prayer

Q 9 *Copy the illustration about John Wesley and prayer. Put it in your file on prayer.*

Second, file it. After you write an illustration, file it as soon as possible! You would put the illustration in Figure 7.4 in the *P* file. Why? The topic "prayer" begins with *P*. Be sure that the topic is written on the file in which you put the illustration. For example, if you file an illustration on *tithing* in the *T* file, write *tithing* on the T file if it is not already there.

Q 10 *Where would you file an illustration on obedience?*

Third, make notes on related topics. These notes are also called cross-reference topics. Some illustrations relate to more than one topic. For example, we wrote the illustration on prayer from the life of John Wesley. But this illustration also relates to fruitfulness. Prayer enabled John Wesley to lead 250,000 to Christ. Prayer made Wesley fruitful. Someday, you will want to preach on fruitfulness. You may forget that you have a good illustration on fruitfulness under the topic of prayer in the *P* file. So, make a *related topic* note. How? On a separate, small piece of paper, make a note on fruitfulness and put it in the *F* file (Figure 7.4).

Q 11 *Why should you write a second note for the prayer illustration and file it under F: "fruitfulness"?*

> **Topic:** Fruitfulness
> Look under "prayer." It was the key to John Wesley's fruitfulness.

Figure 7.4   Written note that relates fruitfulness to the topic of prayer

Making notes on related topics takes only a few seconds. Take the time to do this! Even pastors with the best memories will forget things. And the older you become, the harder it is to remember! As one proverb states it, "He who used to jump the river now wades." Notes on related topics will keep you from losing an illustration in your own files![+]

Now you have your files, and you know how to record illustrations. You are ready to begin asking others to write illustrations for you. Maybe you have asked an elder to write an illustration for you. Write the topic on a piece of paper for him. Also, on that paper, identify him as the source. As you gather illustrations from him and others, complete the details and put them in your files. Planning ahead like this is like storing grain in the barn. It will be there when you need it!

Q 12 *Ask an elderly person to write an illustration for you on a topic you choose. File it.*

+ Some pastors write and file another note, relating each illustration to a biblical text. They set up topical and textual cross-reference files. This requires a file for each book of the Bible. For example, they write a note changing the top line of Figure 7.3 to Text: Mark 1:35, and then file it in the Mark file.

Guidelines for Your Attitude Toward Illustrations

Goal: *Explain 5 guidelines for a pastor's attitude toward illustrations.*

Illustrations are valuable in preaching. They are worth even more when the preacher follows a few basic principles.[2] In the rest of this chapter, we will survey 15 guidelines for using illustrations. Let us begin with five guidelines for the preacher's attitude.

A. Be honest.

Do not tell the experience of someone else as though it happened to you. Jesus told the parable of the Good Samaritan. He began by saying, *"A man was going down from Jerusalem to Jericho"* (Luke 10:30). Jesus never said, "I was going down from Jerusalem to Jericho." He did not say that thieves robbed and beat Him on the journey. Why? Because He was *not* the man who was robbed!

Q 13 *Should a pastor illustrate a sermon with a story that did not happen to him? Explain.*

It is all right to tell a story that happened to someone else. But make sure your listeners understand that you are speaking about someone else. If it did not happen to you, do not start the story with "I." Be honest!

B. Be accurate.

Do not expand or twist the facts. Do not tell a story that people cannot believe. Some pastors are always looking for great signs and wonders in their ministries. If they do not see them, they are tempted to *invent* them. Such men have learned to "multiply," and they do it often! If they saw 6 dogs, they claim they saw 16. Enlarged, expanded, exaggerated stories destroy people's trust in you. Remember that all liars shall have their part in the lake that burns with fire and brimstone (Rev. 21:8). Tell your illustrations as if Jesus were listening. He is!

There is a story about the time General *Napoleon visited his soldiers. One soldier had only one arm.

"Did you lose the arm in battle?" asked the great general.

"Yes, sir, and I'm proud of it," said the soldier with one arm.

"And what were you given?" asked Napoleon.

"A badge of honor," answered the proud soldier.

"You seem to be the type of soldier who would give both arms for his country," said the general.

The soldier responded, "And if I did, what reward would I receive?"

"The double badge of honor," said Napoleon.

At once the wounded soldier drew his sword and cut off his remaining arm.

Q 14 *What is the author's point in the story about the one-armed soldier?*

People told this story for many years as an example of loyalty and commitment. One day, someone asked, "How could a soldier with one arm cut off his own arm?"[3]

You will lose a person's full confidence only once. After that, he will find it hard to trust you again. Be accurate when you use illustrations. Do not just repeat illustrations that other people have used. Check the facts. Make sure that they are true and that people can believe them.

C. Be discreet.

Being discreet means treating personal, private matters with great care. Do not betray the confidence of family members, friends, or those you counsel. Do not share private matters in public. And do not share illustrations that may offend people. If you have a doubt about sharing something, don't!

Imagine a church where the pastor used his church members as sermon illustrations. Those who gossip would love it. For when the pastor told a fault of someone, the gossips would repeat it. But the embarrassed person, who was the illustration, might leave the church! Those who stayed would never share anything personal with their pastor. Be discreet.

Q 15 Why should a pastor not use some details about family members and friends to illustrate his sermons?

A pastor was preaching on the topic, *God Is My Hiding Place*. He told a story about a father and daughter. They had collected money at church for a new building, and were taking it to the bank in two large bags. The daughter was in the back seat of the horse and buggy, and the father was driving. Far away, the father saw some robbers coming. How had they known about the money? Perhaps they were present when the church collected it. He gave the two big bags to his daughter and told her to hide them. When the robbers came, they searched the wagon but could not find the two bags of money. After much searching, the robbers left with the wagon and the horses. The father turned to the girl and asked, "Where did you hide the money?" She smiled, and then pulled both of the big bags out of her mouth. "Very good hiding place," said the father. "And if your mother had been here, we could have hidden the horses and the wagon in her mouth!"

Many people laughed at the funny story. But it hurt the feelings of some of the women. The story was making fun of women with "big mouths." This is an idiom about people who talk too much or gossip. Many women are not like this. Never tell a story that will hurt the feelings of any person, gender, tribe, or race. Hurt feelings are too big of a price to pay for a laugh.

D. Be humble.

You should not be afraid to use your personal experiences. At times, you can help others by telling events from your life. This is especially true of humorous events. People will usually laugh with you if you laugh at yourself.

Q 16 Preachers should not boast about themselves. Why not?

But if you tell a story about yourself, never boast or brag. Do not be like the hypocrites, who loved to be seen by others (Matt. 6:5). People soon tire of stories in which the pastor always turns out to be the hero. Avoid telling illustrations to show that you are clever. *A person wrapped up in himself makes a small package.* Preach Christ and no one else—especially not yourself (2 Cor. 4:5). Be humble.

E. Be prepared.

Q 17 How can a pastor know whether he is ready to tell an illustration?

Know your illustrations well. Do not use 10 minutes to tell an illustration that you can tell well in 2 minutes. Practice telling the illustration to God, to yourself, and to your spouse. Tell the illustration to your children, and then have them tell it to you. Practice telling the illustration until you can tell it easily with feeling.

The leader of a school invited a pastor to talk to the teachers. He wanted the pastor to speak on the subject of influence. The leader asked, "When can you come?" "That depends on how long you want me to speak," the pastor replied. "If you want me to cover the subject in 3 minutes, I will need 2 weeks to prepare. If you want me to speak for 15 minutes, I'll need a week to prepare. If you do not mind if I speak for an hour, I can start right now!" The more you prepare, the less time it takes to say something.

Q 18 Explain: The more you prepare, the less time it takes to say something.

Some pastors speak for an hour and say little. If they prepared more, they could say twice as much in half the time! Be prepared.

Lesson 20 Guidelines for Preparing Illustrations
Goal: Describe 5 guidelines for preparing illustrations.

A. Be wise.

Avoid using too many cultural illustrations, such as animal stories or fables. Wisdom in this area is important. Some cultural illustrations can be helpful. But too many humorous illustrations may cause people to think that you are not serious.

Q 19 Should a pastor use animal stories or fables? Explain.

Q 20 ✎ *Explain Figure 7.5*

Be in step with your people. One pastor says he imagines specific members of his church when he is preparing a sermon. He imagines them gathered around his desk. This pastor pictures the face of a certain old man and asks, "What do you think of this illustration?" Then he pictures an elderly woman. He asks, "Am I raising questions that trouble or confuse you?" Next the pastor imagines the face of a teenage boy. He mentally asks him, "Do you understand what I am saying?" This pastor continues the process, thinking about farmers, businessmen, housewives, and others. In this way, he prepares spiritual food that will feed all of his sheep.[4]

Use illustrations that will help everyone and offend no one. Be wise.

B. Be purposeful.

Do not use illustrations just to fill your sermons. Some pastors tell illustrations to use up time. If an illustration does not add something to a message, it subtracts from it!

Q 21 ➤ *How do some pastors waste time with illustrations?*

Q 22 ➤ *Which 2 are the best illustrations on obedience? a) Mary's response to the angel's visit (Luke 1:26-38); b) Noah (Gen. 8); c) Simeon in the temple (Luke 2:25-35); d) Balaam (Num. 22:21-28); e) the 10 lepers (Luke 17:11-19); f) Saul waiting in Damascus (Acts 9); g) David killing Goliath (1 Sam. 17)?*

Q 23 ✎ *In Q 22, explain which topics each person could be used to illustrate.*

Lazy pastors tell stories to avoid studying. Such men will be judged by God. Remember the slothful servant Jesus described in the parable of the talents (Matt. 25:24-30). The master judged him harshly. Work hard on your sermons. Then, on the Day of Judgment, you will not stand next to the lazy servant of Matthew 25.

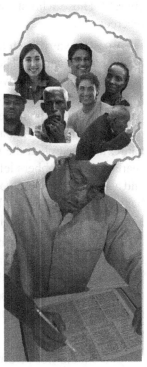

Figure 7.5 As you plan illustrations, think of the people you want to reach.

Do your best to present yourself to God as one approved, a workman who does not need to be ashamed and who correctly handles the word of truth (2 Tim. 2:15).

Wasting people's time is a sin. Illustrations should be told only to reach a goal. Keep searching until you find an illustration that will teach the exact truth you want to share. Use illustrations that will help you reach your goal. Be purposeful. Shoot an arrow straight to the center of your target!

Q 24 ➤ *Which 3 illustrations in Figure 7.6 are good ones?*

> **A. Illustrations of people who repented**
> 1. Saul of Tarsus
> 2. Mary Magdalene
> 3. Pharaoh
> 4. David
> 5. Abel

Figure 7.6   Practice choosing illustrations for a purpose.

C. Be efficient.

Q 25 ➤ *Why should you not use many (or any) words to announce an illustration?*

Q 26 ➤ *How did Jesus introduce each of the 7 parables in Matthew 13?*

Do not begin an illustration by saying, "This is an illustration" or "Let me give you an example of what I'm talking about today, so that you will have a better understanding of what I am trying to tell you!" Study the illustrations Jesus told. Most of the time He used few or no words to introduce an illustration. A long introduction for Jesus was, *"The kingdom of heaven is like...."* Those listening to Jesus knew when He was illustrating a truth. And people will know you are giving an illustration once you begin. You would dull a knife by trying to cut metal with it. Likewise, you will dull the effect of an illustration by introducing it. Just *tell it!* Jump into it. Be efficient. Do not waste words. Do not use more details than necessary. Move straight ahead!

D. Be creative.

Do not repeat the same illustrations over and over. One believer was stirred to tears the *first* time he heard a certain illustration. The *second* time he heard it, he still thought it was good. But his reaction to the same illustration in a *third* sermon was different. He could hardly wait until it was over. The *fourth* time he heard it, he was again moved to tears. But this time he was crying because he was so tired of hearing the illustration! Be creative. Wait a long time before you repeat an illustration to the same listeners.

Q 27 What happens when a pastor repeats an illustration too often?

E. Be focused.

Focus on only one lesson in each illustration. Do not emphasize more than one point with one illustration.

Q 28 How does an illustration with several lessons affect the listeners?

One night a young man stood at the steps of a bridge. It was built so that people could cross above two sets of train tracks. He decided to walk across the tracks instead of using the bridge. He knew this was illegal, but he thought he would not get caught. Crossing the tracks would save him time. As he approached the last track, a watchman with a guard dog stopped him. The watchman grabbed the man's arm and demanded a bribe to let him go free. The young man quickly placed a folded piece of paper into the watchman's hand. Since it was dark, the watchman thought the folded paper was money. So he let the young man go free. Later, the watchman discovered that the youth had given him a piece of newspaper.

The story above would not be a good illustration about sin. It tells about breaking the law. But it confuses the listeners by adding the topics of bribery and deceit. However, you could change the story to illustrate sin. To do so, you could end the story when the young man gets caught. That would make the point that those who commit sin will be judged. Shoot at only one target at a time. Be focused.

Lesson 21

Guidelines for Presenting Illustrations
Goal: *Summarize 5 guidelines for presenting illustrations.*

A. Be personal.

Bedtime is a good time to *read* illustrations. But pulpit time is not bedtime! Do not read illustrations when preaching! Review them in private until you can tell them naturally.

Q 29 Why is it bad to read illustrations?

There is a joke about a pastor who fell asleep behind his own pulpit while reading an illustration. The congregation fell asleep too! Read illustrations in the pulpit *only* if you want people to go to sleep. Otherwise, look at the people as you preach and share your illustrations. Preach to the people, not to the pulpit. Be personal!

B. Be moderate.

Avoid telling illustrations so s-l-o-w-l-y that people lose interest. Some pastors give so many small details that people's minds begin to wander. Do not tell an illustration so slowly that even a turtle would pass you. In contrast, do not tell an illustration so quickly that even a cheetah could not keep up with you. Talk at a speed that people can easily follow. Be moderate—somewhere between a turtle and a cheetah.

Q 30 When telling illustrations, what happens if a pastor talks too slowly? Too quickly?

Figure 7.7
Tell an illustration between the speeds of a turtle and a cheetah—not too slow and not too fast.

Q 31 How can a pastor know what level of language to use?

C. Be clear.

Do not use words your listeners do not understand. Earlier in this book, we referred to John Wesley. He was a Methodist pastor who led 250,000 people to Christ. It is said that before preaching a new sermon in public, he preached it to his house cleaner. She had very little education. He wanted to be sure that she understood every word. Only then would he preach the message in public. Wesley also encouraged the preachers that he taught to use common words, short words, clearly understood words.[5]

Make sure that the person with the least education can understand what you say. Augustine, a famous bishop of North Africa, had a good view on this. He said that he would rather have his professors criticize him than to have his listeners misunderstand him. Be clear.

Do not say, "A conflagration threatens the edifice." Say instead, "The house is on fire!"

D. Be sincere.

It is important to use emotion when you tell illustrations. But avoid showing false emotions. Those who show too little emotion are like a stalk of corn that has dried up and died. But to have tears in your voice with none in your eyes appears fake. Pastors must be sincere!

Q 32 Explain: You should not have tears in your voice if they are not in your eyes.

Try to get inside an illustration and feel the honest, sincere emotions in it.[6] In the illustration that follows, notice how the pastor *gets inside* the leper's mind and heart. He helps us experience the leper's feelings.

Q 33 Does the story of the leper help you feel what he felt? Explain.

Once there was a man who made a fearful discovery. At first, he could not believe what he had seen. He was shocked—stunned! He knew it had happened to other people. But he could not believe it was happening to him. The awful discovery kept him awake at night. When he did sleep, he had bad dreams. He awoke in the darkness, overwhelmed with fear. Again and again in the darkness, as his mind cleared, he would have to face the truth. The bad dream was true. This terrible thing was happening to him! He could no longer pretend it was not true. His wife noticed. His friends noticed. He looked tired and worn-out.

This troubled man knew he must make a journey. It was all so strange, so mysterious. He told his wife and children not to worry. He would be gone a few days. Everything would be all right. He would return.

The long, lonely journey began. His family waved good-bye as the man turned away down the road. His eyes filled with tears. He walked alone, carrying in his heart the knowledge of his fearful discovery.

Finally, he reached the city. He went to a certain room in a great building called the temple. There he met a man he had never seen before—a priest. The frightened man described his awful discovery. Then he showed the priest the white spots on his legs and arms. The priest shook his head slowly, because he had seen spots like these before. The man had leprosy. The priest was careful not to touch him.

The priest looked very serious. He said, "I declare before God that you are now unclean. The Scriptures say:

[45]*"The person with such an infectious disease must wear torn clothes, let his hair be unkempt, cover the lower part of his face and cry out, 'Unclean! Unclean!'* [46]*As long as he has the infection he remains unclean. He must live alone; he must live outside the camp"* (Lev. 13:45-46).

"May God have mercy on you," said the priest as he left the room. The man stood alone. Tears flowed down his cheeks. His body slumped.

He knew what this meant. He could no longer hold his children in his arms. He could no longer embrace his wife. He could no longer give or receive the handshake of a friend. He could no longer worship in the synagogue, nor earn his living at his job. What would happen to his wife and children? They would be left alone. Slowly he began to tear his clothes so they were like rags. Then he took his hand and messed his hair up. Dragging his feet in despair, he stepped out into the street. His shoulders were down. He put his hand to his mouth, covering his upper lip, and cried, "Unclean! Unclean!"

For the first time in his life people were afraid of him. They stepped back. They looked at him with disgust. Parents grabbed their children. His voice sounded through the streets: "Unclean! Unclean!" The way opened before him. He walked alone toward his own village. He saw it in the distance. This would be the hardest part of all. His children would want to rush out to hug him. His wife would want to kiss him, leprosy or not. But he must be strong. He must protect them, even if it broke their hearts. He must not allow them to touch him.

Q 34 ✎ *Write an illustration about how Mary felt, explaining that she was pregnant.*

So the tragic scene continued. The children thought their father was angry with them. He told them to keep away. He told his wife to come no closer. His appearance frightened them. He seemed like a crazy man. In reality, his heart was breaking as he turned to go to the leper's cave. And his family went back to their lonely home.

Q 35 ✎ *Write an illustration about Abraham's struggles as he considered sacrificing Isaac.*

Then, one day, something wonderful happened!

²A man with leprosy came and knelt before him [Jesus] *and said, "Lord, if you are willing, you can make me clean." ³Jesus reached out his hand and touched the man. "I am willing," he said. "Be clean!" Immediately he was cured of his leprosy* (Matt. 8:2-3).

E. Be spiritual.

Figure 7.8 As a boat with sails needs the wind, an illustration needs the anointing of the Spirit.

The best illustration, used without the Holy Spirit's blessing, is like a sailboat without any wind. Prepare your illustrations well; then depend on the anointing of the Holy Spirit. Be spiritual.

Q 36 ⤳ *How is an illustration like a boat with sails?*

Under God's anointing, Samson was a mighty defender of Israel (Judges 13–16). Before he was born, an angel appeared to his mother, and told her that Samson was to be a *Nazirite. That is, he would be dedicated to God from birth. He was not to cut his hair. It was an outward symbol of his commitment to God. While Samson was obedient, the Holy Spirit anointed him with power. He delivered Israel from the Philistine enemies. But Samson told a Philistine woman the secret of his strength. *"No razor has ever been used on my head…because I have been a Nazirite set apart to God since birth. If my head were shaved, my strength would leave me, and I would become as weak as any other man"* (Judg. 16:17). This woman, Delilah, deceived Samson. While he was asleep, she had someone shave Samson's hair, and the LORD left him (Judg. 16:19-20). Samson was powerless, and was taken as a prisoner. He died because of his disobedience. Samson's power was not in his hair, but in the Spirit. Likewise, pastor, the power you need is not in an illustration or in any words. What makes the difference? The words or illustrations you use will only have power as God anoints them. Depend on the Holy Spirit!

Q 37 ⤳ *What lesson does Samson's hair illustrate?*

Test Yourself: Circle the letter by the **best** completion to each question or statement.

1. Which is a good source for illustrations?
a) Bible school
b) The dictionary
c) People
d) All of the above

2. The number of sermon files needed
a) is the same for each pastor.
b) depends on the number of sermons.
c) is less for the young than the old.
d) depends on the language of preaching.

3. Illustration files DO NOT need
a) a Scripture reference.
b) a topic.
c) an outline.
d) a source.

4. A preacher should tell few illustrations
a) that are personal.
b) that are from the Bible.
c) that exalt himself.
d) that are from books.

5. Most of all, a *pastor* should be _____ with illustrations.
a) original and funny
b) honest and discreet
c) serious and academic
d) confident and emotional

6. You should not tell an illustration if
a) it does not come from the Bible.
b) it does not relate to your goals.
c) it did not happen to you.
d) it did not happen recently.

7. An illustration with many topics will
a) relax people.
b) relate to people.
c) confuse people.
d) comfort people.

8. Which is NOT a guideline for presenting illustrations?
a) Be loud.
b) Be clear.
c) Be personal.
d) Be spiritual.

9. When telling illustrations,
a) do not use emotion.
b) show less emotion than you feel
c) show emotion that you feel.
d) show more emotion than you feel.

10. When you tell illustrations, speak
a) at a normal speed.
b) at a fast pace.
c) in a low voice.
d) in a powerful way.

 Essay Test Topics Write 50-100 words on each of these goals that you studied in this chapter.

Guidelines for Finding and Managing Illustrations

Goal: *Identify 5 sources of illustrations.*

Goal: *Explain 5 steps to make illustration files, and 5 details for writing illustrations.*

Guidelines for Your Attitude Toward Illustrations

Goal: *Explain 5 guidelines for a pastor's attitude toward illustrations.*

Guidelines for Preparing Illustrations

Goal: *Describe 5 guidelines for preparing illustrations.*

Guidelines for Presenting Illustrations

Goal: *Summarize 5 guidelines for presenting illustrations.*

Unit 3: Preparing Expository Sermons With Methods A and B

In this unit we make a big change. In Unit 1 we discussed the pastor—his character, message, passion, and anointing. In Unit 2 we studied illustrations—14 types of illustrations, 19 reasons to use them, and 15 guidelines for sharing them. But this unit shifts from talking about preaching to *practicing* it! From this point on, you will read *less* and speak *more*.

Chapter 8 is about understanding expository sermons. We will guide you to:
- *Contrast a topical and expository sermon.*
- *Explain seven advantages of planning a group of expository sermons.*
- *Explain the purpose and parts of a sermon outline.*
- *Analyze the characteristics and advantages of stating main points as principles.*
- *Summarize three steps for finding and creating principles.*
- *Explain six guidelines for creating principles. Illustrate each.*
- *Explain the differences between a good and bad sermon title.*
- *Define the proposition of a sermon and explain its importance.*
- *Explain the purposes, challenges, and types of introductions.*

Chapter 9 focuses on presenting the Problems and Solutions. By the end of this chapter, you will be able to:
- *Explain how a pastor can prepare sermons that are logical, wise, successful and helpful.*
- *Respond to four common questions students ask about presenting Problems.*
- *Identify the Problem and Solution in a given passage of Scripture.*

Chapter 10 focuses on presenting the Problems and Solutions using Method A. By the end of this chapter, you will be able to:
- *Summarize how to develop the Problem and Solution parts of a sermon using Method A.*
- *Explain the need for transition sentences, and give an example.*
- *Create the Problem and Solution parts of an expository sermon using Method A (P_1P_2–S_1S_2).*

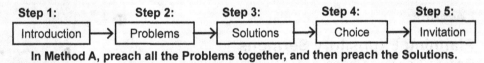

Step 1: Introduction → **Step 2:** Problems → **Step 3:** Solutions → **Step 4:** Choice → **Step 5:** Invitation

In Method A, preach all the Problems together, and then preach the Solutions.

Chapter 11 teaches you to present the Problems and Solutions using Method B. We will guide you to:
- *Contrast Method A and Method B of preparing an expository sermon.*
- *Prepare an expository sermon using Method B (P_1S_1–P_2S_2–P_3S_3).*

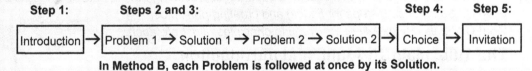

Step 1: Introduction → **Steps 2 and 3:** Problem 1 → Solution 1 → Problem 2 → Solution 2 → **Step 4:** Choice → **Step 5:** Invitation

In Method B, each Problem is followed at once by its Solution.

Chapter 12 is about the Choice. You will discover how to:
- *Illustrate the positive, negative, and contrast methods of the Choice Step.*
- *Use the contrast method to create Step IV of a sermon.*

Chapter 13 emphasizes the Invitation. We will enable you to:
- *Summarize the six rules of an Invitation.*
- *Explain ways to invite people to respond and how to plan time at the altar.*
- *Prepare the Invitation Steps for two sermons.*
- *Write and preach a complete expository sermon using the Five-Step Method.*

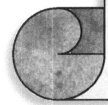

Chapter 8:
Expository Sermons

Introduction

Preaching a series of expository messages will enable you to deal easily with hard topics. Some people close their hearts when they think the preacher is preaching at them. Perhaps two people in the church are fighting. They are bitter and refuse to forgive each other. If you preach on forgiveness, both of them may think you are being too direct. As a result, they may get angry at you. A wise way to handle this type of problem is to preach through a book, like Philippians. Then people will bless you for preaching the Word of God to them. And when you come to Philippians 2 and 4, they will not blame you for preaching about getting along with one another. They will not be upset

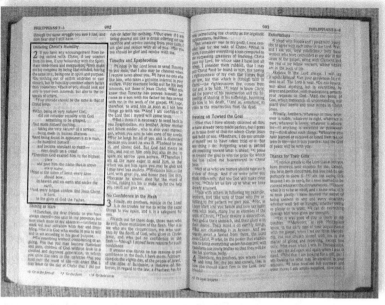

Figure 8.1   In an expository sermon, you preach about the Problem and Solutions of one biblical passage.

with you and will be more receptive to the Holy Spirit guiding them. Wise preachers learn to plan their sermons in groups. This makes it easy to cover many topics, especially the hard ones.

In this chapter we will teach you what expository sermons are and how to create them. Besides the advantage we mentioned above, we will give you six more reasons why every pastor should learn to preach expository sermons. Do your best in this chapter—it will make your ministry more fruitful for the rest of your life.

Lessons:

Planning Expository Sermons

Goal A: *Contrast a topical and expository sermon.*
Goal B: *Explain 7 advantages of planning a group of expository sermons.*
Goal C: *Explain the purpose and parts of a sermon outline.*

State Your Main Points as Principles

Goal A: *Analyze the characteristics and advantages of stating main points as principles.*
Goal B: *Summarize 3 steps for finding and creating principles.*
Goal C: *Explain 6 guidelines for creating principles. Illustrate each.*

The Title, Main Thought, and Introduction

Goal A: *Explain the differences between a good and bad sermon title.*
Goal B: *Define the proposition of a sermon and explain its importance.*
Goal C: *Explain the purposes, challenges, and types of introductions.*

 Key Words

expository

principles
Roman numeral

title

Lesson 22 — Planning Expository Sermons

Goal A: *Contrast a topical and expository sermon.*
Goal B: *Explain 7 advantages of planning a group of expository sermons.*
Goal C: *Explain the purpose and parts of a sermon outline.*

A. Using the Problem/Solution Method to organize a sermon

There are several methods for planning sermons. Preachers do not all organize by the same method. In fact, some preachers do not organize by any method! We have all heard sermons that were as disorganized as a sink full of dirty dishes. Everything was mixed together!

Q 1 How are some sermons like a sink full of dirty dishes?

Our purpose is not to criticize any sermon we may have heard in the past. Rather, our purpose is to teach you the Problem/Solution Method of organizing a sermon. Using a method to organize a sermon makes any message better.

The Problem/Solution Method is neither new nor rare. Some of the world's greatest preachers, such as the apostle Paul, Charles Spurgeon, and F. B. Meyer used it. This method is still used today by well-known preachers of many denominations.

The book of Romans is partly organized by the Problem/Solution Method. It begins with an Introduction (Rom. 1:1-17). Then it presents man's great problem: We have all sinned (Rom. 1:18–3:20). Next, Paul presents the solution in two parts. *First*, we are justified by faith in Christ (Rom. 3:21–5:21). *Second,* we overcome sin daily as we abide in Christ and walk in the Spirit (Rom. 6–8). The rest of Romans gives applications related to the theme of righteousness by faith in Christ.

Q 2 Is the book of Jonah organized around a problem and solution? Explain.

Q 3 What is the big problem and solution in the book of Revelation?

Likewise, famous Psalms, like Psalm 1, are partly organized by the Problem/Solution Method. If you begin to look for it, you will find the Problem/Solution Method throughout the Bible. It is a common method used in Scripture and other books. Most every story you know is organized by the Problem/Solution Method.

Q 4 What 2 problems did Paul write Ephesians to solve?

In this course, we are studying the Problem/Solution Method to develop sermons. Learn this method first. As you become more skilled as a preacher, you will develop this method in new ways, and learn other methods as well.

Learning a method will make preparing sermons less of an art and more of a skill. By art, we mean things like writing a poem or song, or painting a picture. Only a few people are good artists. Their success depends a lot on the talents they were born with, although good artists get better. In contrast, a skill, like sewing or building, is easier to learn than an art. Just as a carpenter must learn to use tools, preachers must learn basic skills to preach.[1] Just as a carpenter can build a weak or strong house, a preacher can prepare a weak or strong message.

If you are called by God, and willing to work hard, we can teach you the skill of preparing and preaching biblical messages. Many of the most famous preachers were like artists. They had unusual gifts and talents that enabled them to paint beautiful word pictures. If your goal is to be a famous preacher, we cannot help you much. An art is hard to teach. But if your goal is to be a fruitful, faithful preacher, we can help you. Do your best to learn the methods in this course, and the Holy Spirit will help you fulfill your calling.

B. Two types of sermons: topical and expository

Books about preaching often contrast topical and *expository sermons.[2] Let us examine these two types of biblical messages.

Q 5 ➤ *Are topical sermons biblical? Explain.*

A topical sermon begins with a topic. *Topic* is another word for subject or theme. Prayer, giving, trials, and worship are examples of topics. A pastor must be *biblical* when preaching a topical sermon. And as John R. Stott has said, there is a sense in which a topical sermon is expository. Stott emphasizes that all sermons should be expository—bringing into the light what the Bible teaches.[3] Yet a topical sermon does not tie a preacher to one text of Scripture. A topical outline may begin with Genesis and end with Revelation. A pastor may find a problem in Exodus and its solutions in Luke, Colossians, or Hebrews. Thus, he is free to choose Scriptures wherever the topic leads him.

There is the need for a preacher to do some topical preaching. For example, every pastor should preach a series of sermons on the great doctrines of the Bible. Will the church members learn the basic truths of Scripture if the pastor does not preach on them?

The great doctrines of the Bible are topics. They are not built upon only one passage of Scripture. Rather, doctrines are based upon several passages. Thus, to preach a complete, broad message on a biblical doctrine, a preacher must preach a topical sermon. In this case, the preacher will start with the topic or doctrine. Then, he will search the Scriptures to see what they teach about the topic. Even in topical sermons, a preacher should discuss the problems (false teachings) before the solutions (correct teachings). For a list of 16 doctrines to preach on, see Figure 8.2.

---

16 Basic Doctrines of the Bible

1. The Inspiration of Scripture
2. The One True God
3. The Deity of the Lord Jesus Christ
4. The Fall of Man
5. The Salvation of Man
6. The Ordinances of the Church
7. The Baptism in the Holy Spirit
8. The Evidence of the Baptism in the Holy Spirit
9. Sanctification
10. The Church and Its Mission
11. The Ministry
12. Divine Healing
13. The Blessed Hope
14. The Millennial Reign of Christ
15. The Final Judgment
16. The New Heavens and the New Earth

Figure 8.2   Pastors should preach a topical series on 16 basic truths of the Bible.

A topical sermon can be a weak sermon if it does not have a basis in Scripture. It must be more than just the opinion of the preacher.

The strongest sermons are expository sermons. Our only authority in preaching is the Scriptures. Preach the Word!

Besides a series on doctrines, there are other topics for which a pastor should plan a series, such as principles for the Christian family or principles for solving life's problems. Remember, in a topical sermon, the preacher bases his sermon on a topic, rather than a passage of Scripture.

In contrast to a topical message, an expository sermon is based on one passage of Scripture. As Dr. George O. Wood states, the passage may be a verse, a paragraph, a chapter, or even a book of Scripture, such as Philemon.[4]

Q 6 ➤ *What is an expository sermon?*

All of the sermon examples used in this course are expository sermons. An expository sermon is a type of sermon. Still, every pastor needs a method to create any type of sermon. Our method is to identify a Problem and a Solution within a biblical text and its context. Then, we will guide you to state the Problems and Solutions as principles, based on the text. Finally, for each principle, you will learn to explain, illustrate, and apply it from anywhere—Scripture or other sources. Figure 8.3 summarizes the difference between topical and expository sermons. The Problem/Solution Method works well to organize both topical and expository sermons.

When preparing a topical sermon, a preacher begins with a topic. Then the preacher searches the Scriptures for verses related to that topic. In contrast, an expository sermon begins with a passage of Scripture. In an expository sermon, the preacher may not discover what the topic is until studying a passage for a few minutes. An expository sermon explains what an entire scriptural passage means. It exposes the text, bringing the meaning of the passage into the light for all to see. As the preacher studies the passage, he or she identifies the topic or theme in it.

To create an expository sermon, you will learn to identify the Problem a passage deals with and the Solution that passage offers. For example, you may choose to preach an expository sermon on the resurrection from 1 Corinthians 15. Then, the only Problems and Solutions you will talk about are those you find in that chapter. Remember this: In an expository sermon, you must preach only about the Problems and Solutions found within the passage and context of Scripture you choose.

Q 7 ➤ *In an expository sermon, can the Problem and Solution come from different passages? Explain.*

Biblical authors always wrote for a purpose. They wrote to help their readers with problems or needs. Sometimes those problems are clearly stated in a text. At other times, a preacher must search the historical background to identify and understand a problem. Expository preaching answers two questions: How did the text help readers then? And how can it help us now?[5] We will teach you how to organize your sermons to answer these two questions.

Sermon Type	Subject	Problem and Solution	Illustrations and Applications
Topical	Subject is chosen without a text.	These come from the *subject* or any texts related to it.	May come from anywhere in the Bible or from other sources.
Expository	Subject comes from the text.	These come only from one *passage* or *its context*.	May come from anywhere in the Bible or from other sources.

Figure 8.3   A comparison of topical and expository sermons

C. Seven advantages of planning a series of expository sermons

In chapter 2, we discussed planning a series or group of messages. There are at least seven advantages to planning a series of expository sermons.

1. When we plan, we are like God.   He planned for the stars to be above us and the earth to be below us. He planned for fish to swim and birds to fly. He planned for the cows to eat grass and the lions to eat meat. He planned each day and each night. He planned for your eyes to be on your face and your toes to be on your foot! Imagine what people would look like if God had not planned! Not planning is unspiritual. In contrast, God planned for your heart to be in your chest and your teeth to be in your mouth! Before He created us, He planned to save us. He has planned a day when He will judge the world. He planned heaven for those who obey Him and hell for those who reject Him. He plans ahead at least 9 months before each person is born. He will not be upset with you for planning your sermons!

Q 8 ➤ *Is it unspiritual to plan a group of messages? Explain.*

Pastor, do not let anyone tell you that it is not spiritual to plan. God is the most spiritual of all, and He plans more than anyone does. To plan is to be like God. But as you plan, ALWAYS depend on the Holy Spirit to guide you. NEVER plan without God. Fast and pray as you plan.

2. Planning a series of expository messages helps a pastor stay longer at one church.   Some preachers move from church to church. One of the reasons is that they preach on the same topics over and over. People tire of eating beans and rice every meal!

Q 9 ➤ *Why does planning expository messages help a pastor stay longer at a church?*

W. A. Criswell was a famous preacher. He pastored one church for 50 years. When asked the secret, he said that it was planning groups of expository sermons. In his first year, he began preaching through Genesis. He kept preaching groups of sermons through books of the Bible. After 25 years, he finished preaching through the book of Revelation.[6] Pastor, if you want to stay for many years at the same church, you need a plan. For every 10 years, you may preach about 1,500 messages! Do you see the wisdom of planning your sermons in groups?

Pastor George O. Wood is the General Superintendent of the Assemblies of God in America. He pastored one church for 17 years. He let the Spirit lead him to plan groups of expository sermons. Dr. Wood says this type of planning is a key to staying for a long time at the same church.

Pastor John Lindell is pastor of James River Assembly of God in Springfield, Missouri. When he first came, there were fewer than 100 people. After 10 years, the church had grown to about 5,000 people. He likes to plan groups of expository sermons. In 10 years, he has preached through entire books of the Bible such as Matthew, Acts, Genesis, Ephesians, and Hebrews.

Q 10 ✎ *Why will a series of expository sermons help your people learn Scripture better?*

3. Planning a series of expository messages helps people learn the Bible.   People learn better when there is a plan of study. Do you like the way we have put the pages of this book in order? How much do you think you would learn if we mixed up all of the pages? What if we put page 152 after page 7 and page 128 before page 2? Does it help you that the days of the week are in order, and that we number the hours of each day?

So why do some preachers jump from A to Z and from 1 to 68? Why do some preach from Genesis 1 on Sunday and Colossians 3 the next Sunday, and then skip to Leviticus 21? What would happen to a schoolteacher who did not follow a plan for teaching through a book or subject? We all learn best line upon line. One of the reasons people have not learned the Bible well is that preachers jump from book to book. Preach through an entire book of the Bible. Challenge your people to read the book you are preaching. Invite them to write questions about the book you are preaching. From time to time, you can answer some of the questions in your sermons. This will encourage your people to read the Bible more. If you preach through a book like Philippians, your people will learn a lot about that book.[7]

Q 11 ✎ *What is one of the greatest pressures a pastor faces?*

4. Planning a series of expository messages will help you listen better to the Spirit.   Most preachers will admit that finding a message to preach puts a lot of pressure on them. The closer they get to a service, the more pressure they feel. Some refer to the *Saturday night panic!* Unfortunately, the hardest time to hear God's voice is when we are feeling nervous or under pressure. Hearing the Spirit's voice when we are under pressure is like trying to hear a friend whisper when a train is passing by! Pressure creates noise within us that makes it hard to hear the gentle voice of the Spirit. In contrast, planning a group of messages on a book of the Bible enables us to be at peace spiritually. Then, it is easy to hear the Spirit's voice.

Q 12 ✎ *How does planning a series of expository sermons save you time?*

5. Planning a series of expository messages gives you more time to study and pray.   Some preachers spend more time worrying about what to preach than they spend preparing the sermon itself! Pray until you feel peace and direction about preaching a series of expository sermons from a certain book of the Bible. Then spend your time preparing several sermons instead of just finding a topic.

The time you spend on the first sermon of a series will save you time on the next sermon in that series. For example, suppose you are preaching a series on Colossians. The first week, you must study about the location of the town and the problems the people were facing. But the next week, when you return to study Colossians, you will remember some things that will help you. Preaching a series of sermons is like planting a garden in the same place year after year. You only need to remove the stumps and rocks once.

6. Planning a series of expository messages will make it easier for you to find illustrations. Many preachers cannot find illustrations for their sermons because they start looking too late. If you know early in the week what you are going to preach about on Sunday, you have time to think about it. As you pray and meditate on your message, the Holy Spirit will show you illustrations about the problems and solutions of your sermon. If it takes an hour to reach the bus stop, and you want to be there at 8:00, don't leave the house at 7:30! Plan ahead!

Q 13 ⤴ *Why is it easier to find illustrations for a series of expository sermons?*

7. Preaching a series of expository messages will enable you to deal easily with hard or sensitive topics. We put this benefit in the Introduction of this chapter. Take a moment to review it.

Q 14 ⤴ *How can a pastor preach on hard topics without causing people to be angry with him?*

We have considered seven reasons why a pastor should plan some messages as a series of expository sermons on one book of the Bible. We could give you seven more reasons, but we think this is enough! Now let us move a step closer to creating an expository sermon.

D. The purpose and parts of an expository sermon outline

The purpose of an outline is to organize thoughts. We have many things that help us organize. For example, most people have wardrobes or closets in their homes. The purpose of a wardrobe or closet is to organize clothes.

Q 15 ⤴ *What is the purpose of a sermon outline?*

It is not *necessary* to use a closet to arrange clothes. You could throw your clothes into a corner of a room. But finding the clothes you want would take longer if you threw them in a corner. And what you found to wear would not look very nice.

Figure 8.4 Two different methods of keeping clothes

You can learn to organize thoughts in an outline as you organize clothes in a closet. Then your sermon thoughts will be easy to find when you need them. And they will look better to your people!

Q 16 ⤴ *How is an outline like a closet?*

The parts of an outline. Sermons in this course have an introduction, a body, and an invitation. In this course, we use *Roman numerals *only* in the body of the sermon. We do *not* put Roman numerals beside the Introduction or Invitation. The body of the sermon is the part between the Introduction and the Invitation. The body of a message includes the Problems, Solutions, and the Choice parts of the message. We will teach

Q 17 ⤴ *What are the 3 parts of a sermon outline?*

you to prepare each of these parts. And you will learn always to state your main points as principles.

~~Wrong~~	Right!
I. A. Problem: 1. 2. B. Solution: 1. 2.	I. A. Problem: 1. 2. B. Solution: 1. 2.

Figure 8.5   There is a wrong way and a right way to outline.

- The Introduction
- The Body
- The Invitation

Figure 8.6   The three parts of a sermon

Q 18 *Write the Roman numerals for 1 through 5.*

Capital letters come under Roman numerals. Recall that we *indent capital letters for two reasons. *First,* this makes the capital letters easier to find because it separates them from the Roman numerals. *Second,* we indent capital letters to show that they explain something about the Roman numeral topic above them. In an outline, whenever a letter or number is indented, this means it explains or illustrates something above it.

Q 19 *Put these where they belong in Figure 8.7: Love; The Holy Spirit bears fruit; Peace*

B. Solution: _____
  1. Illustration: _____
  2. Illustration: _____

Figure 8.7   Practice using the parts of an outline.

Lesson 23

State Your Main Points as Principles

Goal A: *Analyze the characteristics and advantages of stating main points as principles.*
Goal B: *Summarize 3 steps for finding and creating principles.*
Goal C: *Explain 6 guidelines for creating principles. Illustrate each.*

A. Characteristics of principles

Principles are like handles. They give people something to grab and hold on to. Imagine a suitcase with no handle! It would be hard to pick up or carry. But a handle makes a suitcase easy to use. Likewise, stating your main points as principles enables your people to use your message. People will take hold of principles, remember them, and apply them day by day.[8]

Definition: A *biblical principle* is a broad, cross-cultural, timeless truth. It is a truth from God's Word that will work anytime, anywhere in the world. A principle is like a roof—it is a broad **general** law, rule, or truth that covers many lesser, **specific** truths. For example, a principle from Matthew 6 is: **Do not do righteous deeds to be seen by others** (Matt. 6:1). This principle is like an umbrella. It covers lesser, specific truths like, **Do not give, pray, or fast so others will see you** (Matt. 6:1-18).

In this course we teach that you may state a principle in *four* different ways:[9]

1. A command

- *"You shall not commit adultery"* (Exod. 20:14).[10]
- *"Do to others what you would have them do to you"* (Matt. 7:12). Note that the Golden Rule is a Golden Principle.
- *"Do not be anxious about anything"* (Phil. 4:6).
- *"Go and make disciples of all nations…"* (Matt. 28:19-20).
- *"Faith without deeds is dead"* (James 2:17, 26).[11]
- *"God opposes the proud but gives grace to the humble"* (James 4:6).
- *"Resist the devil, and he will flee from you"* (James 4:7).

2. A warning (Note that a warning is a form of a command.)

- *"Watch out! Be on your guard against all kinds of greed; a man's life does not consist in the abundance of his possessions"* (Luke 12:15).
- [4]*"Watch out that no one deceives you.* [5]*For many will come in my name, claiming, 'I am the Christ,' and will deceive many"* (Matt. 24:4-5).
- *"We must pay more careful attention, therefore, to what we have heard, so that we do not drift away"* (Heb. 2:1).

3. A promise

- *"Surely I am with you always, to the very end of the age"* (Matt. 28:20). [Note that it is easy, and often better to change a promise to a timeless truth. We have restated Matthew 28:20 as a timeless truth in Number 4 below.]
- *"If I go and prepare a place for you, I will come back and take you to be with me…"* (John 14:3)

Q 20 *State John 14:3 as a timeless truth.*

4. A timeless truth or proverb

- Jesus is with us always, to the very end of the age (Matt. 28:20).
- It is not good for man to be alone (Gen. 2:18).
- *"A student is not above his teacher, nor a servant above his master"* (Matt. 10:24).
- All authority in heaven and on earth has been given to Jesus (Matt. 28:18).
- Those who love Jesus obey Him (John 14:15).
- Jesus is the true vine (John 15:1).
- The wicked will not inherit the kingdom of God (1 Cor. 6:9).
- *"Knowledge puffs up, but love builds up"* (1 Cor. 8:1).
- *"Love is patient"* (1 Cor. 13:4).
- *"Whoever sows sparingly will also reap sparingly"* (2 Cor. 9:6).
- Temptation is linked to evil desires within us (James 1:14).
- *"God is light; in him there is no darkness at all"* (1 John 1:5).

Q 21 *What comes immediately after every principle?*

B. Five Benefits of principles

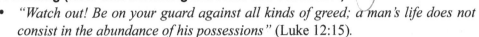

Grade C: Main Points Stated as Topics	Grade A: Main Points Stated as Principles
I. The Call of Joshua (Josh. 1:1-2)	I. God has tomorrow's leaders in training today (Josh. 1: 1-2).
II. The Command of Joshua (Josh. 1:3)	II. God keeps His promises (Josh. 1:3).
III. The Conquest of Joshua (Josh. 1:4)	III. God already has a plan for your future (Josh. 1:4).
IV. The Courage of Joshua (Josh. 1:5-7)	IV. God never abandons those who obey Him (Josh. 1:5-7).

Figure 8.8   First contrast between stating main points as topics and as principles (Josh. 1:1-7)[12]

1. Principles attract attention.   There are many preachers today, like Rick Warren,[13] George O. Wood, and John Lindell, who often state their main points as principles. In contrast, many preachers make a big mistake. They state their main points as topics instead of principles. A topic by itself rarely creates much interest. For example, the four topics about Joshua are biblical, but they are not interesting (Figure 8.8). But a principle

Q 22 *Do you disagree with any of the 5 benefits of principles? Explain.*

Figure 8.9   There are many ways to do your work, but some are quite unnecessary!

grabs the attention of people. Notice how the principles in Figure 8.8 create interest. State your main ideas as principles and people will stay awake during your sermons!

2. Principles are relevant.   They are up to date and ready to use. The main points of some preachers face the past instead of the future. For example, look at the topics about Joshua (Figure 8.8). They face the past. This makes it look like a "B.C. message"[14]—old, dusty, and out of date. State your points as principles, and avoid using any names except God. This will make your sermon sound like it will help people with today's problems.[15] In contrast, hearing the main point "Balaam sought" leaves you asking, "So what?" (Figure 8.10).

3. Principles are easy to illustrate.   If your main point is a topic like "The Call of Joshua," how will you illustrate that point? It would be hard! In Luke 15, Jesus stated a principle: **Heaven rejoices when one sinner repents** (Luke 15:7, 10, 32). He illustrated this principle with the stories of the lost sheep, the lost coin, and the lost son. In this course we will teach you to state your main points as principles. Then, it will be easy for you to illustrate them. One of the biggest reasons preachers do not use more illustrations is that they do not use more principles. It is either hard or impossible to illustrate a topic, but principles are easy to illustrate. And we want to make your work easier, not harder!

4. Principles are easy to apply.   All sermons should be purpose-driven, that is, preached for a purpose. We preach to help people with their problems. There is never more than one step from a principle to the place people live. Look again at the examples in the four types of principles above. All of them are easy to apply.

5. Principles call for a response.   After you apply the truth, you want your listeners to respond. How can people respond to "Balaam fought"? Perhaps they can smile, frown, or go to sleep! But these are not the types of response a preacher wants. In contrast, stating main points as principles enables the preacher to ask the listeners to respond to the truth.[16] Preaching principles makes it easy for you to invite people to pray at the altar. They must choose to accept or reject the biblical principles you preach. Some pastors do not invite people to respond after a sermon because their sermon had no purpose. Learn to preach principles. Then invite people to embrace them.

Q 23 *Which main points from Numbers 22 sound like they will help people today (Figure 8.10). Explain.*

Grade C: Main Points Stated as Topics	Grade A: Main Points Stated as Principles
I. Balaam sought (Num. 22:1-7)	I. To know and do God's will—befriend the truth (Num. 22:1-7).
II. Balaam fought (Num. 22:8-22)	II. To know and do God's will—obey God's Word (Num. 22:8-22).
III. Balaam taught (Num. 22:23-35)	III. To know and do God's will—read the road signs (Num. 22:23-35; compare Matt. 16:2-4; John 20:30-31; Acts 26:14).

Figure 8.10   Second contrast between stating main points as topics and as principles (Num. 22:1-35)

C. Steps for finding and creating principles[17]

1. Read, study, meditate on, and pray over your passage.   Do this without the help of any other books—just you, the Holy Spirit, and your Bible. You may want to spend an hour or more on this step. Discover its topic or theme. Sometimes the topic is stated in the subheading. Identify the author and the readers. *Exegete your passage.[18] Answer questions like: "What did the passage mean to the first readers? How did it help them? What problems does the passage deal with? What caused the problems? Are there any solutions?" There is gold in your text, but you must dig to find it. Squeeze every drop of juice from your text as a person squeezes juice from an orange. Write down key words, thoughts, or questions that come to you. Analyze the passage, finding the subjects, verbs, and word relationships. Try to restate the passage in your own words. Ask the Holy Spirit to apply it to your life. Find the original reasons why the Holy Spirit inspired the passage.[19]

2. Use other books, such as commentaries, Bible dictionaries, study Bibles, other versions of the Bible, and a concordance. If possible, find sermons others have preached on your text. It is easy to see a lot if you stand on the shoulders of a great man. Take notes as you study.

3. State each insight, problem, or solution as a principle. Realize that you may need to restate your principles several times to perfect them. Sometimes you will combine two principles into one. If you have too many principles, you will need to omit some. Getting good principles is like sharpening a knife. Keep working for the change from dull to sharp. As a wise man once said, there is no such thing as good writing, just good re-writing! We have already re-written this page ten times trying to make it better.

Q 24 ↖ Finding good principles is like what?

As an example, consider the temptation, fall, and judgment of man in Genesis 3:1-24. Open your Bible and read this passage. Through much study, meditation, and prayer, we come to know this passage. There are at least four reasons these verses are in our Bible. They give us a record of how the problem of sin came to us. The passage helps us understand the enemy of our souls. These verses help us recognize the results of sin and show us that God makes a provision for salvation.

We may choose to preach five principles based on this passage:

- **Satan likes to *emphasize* what God forbids and *ignore* what God commands** (Gen. 3:1).
- **Satan likes to hide the results of sin** (Gen. 3:4).
- **Satan likes to tempt us by mixing good with evil** (Gen. 3:4-6).
- **Satan knows sin brings separation from God, judgment, and a curse** (Gen. 3:8-19, 22-24).
- **God provides a way for us to return to Him and overcome sin** (Gen. 3:15, 21).

D. Guidelines for stating principles[20]

1. State principles that are true to what the author of your passage meant. Sometimes this is easy, as in Matthew 28:18, where the principle is stated directly. But it is harder to state principles that are based on a story, such as Genesis 3:1-24. The historical setting and context will guide you to state principles that are true to the text. Practice good hermeneutics—follow the rules for interpreting a text. Then you will have the authority from God as you preach His Word.

Q 25 ↖ What principle did Jesus want us to learn from John 13:1-17?

Q 26 ↖ Explain: A principle should be based on the heart and soul of a passage.

You have already seen the principles we gave on Genesis 3:1-24. We feel that these are true to the meaning of the passage. In contrast, here are some bad examples of stating principles that claim to be based on Genesis 3:1-24.

- **Bad** principle: Satan usually tempts people by speaking through snakes or other animals (Gen. 3:1).
- **Bad** principle: The first, forbidden fruit was sex (Gen. 3:3).
- **Bad** principle: Satan has more success tempting women than men.
- Another example of a **bad** principle falsely based on Scripture:
- **Bad** principle: Killing an animal is like killing a man (Isa. 66:3).

Isaiah 66:1-4 records that God did not accept the sacrifices of bulls, lambs, grain, or incense. The reason he rejected these sacrifices was because the people's heart were not right (Isa. 66:3). They had chosen their own ways. So the principle stated above is bad because it is not true to the meaning or context of the text. A good principle is: **God only accepts offerings from those whose hearts are right** (Isa. 66:1-4).

Before leaving this point, we will give one more example of five good principles. These are based on Ephesians 5:25-33:

- **A husband's love should sacrifice for his wife** (Eph. 5:25).
- **A husband's love should make his wife better** (Eph. 5:26-27).

- **A husband's love should care for and nourish his wife** (Eph. 5:28-29).
- **A husband's love should unite him to his wife** (Eph. 5:30-31).
- **A husband's love should be faithful to his wife until death** (Eph. 5:25-33).[21]

Q 27 ✎ *Explain: Biblical principles will work anywhere, anytime.*

2. **State principles as truth that applies across times and cultures to anyone, anywhere, anytime.**   The details may change, but the principles remain the same. For example, we are not in the Garden of Eden. And Satan may not tempt us to eat a certain fruit. But he will continue to emphasize what God forbids, and ignore what God commands. Some examples of bad principles are:

- **Bad** principle: God will give you the land—every place you set your foot (Deut. 11:24-25). This was a specific promise to Abraham. It is not a promise or principle that is true for every believer, unless you are talking about our inheritance after this life!
- **Bad** principle: God wants all believers to have 14,000 sheep and 6,000 camels (Job 42:12). The amount of wealth God desires for people varies. Some, like Abraham and Job, were greatly blessed financially. Others, like the apostles, or believers at Smyrna, were very spiritual, but very poor (Rev. 2:8-11).
- Good principle: **Seek God's kingdom and your relationship with Him first, and He will meet your needs** (Matt. 6:33).
- **Bad** principle: Believers should greet each other with a kiss of love (1 Pet. 5:14). In some cultures, this might be acceptable. In others, it would be ridiculous!
- Good principle: **Believers should show love in the way they greet one another** (1 Pet. 5:14).

Q 28 ⚒ *How long should a principle be?*

3. **State a principle in one, short sentence.**   Review the length of the principles we have given as examples. Each of our examples is only one sentence. Often, the length of principle is 8–12 words. Most of the time, you can state principles in fewer than 15 words. But if the principle is too short, it may not be clear. And if it is too long, people may not grasp it well. The principle of Luke 12:15 is over 20 words, but it seems to be easy enough to grasp. The latter part of Luke 12:15 explains the first part. But a length of 20 words is too long for most principles.

Q 29 ⚒ *Can a principle based on Paul's writings contradict a principle based on James's writings? Explain.*

4. **State principles that agree with all other parts of the Bible.**   Never create principles that contradict other Scripture. If your principles are true, they are in harmony with *all* of God's Word. We have given you examples of good principles. Some examples of principles that are bad because they contradict other verses are:

- **Bad** principle: The gospel is only for Jews, not Gentiles (Matt. 10:5-6).
- Good principle: **God does not want anyone to walk away from Him, but all to walk toward Him** (2 Pet. 3:9).
- **Bad** principle: Your enemies will flee seven different ways before you (Deut. 28:7). This may be true at times today, as it was at times in the Old Testament. But it contradicts many verses in the New Testament. In Acts 8, it was the believers who fled seven different ways. Jesus told his followers that when persecution came in one place, they should flee to another (Matt. 10:23).
- Good principle: **God is with His children at all times** (Matt. 28:20).
- Good principle: **"God opposes the proud, but gives grace to the humble"** (James 4:6).
- Good principle: **Sin desires to master us, but we must master it** (Gen. 4:7).

Q 30 ✎ *Give an example of a main principle and a secondary principle from a passage.*

5. **State the main principles, not the lesser, secondary principles.**   There are several reasons why you should only preach the main principles. The bigger the principle, the more authority it has. There is not time to preach all of the principles in a long passage. For with each principle, you must take time to explain, illustrate, and

apply it. If you preach too many principles in a sermon, people will not remember any of them. So choose only the main principles.

For example, in Genesis 3:1-24, we chose not to emphasize lesser principles, such as:
* Lesser principle: Those who sin like to blame someone else (Gen. 3:12).
* Lesser principle: As humans and snakes are enemies, humans and Satan are enemies (Gen. 3:15).
* Lesser principle: Eve is the mother of all except Adam.

You will spend a lifetime learning to state your main points as principles. It is hard work and requires much skill. So we will begin by stating the principles for you. In these *Faith & Action Series* courses, we state many principles as headings and subheadings. Observing how we do this will help you find principles and learn to state them. Also, since most of our headings are principles, it will make our lessons easy for you to preach and teach.

6. State the principles within a sermon as parallel as possible.   This will make your message easier to preach, follow, and remember. Review the principles in the sermons about Joshua, Balaam, the temptation, the rich young ruler, and a husband's love. First, we developed the principles in each of these sermons. Then, we rewrote them to make them as parallel as possible.[22]

Q 31 ↖ *Change the principles in Figure 8.11 to be parallel.*

Principles That Are Not Parallel	Principles That Are Parallel
1. Bad trees bear bad fruit, and good trees bear good fruit.	1. Teachers are known by their fruit.
2. False teachers come in sheep's clothing.	2. Teachers are not known by appearance alone.
3. Many will do great works, but be lost forever.	3.
4. False teachers lack the fruit of good character.	4.

Figure 8.11   Principles based on Matthew 7:15-20

Some preachers strengthen a parallel form, and aid memory, by adding a word in front of each principle. First, they write their principles or main points. Then, they introduce each principle with a key word. For example, recall that Israel defeated Jericho as they obeyed God. But Israel was defeated at Ai, because of Achan's sin. Consider these three principles from Joshua 6–8.[23]

Q 32 ↗ *What are 2 benefits of introducing a principle with a key word?*

Q 33 ↖ *Why should each key word begin with the same letter, or perhaps rhyme?*

Parallel, Memory Words	Principle	Scripture
Remember:	The blessings of God are not cheap—they come only through the price of obedience.	Joshua 6–7:5
Return:	To receive God's blessings, we must come back to Him if we have sinned.	Joshua 7:6–8:29
Renew:	To express thanks for God's blessings, we should often commit our lives to Him.	Joshua 8:30-35

Figure 8.12   Key words before principles strengthen parallelism and help memory.

E. Sometimes preachers move from specific truths to principles.

In this chapter and this entire book, we are guiding you to state your main points as principles. We want you to do three things to each principle: explain it, illustrate it, and apply it. This is the method we will teach you in this course. However, there are times when preachers use truths that are not principles.

For example, Billy Graham once preached a sermon on the Rich Ruler (Luke 18:18-30). Look at Figure 8.12. On the left it shows the five specific truths Reverend Graham began with. On the right it shows the principles he moved toward so that he could illustrate and apply the sermon.

Specific truths:	Principles:
I. He came to the right person.	I. The right person to come to is Jesus.
II. He came at the right time.	II. The right time to come is today.
III. He asked the right question.	III. The right question to ask is about eternal life.
IV. He got the right answer.	IV. The right answer comes only through Jesus.
V. He made the wrong decision.	V. The right decision can only be made by you.

Figure 8.13   Five truths and principles about the rich ruler in Luke 18:18-30

We recognize that stating main points as principles is not the only good way to preach a sermon. For example, funerals and weddings may call for a different type of message.[24] Also, there are times when pastors organize their messages around key questions. But much of the time a pastor will want to preach principles. Learn this method well and it will help you throughout your ministry.

Lesson 24

The Title, Main Thought, and Introduction

Goal A: *Explain the differences between a good and bad sermon title.*
Goal B: *Define the proposition of a sermon and explain its importance.*
Goal C: *Explain the purposes, challenges, and types of introductions.*

A. The *title of a sermon

Q 34 *How is a title like a sign?*

Every sermon should have a title. Its purpose is to tell the listeners what the sermon is about. A title is like a sign—it tells people what is ahead. A title should be interesting and brief. It should give information and attract attention without being silly.

Figure 8.14   A sermon title is like a sign—it tells people what is ahead.

The title should not promise more than the sermon can deliver. It should be short, creative, specific, interesting, and in harmony with the purpose of the sermon.

Let us consider a title for a sermon on Ephesians 2:8-9: [8]*"For it is by grace you have been saved, through faith—and this not from yourselves, it is the gift of God—* [9]*not by works, so that no one can boast."*

Three examples of poor titles for Ephesians 2:8-9 are:
* "Grace." This title is too short. It is not specific enough.
* "We have been saved by grace through faith." This title is too long!
* "The Grace of God." This title is too broad. Like the first title above, it is not specific enough.

Two examples of good titles for Ephesians 2:8-9 are:
* "The Grace That Saved My Life"
* "Saved by Grace!"

Pastors often write a temporary title when they start preparing a message. Later, they improve the title after they complete the message. Many pastors announce a title *after* the Introduction.

Topic	Sermon Title
Grace	Amazing Grace
Repentance	The Way Up Is Down
Love	The Strongest Power in the World
Tithing	The Key to God's Financial Blessings
Forgiveness	
Holiness	

Figure 8.15   Practice choosing sermon titles.

Q 35 ✎ Complete Figure 8.15.

B. The main thought of a sermon

A preacher should seek to identify the main thought of a biblical passage. He should work until he can state this main thought in one sentence. In the past, great teachers often referred to the main thought as the *proposition.*[25] Walter Kaiser refers to the proposition as a topic sentence.[26] The main thought or proposition of a sermon is a summary of the sermon in one sentence.[27] In the next chapter we study a sermon based on Philippians 4:6-8. In that sermon, we will discuss the problem of worry. Then we will show that the passage says we can overcome worry through praying our problems, giving thanks, and thinking good thoughts. We may state the main thought or proposition of the sermon as:

Paul gives us three keys to overcome the problem of worry.

Notice that our summary does not answer the question "How?" Stating the main thought of a passage may not give details. But it summarizes the sermon.

A preacher is not ready to preach until he or she can summarize the main thought in one sentence. The main thought of the sermon should shine as plain as the moon in a sky with no clouds.[28] You will learn to state the proposition after you have studied a passage. Then, as you prepare your outline, you must be sure that each part of the outline relates to the main thought. If not, you must revise your main thought, for it is a summary of your main points and message.

A preacher must always let the main thought come out of a biblical passage. This is expository preaching—exposing the main thought of a text. For example, there are many topics in the parable of the Good Samaritan (Luke 10:25-37). The parable speaks of thieves, religious leaders, trials, love, and sacrifice. But the main thought of the parable is that to be a good neighbor, we must avoid prejudice.[29] The Samaritan was willing to do what the two religious leaders refused to do. So in preaching the main thought on this parable, it would be important to focus on the truth that true love helps anyone in need.

C. The purposes of the Introduction

The Introduction, has two purposes. The *first* purpose is to gain the attention of the listeners.

Imagine a pastor starting to preach. He holds up a bag in front of the people. Something is alive in the bag, and it is trying to get out! Is it a snake? Is it a cat? Something in the bag is moving. The eyes of every person in the building are watching the pastor and the bag. Everyone wants to know what is in the bag. A sermon should start like this. That is, the Introduction should capture people's attention.[30]

The *second* purpose of the Introduction is to gain the favor of the listeners. The pastor must build a bridge from himself to his people. That is, he must gain their favor and build *rapport—a

**Figure 8.16
An Introduction
should gain people's
attention.**

Q 36 ↗ How should Step I (the Introduction) be like a pastor holding a bag?

Q 37 ↗ What is the second purpose of the Introduction?

good relationship with the listeners. The pastor wants the people to have good feelings toward him and his sermon. The Introduction brings the preacher and the people closer together.

D. The challenges of the Introduction

There are three reasons why gaining people's attention and favor may be harder than you think.

Q 38 ✎ *What are the most common types of distractions in your church?*

1. People are often distracted by things in the church.   If a baby cries, they may look that direction and listen to it instead of the pastor. If someone walks into or out of the church, people may turn their thoughts in that direction. Small things can pull the attention of people away from God's messenger.

Q 39 ✎ *Do a person's eyes always tell you whether he or she is paying attention? Explain.*

2. People's minds may go on a mental safari.   People can fool you. They can be looking at you, but thinking about something else. They can be looking straight ahead, but thinking about food instead. They can be eye-to-eye with the pastor, while thinking about problems at home or at work. They can be present in body, but not in mind! Usually, there has been singing before the preaching begins. Singing is more exciting than sitting and listening. So the pastor needs a good introduction to pull people's thoughts to God's Word.

Q 40 ↗ *Name at least 3 things that we preach in order to change.*

3. People resist change.   We should always preach to change something.
* We preach to *change* sinners into saints;
* We preach to help Christians *change* and become more like Christ;
* We preach to *change* wrong beliefs and bad patterns of thinking;
* We preach to *change* depression, unforgiveness, discouragement, and bitterness.

We are studying reasons for the sermon's Introduction. The pastor who does not want to change something can leave out the Introduction. In fact, if a pastor does not want to change something, he should cancel every sermon! Any sermon that does not aim at changing something is wasting people's time. It should not be preached at all. Only preach messages that aim to bring good changes![31]

But be aware that people resist change. We are often content to let things remain as they are. The greatest hindrance to becoming more like Christ is not being willing to change.

Q 41 ↗ *Which 2 types of pastors do people naturally resist?*

Q 42 ↗ *State 3 reasons why it may be hard to gain the favor and attention of people.*

If we think someone is trying to change us, we resist. This puts the pastor in a difficult place at the beginning of his sermon. Listeners especially resist if they do not know the pastor. But they also resist if they do know the pastor! Listeners resist two types of pastors: those they know and those they do not know! So it is important for the pastor to gain the favor and attention of those who are listening.

E. Four types of introductions

Q 43 ✎ *Why do you think praising people helps gain their favor?*

1. Praise.   One way to gain favor and attention is by giving praise. Give the listeners sincere praise on anything that is good. Thank them for attending. Praise them for the way they look or sing. Say something good about their church building. Praise them for their children or their reputation. Jesus sent letters to seven different churches (Rev. 1–3). He did His best to praise each of them for something. So when we praise believers, we are following the example of the Good Shepherd.

Q 44 ✎ *Can you remember any good things people have said about you?*

Most believers deserve much more praise than they receive. They work hard and love God. So pastors can encourage them by giving compliments. Most of us never tire of receiving sincere compliments. We feel warm toward those who appreciate us. And some of us can remember praise that people gave us in past years. On the other hand, we feel cold toward those who criticize us. Begin some of your sermons with a sentence that everyone will be happy to hear. Give praise! Give honor to whom honor is due. Give thanks to those who deserve it. A compliment alone is not a sufficient introduction, but it is a step in the right direction.

2. Humor. Humor is one of the best ways to "warm up" a group of listeners. People may not like it if a pastor laughs at another person. But people will normally laugh with him when he laughs at himself. When people laugh with a pastor, they tend to open up to him. They allow him to be a part of their group. They are more willing to hear his ideas.

Q 45 ↗ *What 3 things happen when people laugh with a pastor?*

Still, do not use humor too much. In most cases, the humor should be directly related to the sermon. Do not use humor that serves no purpose in the message.

A pastor once preached on forgiveness. He introduced his message by telling a humorous story about himself. As a child, he had a dog that was dear to him. One day the dog died, so he buried it. But he left the tail sticking out of the ground! Every few days, he went to the grave to see his beloved dog. He grabbed the tail and pulled the dead animal out of the ground. What a terrible odor! What an ugly sight! He always re-buried the dog—except for the tail. After some days of this, his father stopped him from digging up the dog's body again.

Q 46 ↗ *Why was the dog story a very good introduction?*

What was the pastor's point in this humorous illustration? People should *completely* forgive and bury past hurts and wrongs. Digging up bad things from the past only creates a bad odor all around us. This pastor shared a past event that was once painful to him. He was able to laugh at himself about it and to invite people to laugh with him. His use of humor helped his listeners face the need to forgive completely.[32]

Some pastors are afraid to laugh at themselves. They will never admit their own faults. Such men are not secure. They fear that if they admit their faults, their listeners will think less of them. But the opposite is true. Pastors who can laugh at themselves and admit their faults appear real and human. People relate to spiritual men who live the same type of lives they do.

Q 47 ↗ *Do you think less of a leader who can laugh at himself? Explain.*

A preacher must use wisdom to discern what he should share. No church wants a pastor who does not respect himself or who tells too much about himself. Still, an effective preacher is sometimes like the turtle. He moves forward when he sticks his neck out!

Q 48 ↗ *How is a pastor sometimes like a turtle?*

Figure 8.17
Sometimes a preacher is like a turtle.

People who laugh with you during the Introduction will probably cry with you over life's problems. This is what every preacher wants—to touch people's emotions with God's concerns. When people's hearts and emotions are touched, they open up to God.

Q 49 ↗ *Why should a pastor try to touch people's emotions?*

3. Help from the listeners. A third way of gaining favor and attention is to ask the listeners for help. The preacher wants his listeners to become involved in the sermon. Why? This brings the preacher and listeners closer together. Listeners can become involved in many ways. These include answering questions, raising their hands, saying amen, giving testimonies, and helping with dramas.

Q 50 ↗ *Explain 4 ways listeners can become involved in a sermon.*

A pastor once asked for a volunteer from the listeners. A deacon agreed. He played the role of the wounded man in the parable of the Good Samaritan. The pastor then got another volunteer to be the Good Samaritan. The pastor acted out the roles of both the Levite and the priest. He walked past the man in need. What was the result of this drama? Since some of the people were helping with the sermon, everyone paid close attention.

Q 51 ↗ *Why is it better to get people involved in the message?*

The pastor's Introduction was wise. He found a way for the people to participate with his sermon. This lowered the people's resistance to his message about prejudice. The people and the pastor looked at the story together. Instead of him facing one way and them another, they all faced the same direction. This method worked better than the pastor just telling the story to them. All of them were involved. Attention went up; resistance went down.

Q 52 *Which types of illustrations may a preacher use to introduce his message?*

Q 53 *In which 2 directions should the Introduction move the listeners?*

Q 54 *How long should the Introduction be?*

4. Illustrations. A preacher may use many other ways to gain favor and attention. He may begin with a question, a story, a proverb, a testimony, a song, a poem, an object lesson, or a newspaper story. *Any* illustration may serve as a good introduction. It should always move listeners toward the speaker and the subject.

The length of the Introduction depends on two things:

- • the subject, and
- • the relationship of the preacher to the people.

The Introduction should be as short as possible. It should be just long enough to prepare people for the main part of the sermon. Too much time in the Introduction confuses the listeners—causing them to wonder what the purpose of the sermon is. A long Introduction sounds like the first point of a sermon. Then, when it is time to move into the first main point, the listeners are confused. This can cause them to lose interest. So keep the Introduction short!

Often, the preacher prepares the Introduction last. Be sure you plan the Introduction well. The rest of the sermon may be wasted if the preacher fails to gain favor and attention in the Introduction.

F. A sample Introduction

Sermon Title: Trade Your Worry for Peace

Main Thought: The Bible gives us 3 keys to overcome worry.

Text: Philippians 4:6-8

Introduction:

A small boy came home troubled from school. He told his mother that his teacher had warts on her left hand. The boy had heard someone say that warts were caused by worrying. The boy asked his mother, "Are warts really caused by worrying?" She smiled and said that warts were not caused by worrying. However, with a serious face she warned her son that worrying is a bad problem. It does not cause warts, but it causes many things that are worse than warts.

Figure 8.18 Introduction to the sermon: Trade Your Worry for Peace (Phil. 4:6-8)

Test Yourself: Circle the letter by the ***best*** completion to each question or statement.

1. An expository sermon is based on
a) a topic.
b) a recent event.
c) an expositor.
d) a biblical passage.

2. Preaching through a book will help a pastor
a) know the Old Testament.
b) memorize the Bible.
c) deal with hard topics.
d) All of the above

3. What is the purpose of an outline?
a) To help the preacher end on time
b) To organize thoughts
c) To entertain the audience
d) To provide illustrations

4. Principles include
a) topics and themes.
b) facts and numbers.
c) warnings and promises.
d) stories and riddles.

5. A good Introduction will
a) present a solution.
b) make people cry.
c) list the main points.
d) gain people's interest.

6. A sermon title is like
a) a sign.
b) a bridge.
c) a meal.
d) a question.

7. It is hard to gain attention and favor because
a) most people do not like preachers.
b) people are all thinking about work.
c) people resist change in any form.
d) All of the above

8. One goal of preaching is to always
a) sound prepared.
b) change people.
c) explain questions.
d) teach Bible stories.

9. Which is FALSE?
a) Humor should relate to the sermon.
b) Illustrations should be as short as possible.
c) A compliment is a sufficient introduction.
d) Giving praise will help you gain favor.

10. If a preacher admits some of his faults,
a) people will think less of him.
b) people will question his faith.
c) people will think he is unspiritual.
d) people will relate to him better.

 Essay Test Topics Write 50-100 words

on each of these goals that you studied in this chapter.

Planning Expository Sermons

Goal: *Contrast a topical and expository sermon.*

Goal: *Explain 7 advantages of planning a group of expository sermons.*

Goal: *Explain the purpose and parts of a sermon outline.*

State Your Main Points as Principles

Goal: *Analyze the characteristics and advantages of stating main points as principles.*

Goal: *Summarize 3 steps for finding and creating principles.*

Goal: *Explain 6 guidelines for creating principles. Illustrate each.*

The Title, Main Thought, and Introduction

Goal: *Explain the differences between a good and bad sermon title.*

Goal: *Define the proposition of a sermon and explain its importance.*

Goal: *Explain the purposes, challenges, and types of introductions.*

Chapter 9:

Present the Problem Before the Solution

Introduction

The Problem comes before the Solution.

The Problem Comes First	The Solution Solves the Problem
People get hungry	before they want to eat.
People get thirsty	before they want to drink.
People get tired	before they want to rest.
People feel an itch	before they want to scratch.
People have a question	before they look for an answer.
People must feel a need	before they seek to fulfill it.

Figure 9.1   The Problem comes before the Solution.

In this chapter we will teach you to be wise by always preaching about the Problem *before* you preach about the Solution.

Figure 9.2   A farmer succeeded when he thought about what his donkey wanted.

Lessons:

 Cooperate With the Way People Think
Goal: *Explain how a preacher can prepare sermons in a way that is logical, wise, successful and helpful.*

 Four Questions and Answers About the Problem Step
Goal: *Respond to 4 common questions students ask about presenting Problems.*

 Practice Identifying Problems and Solutions in a Biblical Passage
Goal: *Identify the Problem and Solution in a given passage of Scripture.*

Cooperate With the Way People Think

Goal: *Explain how a preacher can prepare sermons in a way that is logical, wise, successful and helpful.*

A. Be *logical: Plow before you plant!

Prepare a sermon in harmony with the way people think. Always present a Problem before you present the Solution. This matches the way people think. A man once saw a sign on a car. The sign said, "Christ is the answer." The man asked, "What is the question?" People do not look for answers *before* they have a question. Solutions logically come *after* problems. Have you ever seen someone seeking the answer to a math problem *before* he knew the problem? Of course not! It is natural to look for solutions *after* we face a problem. Therefore, we preachers should always discuss the problem before the answer.

Figure 9.3   A wise preacher is like a farmer—he plows before he plants.

After the Introduction, state a Problem. In fact, a Problem may serve as its own Introduction. Stating the Problem *before* giving the Solution is like plowing the ground before planting the seed. How foolish it would be to plant seed in ground that had not been plowed. How unwise to tell people what the Solution is before you discuss the Problem!

Q 1 ⋏ *What should a preacher always describe before the answer?*

Q 2 ⋏ *Describing the Problem before the Solution is like _____.*

B. Be wise: Make people thirsty before you offer them water.

Figure 9.4
Sheep drink after they become thirsty.

You can lead an animal to water, but you cannot make it drink. If a sheep is not thirsty, getting it to drink is very hard. You can lead it to the water—even pour buckets of water on its head. But it will not drink if it is not thirsty. The water will go *on* it but not *in* it! The water will just roll off its back. But take that same sheep for a long walk over dry, dusty ground in the hot sunshine. Then lead it to water. It will be hard to stop the sheep from drinking!

You must make people thirsty if you expect them to *drink* the solution to a problem.

Q 3 ⋏ *How do you make your "sheep" thirsty for your solution?*

Q 4 ⋏ *Why is it a mistake to offer people a Solution before the Problem?*

C. Be successful: Discern what people need before you offer help.

Q 5 ⋏ *When do we resist the most?*

One of the hardest things in the world is to *force* people to do something. People can be stubborn. They resist if they think someone is trying to force them to act in a certain way. In contrast, people gladly do things that they *want* to do.

What people want is closely related to what they need. So a preacher should plan his messages based on the desires and needs of his people. He should never try to force them to act.

A father and son tried to force a calf to move from one place to another. The father was in front of the calf, pulling it. The boy was pushing the calf from behind it. Still, the calf refused to move. A little girl came along and was able to move the calf easily. How did she do it? She stuck her finger in the calf's mouth. It thought she had milk!

Figure 9.5   Two methods of moving a calf

So the animal gladly followed her. The girl persuaded the calf to move because she thought about what the calf wanted![1]

A sermon should help people get what they want and need. A pastor will lead many people in God's ways if he plans sermons with this in mind. Let us look at how to know the needs and wants of people.

People want many things in life. They want God to meet their physical needs for food, clothing, shelter, finances, and health. And they want to live in safety, free from fear. All human beings want to feel protected…accepted…loved…happy…free from guilt…needed…appreciated…respected…peaceful…and successful. People want to know that their lives have purpose and meaning. And deep within, people want to know their Creator and have fellowship with Him.

None of these human desires is wrong. God created us this way. All of us are naturally concerned about these desires and needs. All listeners have two questions:

Q 6 ➢ *Why did the father and son fail? Why did the girl succeed?*

- "How will this sermon help *me*?"
- "What will *I* get out of this message?"

Q 7 ➢ *What are some things all people want and need?*

We all move *toward* the good things we want.[2] A successful preacher plans his sermons to help his people solve their problems, meet their needs, and receive the good things that they want.

Q 8 ➢ *Why should a pastor's solution answer the questions of his people?*

D. Be helpful: Present biblical solutions *after* you preach about a problem.

After preaching about problems people face, you must give the biblical solutions.[3] There are three things to do in this step. *First,* you show that this solution solves the problem. This is like offering water to people who are thirsty. Use as many types of illustrations as you need to persuade the head and heart.

Second, you show *how* to put the solution into action. For example, it is not enough to tell believers they should not worry. You must show them *how* to avoid worrying.

Third, you deal with any questions or objections that listeners might have. Do not ignore the questions people have. And do not expect them to ask the questions during the church service. You, the pastor, must learn to understand your people. In private, they may ask you some of their questions as you talk together. You must learn to recognize the questions that they have. Then, you must help them find answers that will satisfy them. Otherwise, the questions people have may prevent them from accepting your solution.

Lesson 26

Four Questions and Answers About Presenting Problems

Goal: *Respond to 4 common questions students ask about presenting Problems.*

A. First question

Student A: Why are you telling me always to preach about a problem? I might want to preach on something that is not a problem.

Q 9 ➢ *Why should a pastor always preach on a real problem?*

Teacher: Students may be pulled toward a topic just because it is interesting. Some students have a lot of time to read, sit, and think. In contrast to such students, many adults struggle to survive. Some must work hard to keep their jobs. Others do not have jobs and need to find work. They must buy food and cook meals. They must wash dishes and clothes. People have bills to pay and children to educate. They must care for sick family members at times. Adults must conquer discouragement and temptations. They struggle to relate to difficult people. There are arguments and quarrels to solve. Adults with children or aged parents have concerns for many people other than themselves. They care for the needs of their family.

The people of *Athens, in ancient Greece, were unusual. *"All the Athenians... spent their time doing nothing but talking about and listening to the latest ideas"* (Acts 17:21).

Q 10 *How are most church members different from the citizens of Athens?*

Hell is full of people like the citizens of Athens. They spent their time talking about ideas. They never realized that earth is a spiritual battleground. They did not discern that God and Satan are fighting for men's eternal souls.

Pastor, the people in your church are *not* like the citizens of Athens. Several times each week you will preach to hard-working, struggling people. These people come to church to be renewed and encouraged. They come to meet God, to sing, worship, and receive spiritual food for another hard week in the world. Your preaching must meet their needs.

Q 11 *List some reasons why sincere people come to church.*

Satan does not want even one person to escape the flames of everlasting hell. He tries to lead people away from the cross and into the brief pleasures of sin. Satan whispers temptations to men on the street corners. He discourages people at work, and brings trouble to their homes. The devil leads multitudes of youth away from Christ. And he laughs when children grow up outside of the church.

Without a pastor, these people will be helpless, *"like sheep without a shepherd"* (Matt. 9:36). God calls pastors to lead and care for these sheep. People must get solutions to the problems they face every day. A pastor's sheep will love and appreciate him if his messages help them and minister to their needs. Such church members will have healthy spiritual appetites. They will attend regularly, bring visitors, and support the church with tithes and offerings.

Pastors must help people with life's problems. They should serve their flock, as the Good Shepherd served all of us. Jesus spent His life helping people with their problems. Pastors should preach what the Bible says about people's problems. This is like bringing Christ to the table where they eat. Otherwise, they will eat alone.[4]

Q 12 *Who is the key person God has chosen to help people with their problems?*

So do not consider preaching about something that is not a problem. People are desperate. Their problems are like a group of thieves. Help your people overcome, or they will perish!

Student A: Thank you. As a student, it is easy for some of us to forget the problems many people face. I promise before God that I will fulfill His call on my life. As a shepherd, I will preach to help His sheep live in victory over their problems!

B. Second question

Student B: Why waste time convincing people that something is a problem when they already know it is a problem?

Q 13 *How would you answer the question of Student B?*

Teacher: Not everyone agrees about what is a problem. For example, alcohol leads to drunkenness, disease, and poverty. It causes thousands to die in road accidents. Alcohol makes fools out of many who drink it. Still, some do not consider alcohol to be a problem. It will shock you to discover the things that believers are not aware of.

- About half of the world does not read. Do all the believers in your church know that illiteracy is a huge problem?
- Half of the world has never heard the gospel. Do all believers realize what a big problem this is?
- Perhaps many of the members in your church earn good wages. They may not realize that poverty is a big problem. They may not know that 2.8 billion people, almost half of the world, live on less than $2 per day![5]
- Perhaps many of your church members are safe. Do they realize that 160,000 people are killed each year for their faith in Christ?[6]

- Perhaps your people eat well. Do they realize that hunger is a problem? Every day, more than 800 million people (300 million children) suffer the gnawing pain of hunger, and the diseases caused by it. Some estimate that as many as 24,000 people die every day as a result.[7]

A giraffe and a turtle stood near each other. The turtle was very discouraged. The rain had created a big ditch between him and the lake. At first, there was enough water in the small puddles. But after a week, the hot sun dried up all of these small water holes. Now, the only water was in the lake, and the ditch was too deep for the turtle to cross. He needed water to live.

The giraffe stood with a foot on each side of the ditch. His stomach was full of cool water. He did not realize that the turtle was only a day away from death. Then a small bird lit on the giraffe's head. The giraffe was alarmed. He thought the bird was trying to steal a hair for a nest. Then the tall animal heard the bird whisper about the turtle's need. The giraffe looked down. For the first time, he considered the turtle's point of view. Like a mother cat carries a kitten, the giraffe lifted the turtle across the ditch and close to the lake. Soon, the turtle was smiling again.

Do not assume that everyone agrees on what is a problem. Be certain your listeners are convinced that something is a serious problem. Like the giraffe and the turtle, people see things in different ways. One steps over what another sees as a deep valley.

C. Third question

Q 14 *Explain: It is harder to reach the heart than the head.*

Student C: Suppose I am sure that everyone in my church knows that something is a problem. May I skip over talking about the problem and go on to the solution?

Teacher: This is an important question. Also, I can tell from your voice and your face that you are sincere. Every good teacher welcomes sincere questions. I will answer your question in two parts. *First*, it would be hard to know for sure what everyone in a church thinks about a topic. *Second*, keep in mind that you are aiming for the heart, not just the head. Reaching the heart is harder than reaching the head.

For example, suppose you want to preach about overcoming discouragement. Most people would agree that discouragement is a problem. But only those who have had a discouraging week would be ready for a solution. Those who had not recently struggled with discouragement would not be ready for your solution. Offering them a solution would be like offering water to someone who is not thirsty. So emphasize the problem until everyone feels the need for help. Then your solution can reach every heart. Keep in mind that you will need to emphasize some problems more than others. The more aware people are of a problem, the less you need to emphasize it.

D. Fourth question

Q 15 *Do people get tired of a newspaper that is prepared by the same methods? Explain.*

Student D: Won't people get tired of hearing the same method if I always emphasize the problem before the solution?

Teacher: We use the same methods over and over in daily life, yet people do not get tired of them. Why? Most people do not recognize or analyze a method.

Consider the daily newspaper. Every newspaper is prepared by the same method. People type headlines. They use the same machines day after day. Each page is the same size. Each newspaper is printed on the same kind of paper with the same black ink. The text is always printed in columns. Certain types of articles are usually found each day in the same location in the newspaper. The paper is folded the same way every time. In other words, the method of preparing a newspaper is the same every day. Yet many people buy newspapers every day!

Why do people like newspapers so well? People do not analyze the method by which a newspaper is prepared. All they are interested in is the *content*. They want the news!

If today's newspaper has new headlines and new stories, people want it. The method of preparing the paper is not important to them.

Likewise, meals are prepared by the same method day after day. A cook uses the same stove and the same pots. She serves food in the same plates and bowls. No one will question this method. The food is what they care about! Those who eat are not concerned about the method used to organize the meal. In fact, the cook is normally the only one who thinks about it. After years of cooking, even the cook may not realize that he or she is using a method.

Q 16 ⟩ *Do people get tired of the method a cook uses to prepare a meal? Explain.*

The number of methods you use daily that were once hard to learn might surprise you. What method do you use for walking? Reading? Writing? Eating? Talking? Studying for an exam? Perhaps you have forgotten how many methods you use. Like most people, you do not often analyze your methods of doing things. When you do analyze methods, you are thankful for them. Try to write by a different method than the one you use now. It is very hard! Try to prepare a sermon *without* using a method. No, please don't! Methods help!

Q 17 ⟨ *Name some methods you repeat and do not want to change.*

We stated earlier that a preacher's outline should be hidden like an animal's skeleton. Your listeners will not grow tired of the Problem/Solution Method if you use it correctly. In fact, they will not even know that you are using a method! They will be blessed by the message, but will seldom analyze it.

Q 18 ⟩ *State 2 reasons why people will never grow tired of the Problem/Solution Method.*

Keep in mind that you should *never* announce all the parts of your sermon. Your outline will have an *Introduction.* But you will never say, to your listeners, "Here is the Introduction to my sermon!" Rather, you will just give the Introduction. You probably will not say, "Next I want to talk to you about a problem." Instead, you will just state what the problem is.

You have heard many sermons that used a Problem/Solution Method. But you did not recognize or analyze the method. You just enjoyed the sermon. The same will be true of your listeners.

Lesson 27 — Practice Identifying Problems and Solutions in Biblical Passages

Goal: *Identify the Problem and Solution in a given passage of Scripture.*

With practice, it will become easy for you to discern the Problems and Solutions in biblical passages. We have completed some of the chart that follows (Figure 9.6). Some students may complete it by themselves. Others may work on it in class with a teacher. Note that the biblical passages follow the chart.

Q 19 ⟨ *Complete Figure 9.6 by identifying the Problems and Solutions in biblical passages.*

Passage	Theme	Problem(s)	Solution(s)
Matt. 4:1-11	Temptation	1. Satan tempts us to meet our needs in the wrong ways. 2. Satan tempts us to test God by doing foolish things. 3. Satan tempts us to compromise—to use wrong methods to reach good goals.	1. We do not live by bread alone—by thinking only about our needs—but by fullfilling our needs as God's Word directs us. 2. We should trust God, but not tempt Him. 3. Resist the devil by doing right, and he will flee from you.
Matt. 7:1-5	Judging		1. Pay attention to your own faults.
Matt. 15:1-9	Worship		1. Sometimes we must choose between tradition and Scripture.
Matt. 18:21-35	Forgiving		
Matt. 26:6-13			
Acts 1:4-8	Being filled with the Spirit		
Rom. 12:1-2			
Rom. 13:1-7			

Figure 9.6   Practice finding the Problems and Solutions in biblical passages.

Matthew 4:1-11

¹Then Jesus was led by the Spirit into the desert to be tempted by the devil. ²After fasting forty days and forty nights, he was hungry. ³The tempter came to him and said, "If you are the Son of God, tell these stones to become bread." ⁴Jesus answered, "It is written: 'Man does not live on bread alone, but on every word that comes from the mouth of God.'" ⁵Then the devil took him to the holy city and had him stand on the highest point of the temple. ⁶"If you are the Son of God," he said, "throw yourself down. For it is written: "'He will command his angels concerning you, and they will lift you up in their hands, so that you will not strike your foot against a stone.'" ⁷Jesus answered him, "It is also written: 'Do not put the Lord your God to the test.'" ⁸Again, the devil took him to a very high mountain and showed him all the kingdoms of the world and their splendor. ⁹"All this I will give you," he said, "if you will bow down and worship me." ¹⁰Jesus said to him, "Away from me, Satan! For it is written: 'Worship the Lord your God, and serve him only.'" ¹¹Then the devil left him, and angels came and attended him.

Matthew 7:1-5

¹"Do not judge, or you too will be judged. ²For in the same way you judge others, you will be judged, and with the measure you use, it will be measured to you. ³Why do you look at the speck of sawdust in your brother's eye and pay no attention to the plank in your own eye? ⁴How can you say to your brother, 'Let me take the speck out of your eye,' when all the time there is a plank in your own eye? ⁵You hypocrite, first take the plank out of your own eye, and then you will see clearly to remove the speck from your brother's eye."

Matthew 15:1-9

¹Then some Pharisees and teachers of the law came to Jesus from Jerusalem and asked, ²"Why do your disciples break the tradition of the elders? They don't wash their hands before they eat!" ³Jesus replied, "And why do you break the command of God for the sake of your tradition? ⁴For God said, 'Honor your father and mother' and 'Anyone who curses his father or mother must be put to death.' ⁵But you say that if a man says to his father or mother, 'Whatever help you might otherwise have received from me is a gift devoted to God,' ⁶he is not to 'honor his father' with it. Thus you nullify the word of God for the sake of your tradition. ⁷You hypocrites! Isaiah was right when he prophesied about you: ⁸"'These people honor me with their lips, but their hearts are far from me. ⁹They worship me in vain; their teachings are but rules taught by men.'"

Matthew 18:21-35

²¹Then Peter came to Jesus and asked, "Lord, how many times shall I forgive my brother when he sins against me? Up to seven times?" ²²Jesus answered, "I tell you, not seven times, but seventy-seven times. ²³Therefore, the kingdom of heaven is like a king who wanted to settle accounts with his servants. ²⁴As he began the settlement, a man who owed him ten thousand talents was brought to him. ²⁵Since he was not able to pay, the master ordered that he and his wife and his children and all that he had be sold to repay the debt. ²⁶The servant fell on his knees before him. 'Be patient with me,' he begged, 'and I will pay back everything.' ²⁷The servant's master took pity on him, canceled the debt and let him go. ²⁸But when that servant went out, he found one of his fellow servants who owed him a hundred denarii. He grabbed him and began to choke him. 'Pay back what you owe me!' he demanded. ²⁹His fellow servant fell to his knees and begged him, 'Be patient with me, and I will pay you back.' ³⁰But he refused. Instead, he went off and had the man thrown into prison until he could pay the debt. ³¹When the other *servants saw what had happened, they were greatly distressed and went and told their master everything that had happened. ³²Then the master called the servant in. 'You wicked servant,' he said, 'I canceled all that debt of yours because you begged me to. ³³Shouldn't you have had mercy on your fellow servant just as I had on you?' ³⁴In anger his master turned him over to the jailers to be tortured, until he should pay back all he owed. ³⁵This is how my heavenly Father will treat each of you unless you forgive your brother from your heart."*

Matthew 26:6-13

⁶While Jesus was in Bethany in the home of a man known as Simon the Leper, ⁷a woman came to him with an alabaster jar of very expensive perfume, which she poured on his head as he was reclining at the table. ⁸When the disciples saw this, they were indignant. "Why this waste?" they asked. ⁹"This perfume could have been sold at a high price and the money given to the poor." ¹⁰Aware of this, Jesus said to them, "Why are you bothering this woman? She has done a beautiful thing to me. ¹¹The poor you will always have with you, but you will not always have me. ¹²When she poured this perfume on my body, she did it to prepare me for burial. ¹³I tell you the truth, wherever this gospel is preached throughout the world, what she has done will also be told, in memory of her."

Acts 1:4-8

⁴On one occasion, while he was eating with them, he gave them this command: "Do not leave Jerusalem, but wait for the gift my Father promised, which you have heard me speak about. ⁵For John baptized with water, but in a few days you will be baptized with the Holy Spirit." ⁶So when they met together, they asked him, "Lord, are you at this time going to restore the kingdom to Israel?" ⁷He said to them: "It is not for you to know the times or dates the Father has set by his own authority. ⁸But you will receive power when the Holy Spirit comes on you; and you will be my witnesses in Jerusalem, and in all Judea and Samaria, and to the ends of the earth."

Romans 12:1-2

¹Therefore, I urge you, brothers, in view of God's mercy, to offer your bodies as living sacrifices, holy and pleasing to God—this is your spiritual act of worship. ²Do not conform any longer to the pattern of this world, but be transformed by the renewing of your mind. Then you will be able to test and approve what God's will is—his good, pleasing and perfect will.

Romans 13:1-7

¹Everyone must submit himself to the governing authorities, for there is no authority except that which God has established. The authorities that exist have been established by God. ²Consequently, he who rebels against the authority is rebelling against what God has instituted, and those who do so will bring judgment on themselves. ³For rulers hold no terror for those who do right, but for those who do wrong. Do you want to be free from fear of the one in authority? Then do what is right and he will commend you. ⁴For he is God's servant to do you good. But if you do wrong, be afraid, for he does not bear the sword for nothing. He is God's servant, an agent of wrath to bring punishment on the wrongdoer. ⁵Therefore, it is necessary to submit to the authorities, not only because of possible punishment but also because of conscience. ⁶This is also why you pay taxes, for the authorities are God's servants, who give their full time to governing. ⁷Give everyone what you owe him: If you owe taxes, pay taxes; if revenue, then revenue; if respect, then respect; if honor, then honor.

Test Yourself: Circle the letter by the *best* completion to each question or statement.

1. Preaching the Problem before the Solution is like
a) eating before cooking.
b) signing before reading.
c) harvesting after planting.
d) plowing before planting.

2. Preach the Solution after the Problem, because
a) answers should come before questions.
b) people drink after they become thirsty.
c) all of us will reap what we sow.
b) that which is born of Spirit is spirit.

3. All who listen to a sermon want to know:
a) How will this sermon help me?
b) What is the preacher's outline?
c) How long will this sermon be?
d) How clever is the preacher?

4. People appreciate messages that
a) inform them of current events.
b) discuss the latest ideas.
c) help with life's problems.
d) give them political advice.

5. Church members are most like
a) people facing a group of thieves.
b) citizens of ancient Athens.
c) students in Bible school.
d) children on a playground.

6. What do methods help with?
a) Cooking food
b) Writing
c) Preaching
d) All of the above

7. In which step should a sermon answer questions?
a) The Introduction Step
b) The Problem Step
c) The Solution Step
d) The Invitation Step

8. One who preaches about things that are not problems would make a good pastor for
a) Rome
b) Jerusalem
c) Athens
d) Antioch

9. When can a preacher skip the Problem Step?
a) If people already know something is a problem
b) If it takes too much time for the Solution
c) If the preacher is not going to preach a sermon
d) If guests are present who might be offended

10. Preach the Problem Step, even on well-known problems, because
a) it will help your sermon be long enough.
b) your teacher will give you a good grade.
c) every sermon needs to have the same form.
d) it is harder to reach the heart than the head.

Essay Test Topics Write 50-100 words on each of these goals that you studied in this chapter.

Cooperate With the Way People Think

Goal: *Explain how a preacher can prepare sermons in a way that is logical, wise, successful, and helpful..*

Four Questions and Answers About the Problem Step

Goal: *Respond to 4 common questions students ask about presenting Problems.*

Practice Identifying Problems and Solutions in a Biblical Passage

Goal: *Identify the Problem and Solution in a given passage of Scripture.*

Chapter 10:
Present the Problem Before the Solution (Method A)

Introduction

In Exodus 20:3-17, the Ten Commandments tell us we should **not** do several things:

- ³*"You shall have no other gods before me."*

- ⁴*"You shall not make for yourself an idol in the form of anything in heaven above or on the earth beneath or in the waters below.* ⁵*You shall not bow down to them or worship them; for I, the L*ORD *your God, am a jealous God, punishing the children for the sin of the fathers to the third and fourth generation of those who hate me,* ⁶*but showing love to a thousand generations of those who love me and keep my commandments."*

Figure 10.1
The Ten Commandments on tablets of stone

- ⁷*"You shall not misuse the name of the L*ORD *your God, for the L*ORD *will not hold anyone guiltless who misuses his name."*

- ¹³*"You shall not murder."*

- ¹⁴*"You shall not commit adultery."*

- ¹⁵*"You shall not steal."*

- ¹⁶*"You shall not give false testimony against your neighbor."*

- ¹⁷*"You shall not covet your neighbor's house. You shall not covet your neighbor's wife, or his manservant or maidservant, his ox or donkey, or anything that belongs to your neighbor"* (Exod. 20:3-17).

These commandments are well-known, and we are careful to obey them. Since they are grouped together, they attract our attention.

Likewise, God gives us many commands in the New Testament. These are not in a group like the Ten Commandments—they are scattered throughout several books. Still, we should make every effort to obey them. In this chapter we will create a sermon related to one of God's commands:

- *"Do not be anxious about anything, ... "* (Phil. 4:6).

Lessons:

Example 1: Creating the Problem and Solution Parts of a Sermon (Method A)
Goal A: *Summarize how to develop the problem and solution parts of a sermon using Method A.*
Goal B: *Explain the need for transition sentences and give an example.*

Example 2 and Practice Creating the Problem and Solution Parts of a Sermon Using Method A
Goal: *Create the problem and solution parts of an expository sermon using Method A (P_1P_2–S_1S_2).*

Example 1: Creating the Problem and Solution Parts of a Sermon (Method A)

Goal A: *Summarize how to develop the problem and solution parts of a sermon using Method A.*

Goal B: *Explain the need for transition sentences and give an example.*

Step 1:		Step 2:		Step 3:		Step 4:		Step 5:
Introduction	→	Problems	→	Solutions	→	Choice	→	Invitation

Figure 10.2 Sometimes it is best to group the problems together, and then preach the solutions (Method A).

A. Overview

```
I.   Problem 1: (Principle)          III. Solution 1: (Principle)
     A. Explanations:                     A. Explanations:
     B. Illustrations:                    B. Illustrations:
     C. Application:                      C. Application:

II.  Problem 2: (Principle)          IV. Solution 2: (Principle)
     A. Explanations:                     A. Explanations:
     B. Illustrations:                    B. Illustrations:
     C. Application:                      C. Application:
```

Figure 10.3 In Method A, the preacher discusses <u>all</u> of the problems *before* revealing <u>any</u> solutions (P_1P_2–S_1S_2).

After the Introduction, a preacher should state a problem or need in one sentence. State the Problem as a big truth to believe[1] or a principle to live by.[+] Put the Scripture reference just after the principle.

After you state the problem as a big truth or principle, you should do **three things**: explain, illustrate, and apply it.

Q 1 *After stating a problem, which 3 things should a preacher do with that problem?*

- **Explain** the problem or need you have stated. This is a good time in your sermon to describe the **background** and **biblical setting** for your listeners. Give them the details they need to understand what you are talking about. Introduce any **places, biblical characters, words,** or **concepts** related to the problem at hand. Also, if your main points, such as I and II, do not state the **cause** of the problem, take time to explain the cause.

  If you are preaching from a story or event, take time to review it for your listeners. For example, if you are preaching principles from the book of Esther, take a short time to summarize and tell the whole story. Otherwise, those who do not know the Bible well may learn biblical principles, but not learn the Bible story itself.

- **Illustrate:** We have looked at many types of illustrations. Always illustrate the problem you are talking about. This will move truth from the head to the heart. Use as many illustrations as time allows.

- **Apply:** In the explanation, you told what the problem was back then, in Bible times. Now, apply the truth to the present. Show how the problem exists today, here and now. Often, to apply the truth, you must state it as a broad, cross-cultural principle and then give examples of it.

+ Some distinguish between a timeless truth to believe and a principle to live by. These two seem to blend together, since we live by what we believe. So in this course we will treat timeless truths as principles.

Q 2 ⋏ *Must illustrations and applications always be separated? Explain.*

Note: Sometimes it is good to combine the **Illustrations** and **Applications**. Some preachers like to give an illustration, and then apply it at once. For example, Jesus told the illustration of the Good Samaritan (Luke 10:25-37). Then He applied it at once by saying, *"Go and do likewise"* (Luke 10:37).

B. First example of the Problem and Solution parts of a sermon (Phil. 4:6-8)

Note that in this first example, we preach about the problem of worry. Then, in the Solution Step, we give three keys to conquering worry.

> **Problem 1:** The Bible gives several reasons why you should not worry (Phil. 4:6).
>
> -
>
> **Solution 1:** Give your problems to God in prayer (Phil. 4:6).
>
> **Solution 2:** Thank God for your blessings (Phil. 4:6).
>
> **Solution 3:** Think good, positive thoughts (Phil. 4:8).

Figure 10.4   Outline of the sermon: Trade Your Worry for Peace (Phil. 4:6-8)

Q 3 ⋏ *In our sermon on worry, how many problems are there (Phil. 4:6-8)?*

Title: Trade Your Worry for Peace

Text: Philippians 4:6-8

I.   **Problem: (Principle) The Bible gives several reasons why you should not worry (Phil. 4:6).**

   A. **Explanations:**

   1. **Biblical Background:** Philippi was a city in Europe, located 10 miles north on the shore of the Aegean Sea. It was a large, important Roman city in the province of Macedonia.

   2. **Biblical Background:** Acts 16 tells us about Paul's ministry in Philippi. He went there on his second missionary journey, about A.D. 49-53. God guided Paul to Philippi through a vision, in which he saw a man asking him to come and help. Lydia was saved there, and a slave girl was delivered. This put an end to the business of those who owned the demon-possessed slave girl. Set free from the demon, she no longer had power to predict the future (Acts 16:19). So her owners stirred up the authorities, who had Paul and Silas beaten and put in prison.

   3. **Biblical Setting:** Paul wrote to the Philippians, probably from a prison in Rome, about A.D. 62/63. So remember that Paul had many chances to worry or be anxious. He was once in prison in Philippi, and he was chained in Rome when he wrote the letter to the Philippians.

   4. **Explain** Philippians 4:6—*"Do not be anxious about anything."* Use only a sentence or two.

   5. **Causes of worry:** finances, sickness, relationships, conflicts, the future, and such.

   B. **Illustrations and Applications:**

   1. **Quote:** Jesus said we should not worry, because it does not help us (Matt. 6:27).

   2. **Comparison:** Worrying is like digging to get out of a pit. It only makes things worse.

   3. **Contrast:** Knitting produces something good. But worrying is not like knitting.

   4. **Story:** Amnon's thoughts made him sick (2 Sam. 13:1-2). Likewise, worry will cause cavities in your teeth and ulcers in your stomach.

   5. **Story:** One young man in Bible school worried so much that he went bald. A young lady worried so much that her eyebrows fell out. Worry is not the only reason for hair loss. But it is one of the reasons. By the way, in time the students I mentioned stopped worrying and regained their hair! I'm not making any threats about hair loss or promises to bald people, but worrying is your enemy!

Q 4 ⋏ *Summarize the 3 illustrations you like best, showing that worry is a bad problem.*

Figure 10.5   The Problem Step (P₁) in the sermon: Trade Your Worry for Peace (Phil. 4:6-8)

Transition—moving smoothly from one part of a sermon to another part

Before moving from a problem to a solution, a preacher should create *transition sentences. *Transition* comes from the word *transit*, which means "to move." For example, we say bananas are in transit when they are being moved from one place to another. Transition sentences help the preacher move smoothly from one thought to another. Some preachers move roughly from truth to truth like a car rushing over a speed bump or railroad tracks. It is good to move smoothly from the Problem to the Solution.

Q 5 ⤳ *Moving from the problem to the solution without a transition sentence is like _____.*

Transition: It is not enough to know that worrying is bad. You must know *how* to stop worrying. Paul gives us 3 keys to overcoming the problem of worry.

II. Solution 1: (Principle) Give your problems to God in prayer (Phil. 4:6).

 A. Explanations:

  1. Explain what it means to obey Philippians. 4:6—*"present your requests to God."*

 B. Illustrations and Applications:

  1. "Pray your problems to God."[2] Worry is only a step away from prayer. All of us think about problems. But refuse to worry when you think of a problem. Pray it instead.

  2. Imagine a man with a heavy chair he wants to sell. He carries it to a place where furniture is sold. A buyer offers to pay him a good price. But instead of selling it, he carries the chair all the way home! It is just as foolish to carry our problems to God in prayer, and then carry them back home to worry about. Give your problems to God in prayer. *Leave them with Him.* Refuse to take them back. Take your burdens to the Lord and leave them there.

III. Solution 2: (Principle) Thank God for your blessings (Phil. 4:6).

 A. Explanations:

  1. Explain Philippians 4:6—*"with thanksgiving."*

  2. Count your blessings instead of your problems.

 B. Illustrations and Applications:

  1. Psalm 103

  2. A father worried because he did not have enough money to buy shoes for his children. As he was walking, he passed a man who was crippled sitting on the street. This beggar had no feet. The father gave the beggar some money. Then, the dad walked on, thanking God that his children could walk. Even bare feet are better than no feet. Thank God for what you *do* have. Some people have problems so big that your problems look small beside theirs.

IV. Solution 3: (Principle) Think good, positive thoughts (Phil. 4:8).

 A. Explanations:

  1. Explain Philippians 4:8—*"think about such things"* instead of worrying.

 B. Illustrations and Applications:

  1. Fill a bucket with rice to keep rocks out. Fill your mind with good thoughts to keep worry out.

  2. Paul and Silas sang in jail at Philippi, instead of worrying (Acts 16:25). Sing instead of worrying.

**Figure 10.6   The Solution Step ($S_1S_2S_3$) in the sermon:
Trade Your Worry for Peace (Phil. 4:6-8)**

Q 6 ⤳ *How did we illustrate giving problems to God?*

Q 7 ⤳ *Summarize one illustration on thanking God for blessings.*

Q 8 ⤳ *Summarize one of our illustrations on the value of thinking good thoughts.*

Q 9 ⟶ *What happens as you rewrite an outline several times?*

Q 10 ⟶ *Why is it important to have an outline, even after you have memorized it?*

Shorten your outline.   You prepare an outline in stages. First, you write as much as you need to remember your thoughts. Then you go back and outline the sermon in a shorter form. You may have to rewrite an outline several times. Some teachers recommend that preachers write their outlines seven times! Rewriting is not a waste of time. You become more familiar with your message each time that you rewrite the outline. Your final outline should fit on one side of one page. But it must be long enough to remind you of each point. Use a red pen or colored marker to underline or highlight key parts of the outline. If you look at a part of the outline, but cannot recall a point, the outline is too short for you at that time!

After you write an outline several times, practice going over each part in your mind, without looking at it. You should know your sermon so well that you do not need to look at your outline when preaching. Still, always take the outline to the pulpit. Glance at it as a reminder. Seeing the key points that you highlighted will help you remember. Having an outline in the pulpit takes pressure off the preacher. Even when you memorize an outline, you can forget it under pressure. Many preachers take an outline into the pulpit, but rarely need to look at it.

We have worked through the Problem and Solution Steps of a sermon on worry. For a shortened form of the outline, see Figure 10.7.

My teachers chose me to give a speech when I graduated from secondary school. I worked on the speech for several weeks, though it was only 5 minutes long. After going over it many times, I discovered that I had memorized it. The evening came to graduate and give the speech. It was so easy for me to remember that I did not take an outline of it to the podium. Our school was small, but 500 people came to the graduation. When I stood to give the speech, I was surprised to see so many people. I felt a little nervous, but my speech began well. After 1 minute, I said, "Methuselah lived 969 years on the earth. But with the help of others, we can learn wisdom before we reach that age." The people liked this line, and they laughed a little at the humor. While they were laughing, I forgot all of the rest of the speech! This was a terrible feeling! I had no outline, and no way to remember the speech. Five very long seconds passed. The people stopped laughing, and were ready for me to continue. But my mind was totally blank! Suddenly, God gave me grace and I remembered the speech. He enabled me to finish it. But I learned a lesson that day. *Always* take an outline with you to speak! God will help you many times, but it is written, *"Do not put the Lord your God to the test"* (Matt. 4:7).[3]

Title: Trade Your Worry for Peace   **Date:** _____   **Place:** _____

Text: Philippians 4:6-8

I. **Problem: (Principle) The Bible gives several reasons why you should not worry (Phil. 4:6).**

    A. **Explanations:**

        1. **Biblical Background:** Philippi was an important Roman city in the province of Macedonia.

        2. **Biblical Background:** Acts 16 tells us about Paul's ministry in Philippi.

        3. **Biblical Setting:** Paul wrote to the Philippians, probably from a prison in Rome.

        4. **Explain** Philippians 4:6—*"Do not be <u>anxious</u> about <u>anything</u>."* Use only a sentence or two.

        5. **Causes of worry:** finances, sickness, relationships, conflicts, the future, and such.

    B. **Illustrations and Applications:**

        1. **Quote:** Jesus said we should not worry because it does not help us (Matt. 6:27).

        2. **Comparison:** Worrying is like digging to get out of a pit. It only makes things worse.

        3. **Contrast:** Knitting produces something good. But worrying is not like knitting.

        4. **Story:** Amnon's thoughts made him sick (2 Sam. 13:1-2). Likewise, worry will cause cavities in your teeth and ulcers in your stomach.

        5. **Story:** One young man in Bible School worried so much that he went bald.

Transition: It is not enough to know that worrying is bad. You must know *how* to stop worrying. Paul gives us 3 keys to overcoming the problem of worry.

II. **Solution 1: (Principle) Give your problems to God in prayer (Phil. 4:6).**

    A. **Explanations:**

        1. Explain what it means to obey Philippians 4:6—*"<u>present your requests to God.</u>"*

    B. **Illustrations and Applications:**

        1. "Pray your problems to God."

        2. Imagine a man with a heavy chair he wants to sell.

III. **Solution 2: (Principle) Thank God for your blessings (Phil. 4:6).**

    A. **Explanations:**

        1. Explain Philippians 4:6—*"<u>with thanksgiving.</u>"*

        2. Count your blessings instead of your problems.

    B. **Illustrations and Applications:**

        1. Psalm 103

        2. A father worried because he did not have enough money to buy shoes for his children.

IV. **Solution 3: (Principle) Think good, positive thoughts (Phil. 4:8).**

    A. **Explanations:**

        1. Explain Philippians 4:8—*"<u>think about such things</u>"* instead of worrying.

    B. **Illustrations and Applications:**

        1. Fill a bucket with rice to keep rocks out. Fill your mind with good thoughts to keep out worry.

        2. Paul and Silas sang in jail **at Philippi**, instead of worrying (Acts 16:25). Sing instead of worrying.

Figure 10.7   Shortened, revised outline of the sermon: Trade Your Worry for Peace (Phil. 4:6-8)

Lesson 29   Example 2 and Practice Creating the Problem and Solution Parts of a Sermon Using Method A

Goal: *Create the problem and solution parts of an expository sermon using Method A (P_1P_2–S_1S_2).*

Remember that emphasizing the Problem is like plowing before you sow. We have looked at one example of preaching the Problem before the Solution. Now let us look at a second example. This sermon is about discouragement. Take a few minutes to study the partial outline on overcoming discouragement (Figure10.8). Notice that the two problems are stated as principles—the causes of discouragement.

Q 11 *State 2 causes of John's discouragement (Figure 10.8).*

A. Example Two: Creating the Problem and Solution parts of a sermon—P_1P_2–S_1S_2 (Matt. 11:2-6)

> **Problem 1:** People may become discouraged when good things happen to bad people (Matt. 11:2-3; 14:1-12).
>
> **Problem 2:** People may become discouraged when bad things happen to good people (Matt. 11:2-3; 14:3-5).
>
> **Solution 1:** Do not be offended—be patient and wait for God's timing (Matt. 11:6).
>
> **Solution 2:** Trust—Starve your doubts, but feed your faith (Matt. 11:4-5).

Figure 10.8   Outline of the sermon: Dealing With Discouragement (Matt. 11:2-6)

You have looked at the outline of our sermon: Dealing With Discouragement (Matt. 11:2-6). So you realize that we will present two problems and then two solutions. But first, let us consider an Introduction to our sermon.

Q 12 *Summarize how John felt in prison (Figure 10.9).*

Title: Dealing With Discouragement	**Date:** _____ **Place:** _____

Text: Matthew 11:2-6[4]

Introduction:

   John the Baptist once had faith like a roaring fire. Great crowds came to hear him. He saw the dove descend on Jesus (John 1:32-34). Once, John was sure that Jesus was the Messiah. He shouted to the multitudes, *"Look, the Lamb of God who takes away the sin of the world"* (John 1:29). But in prison, John's faith changed from a great fire to being like a small candle in the dark. He could not see the crowds, the clouds, or the Jordan River. This great preacher wrestled with doubts. He sent his disciples to ask Jesus if He really was the Messiah. What had happened to John? Why did this great prophet become confused and discouraged? How did Jesus encourage him? Today we will look at what the Bible says about the problem and solution of discouragement.

Figure 10.9   Introduction to the sermon: Dealing With Discouragement (Matt. 11:2-6)

I. **Problem 1: (Principle) People may become discouraged when good things happen to bad people (Matt. 11:2-3; 14:1-12).**

   A. **Explanations:**
      1. **Biblical Background:** Who was John? A great prophet! Recall that he was born to elderly parents, Zechariah and Elizabeth. His father could not speak for 9 months because of unbelief. John was filled with the Spirit from his mother's womb. All of the people waited and watched to see whether John would become a great prophet (Luke 1). Many repented when John preached and baptized at the Jordan River.
      2. **Biblical Setting:** Who was Herod? Read Matthew 14:1-5. Explain who Herod Antipas was and what John said to him.
      3. **Historical Setting:** Explain what it was like in John's dark, cold, lonely prison.
      4. John expected the ax and the fire of judgment to come at once. He said the ax was already at the root of the tree (Luke 3:9). He thought God would judge sinners like Herod immediately! John waited in prison, but Herod prospered. John wondered why good things were happening to a bad person like Herod.
      5. Explain how a winnowing fork was used to separate wheat from chaff (Matt. 3:1-12). John became discouraged when God did not burn up the chaff—like Herod.
      6. John may not have had many visitors in the prison, but Satan always visits those who face discouragement. Perhaps Satan whispered questions like: "How long does it take a tree to fall after the ax has chopped it? Did God really tell you to say that? Did you really see a dove light on Jesus? If God's promises are true, why are they taking so long?" Satan uses questions like seeds of doubt.

   B. **Illustrations:**
      1. Elijah once became discouraged when God did not kill Jezebel (1 Kings 19). Instead, Jezebel prospered.
      2. Believers in Uganda became discouraged when God did not judge Idi Amin. This evil ruler may have killed a half million people. Many of them were believers. One Bishop became very discouraged. He wrote a book entitled *Uganda, the Nation That God Forgot!* Believers died, but the evil ruler prospered.
      3. Habakkuk cried, *"How long, O Lord, must I call for help, but you do not listen?"* (Hab. 1:2).
      4. Revelation 6:9-10
      5. Jesus warned that because of the rise of sin, injustice, and lawlessness, the love of many would grow cold—*like* the ashes left after a fire (Matt. 24:12). In the last days, many will become discouraged and lose their faith because God's justice is delayed.

   C. **Applications:**
      1. Discouragement is an enemy that knocks on every door. Some day, it will knock on your door.
      2. We may be tempted to become discouraged when God's help does not come as quickly as we desire in hard times.

Q 13 ⚒ *What did John expect God to do to Herod, at once?*

Q 14 ⚒ *Give 2 examples of believers who became discouraged when the wicked prospered.*

Figure 10.10   Problem 1 (P₁) in the sermon: Dealing With Discouragement (Matt. 11:2-6)

Q 15 ⟋ *Describe John's feelings when he suffered instead of Herod.*

II. **Problem 2: (Principle) People may become discouraged when bad things happen to good people (Matt. 11:2-3; 14:3-5).**

   A. **Explanations:**
   1. John wondered why Jesus left him in prison. The ax was for the bad trees like Herod, not the good trees like John. But Herod was feasting while John was fasting. John did not understand why the righteous suffer and the wicked prosper. He wondered why bad things happen to good people.
   2. Once, John was sure who Jesus was, but questions, doubt, and discouragement were pushing faith out of his life. John sent his disciples to ask Jesus, *"Are you the one who was to come, or should we expect someone else?"* (Matt. 11:3).

Q 16 ⟋ *Give 2 examples of believers who became discouraged when they suffered.*

   B. **Illustrations:**
   1. Habakkuk did not understand why God allowed the Babylonians to punish the Jews (Hab. 1:13-17).
   2. Naomi became discouraged when her husband and two sons-in-law died (Ruth 1:20-21)
   3. Christians were tempted to become discouraged when unbelieving Jews stoned Stephen and chased followers of Christ out of Jerusalem. They lost their homes and property. Perhaps many asked, "Why did God allow this to happen?"

   C. **Applications:**
   1. Discouragement knocks at the door when accidents kill or hurt people.
   2. When sickness comes to people like Job, we may be tempted to become discouraged.

   Transition: We have looked at two causes of discouragement. Now let us look at two ways the Bible teaches us to overcome this enemy.

Figure 10.11   Problem 2 (P₂) in the sermon: Dealing With Discouragement (Matt. 11:2-6)

Q 17 ⟋ *Summarize the first solution or key to conquering discouragement.*

III. **Solution 1: (Principle) Do not be offended—be patient and wait for God's timing (Matt. 11:6).**

   A. **Explanations:**
   1. **Biblical Setting:** John was discouraged because God did not judge Herod Antipas at once. Things got worse. Herod executed John the Baptist (Matt. 14:1-12).
   2. Later, after a few years, Jesus Himself stood before this same Herod (Luke 23:6-16). But the day will come when Herod will stand before Jesus (John 5:28-29). Justice may be slow, but it is sure.

Q 18 ⟋ *Give an example of justice after delay.*

   B. **Illustrations:**
   1. God's judgment on the unbelieving Jews was delayed, but it came to Jerusalem. Thirty years after John died, the ax and fire came to Jerusalem. The Roman General Titus murdered the people and destroyed the temple. Over one million Jews died at that time.[5] God's judgment was delayed by His mercy.
   2. This year, about 160,000 Christians will be killed for their faith. But justice is coming.
   3. Second Thessalonians 1:5-10

Q 19 ⟋ *Summarize Galatians 6:9.*

   C. **Applications:**
   1. Galatians 6:9
   2. James 5:7-11
   3. Be faithful unto death and God will give you a crown of eternal life (Rev. 2:10).

Figure 10.12   Solution 1 (S₁) in the sermon: Dealing With Discouragement (Matt. 11:2-6)

IV. Solution 2: (Principle) Trust—Starve your doubts, but feed your faith (Matt. 11:4-5).

A. **Explanations:**

1. **Biblical Setting:** Jesus told John what to think about good things (Matt. 11:4-5). John already knew the miracles Jesus was doing (Matt. 11:2). Jesus guided John to think on these good things, not the bad things he did not understand.
2. Never doubt in the dark what God has told you in the light.
3. As John thought on the miracles of Jesus, he would be encouraged. It was important for John to stop meditating on questions and rejoice for the good things Jesus was doing.

B. **Illustrations:**

1. Trying to answer every question that comes is like trying to count every wave of the sea. Turn away from the questions that are too hard for you.
2. King David knew the secret of encouraging himself in the Lord. There were no friends, but only enemies around him (1 Sam. 30:1-6). His family had been captured. His wealth had been stolen. He was an alien in a foreign land. But he encouraged himself in the LORD. How? Perhaps he thought about the bear, the lion, and the giant God enabled him to conquer. Soon, his faith led him to victory.

C. **Applications:**

1. We must not allow negative thoughts to guide us to discouragement. Rather, we must take captive every thought (2 Cor. 10:5). We do this by *choosing* to think on good things.
2. Put your unanswered questions on the altar. Give them to God in prayer. Then think on the good things you know (Phil. 4:8).
3. Starve your doubts and feed your faith. Count your blessings, not your problems.

Figure 10.13   Solution 2 (S$_2$) in the sermon: Dealing With Discouragement (Matt. 11:2-6)

Q 20 ⟍ *What advice did Jesus give John to conquer discouragement (Matt. 11:4-5)?*

Q 21 ⟍ *How do you think David encouraged himself at Ziklag?*

Q 22 ⟍ *What are some good things that all believers can think about?*

Now we have worked through the sermon on Matthew 11:2-6. We can go back through it to shorten and revise our outline (Figure 10.14).

Title: Dealing With Discouragement   **Date:** _____   **Place:** _____

Text: Matthew 11:2-6

Introduction: John the Baptist once had faith like a roaring fire. Great crowds came to hear him.

I. **Problem 1: People may become discouraged when good things happen to bad people (Matt. 11:2-3; 14:1-12).**

A. **Explanations:**

1. **Biblical background:** Who was John?
2. **Biblical Setting:** Who was Herod? Read Matthew 14:1-5.
3. **Historical Setting:** Explain what it was like in John's dark, cold, lonely prison.
4. John expected the ax and the fire of judgment to come at once (Luke 3:9).
5. Explain how a winnowing fork was used to separate wheat from chaff (Matt. 3:1-12).
6. Perhaps Satan whispered questions to John like.

B. **Illustrations:**

1. Elijah once became discouraged when God did not kill Jezebel (1 Kings 19).
2. Believers in Uganda became discouraged when God did not judge Idi Amin.
3. (Hab. 1:2) *"How long, O Lord, must I call for help, but you do not listen?"*
4. Revelation 6:9-10
5. (Matt. 24:12). In the last days, many will become discouraged and lose their faith.

C. **Applications:**

1. Discouragement is an enemy that knocks on every door.
2. Discouragement may come when God's help does not come as quickly as we desire.

Continued on next page

II. **Problem 2: People may become discouraged when bad things happen to good people (Matt. 11:2-3; 14:3-5).**

    A. **Explanations:**

        1. John wondered why Jesus left him in prison.

        2. (Matt. 11:3) *"Are you the one who was to come, or should we look for another?"*

    B. **Illustrations:**

        1. God allowed the Babylonians to punish the Jews (Hab. 1:13-17).

        2. Naomi became discouraged when her husband and two sons-in-law died.

        3. Unbelieving Jews stoned Stephen (Acts 6–7).

    C. **Applications:**

        1. Discouragement knocks at the door when accidents kill or hurt people.

        2. When sickness comes to people like Job, we may be tempted to become discouraged.

Transition: We have looked at two causes of discouragement. Now let us look at two ways the Bible teaches us to overcome this enemy.

III. **Solution 1: Do not be offended—be patient and wait for God's timing (Matt. 11:6).**

    A. **Explanations:**

        1. **Biblical Setting:** Herod executed John the Baptist (Matt. 14:1-12).

        2. Jesus Himself stood before this same Herod (Luke 23:6-16). But Herod will one day stand before Jesus (John 5:28-29).

    B. **Illustrations:**

        1. The Roman General Titus murdered the people and destroyed the temple.

        2. This year about 160,000 Christians will be killed for their faith. But justice is coming.

        3. Second Thessalonians 1:5-10

    C. **Applications:**

        1. Galatians 6:9

        2. James 5:7-11

        3. Be faithful unto death and God will give you a crown of eternal life (Rev. 2:10).

IV. **Solution 2: Trust: Starve your doubts, but feed your faith (Matt. 11:4-5).**

    A. **Explanations:**

        1. **Biblical Setting:** (Matt. 11:4-5). Jesus guided John to think on good things, not the bad.

        2. Never doubt in the dark what God has told you in the light.

    B. **Illustrations:**

        1. Trying to answer every question that comes is like trying to count every wave of the sea.

        2. King David knew the secret of encouraging himself in the Lord (1 Sam. 30:1-6).

    C. **Applications:**

        1. Take captive every thought (2 Cor. 10:5).

        2. Then think on the good things you know (Phil. 4:8).

        3. Starve your doubts and feed your faith. Count your blessings, not your problems.

Figure 10.14   Shortened, revised outline of the sermon: Dealing With Discouragement (Matt. 11:2-6)

B. Practice creating a Problem and Solution (Method A)

The outline that follows on Romans 6:23 is for students to develop (Figure 10.15). In a class, the teacher may develop this outline together with students. Then the teacher may ask one student to preach this to the other students.

Q 23 ✎ *Complete Figure 10.15.*

If you are studying this course by yourself, complete this sermon and preach it to a friend, family member, or small group. It will be good practice for you. Expand the outline to fit your needs. Your presentation should be 10 to 20 minutes.

Title: _____

Date: _____   Place: _____

Text: Romans 6:23

I. **The Problem: (Principle) The wages of sin is spiritual death (Rom. 6:23).**

   A. **Explanations:**
   1. **Biblical Setting:** Where was Rome? Who were the Romans?
   2. What has Paul shown in chapters 1–3 of Romans?
   3. What are wages?
   4. What is sin?
   5. What is spiritual death?

   B. **Illustrations:**
   1
   2.
   3.

   C. **Applications:**
   1.
   2.

Transition:

─ ─ ─ ─ ─ ─ ─ ─ ─ ─ ─ ─ ─ ─ ─

II. **The Solution: (Principle) The gift of God is eternal life through Jesus Christ our Lord (Rom. 6:23).**

   A. **Explanations:**
   1. Contrast wages and a gift.
   2. What is eternal life?
   3. How is eternal life related to Jesus Christ as Lord?

   B. **Illustrations:**
   1.
   2.
   3.

   C. **Applications:**
   1.
   2.

Figure 10.15   Practice creating the Problem and Solution Steps of a sermon (Rom. 6:23).

Test Yourself: Circle the letter by the ***best*** completion to each question or statement.

1. Which 3 things should a preacher do with each Problem?
a) Research it, apply it, meditate on it.
b) Avoid it, analyze it, condemn it.
c) Contrast it, compare it, summarize it.
d) Explain it, illustrate it, apply it.

2. Which Step comes second in a sermon?
a) The Problem
b) The Solution
c) The Invitation
b) The Introduction

3. An illustration about worry is:
a) Paul told the Philippians not to worry.
b) Worrying is like digging to get out of a pit.
c) The Philippians lived near the Aegean Sea.
d) God gives peace to those who trust Him.

4. From Philippians 4:6-8, we created how many principles to solve the problem of worry.
a) 1
b) 2
c) 3
d) 4

5. How is an outline organized with Method A?
a) P_1S_1–P_2S_2
b) P_1P_2–S_1S_2
c) S_1P_1–S_2P_2
d) S_1S_2–P_1P_2

6. Which is a solution from Matthew 11:2-6 for the problem of discouragement?
a) Count your blessings, not your curses.
b) Ignore your problems and earthly solutions.
c) Pray your problems to get solutions.
d) Starve your doubts and feed your faith.

7. Which is a good transition sentence?
a) "Worrying is a bad habit."
b) "Paul gives three steps to stop worrying."
c) "Worry will destroy your health."
d) "Jesus said not to worry."

8. In the outline, where should you discuss the biblical background?
a) Application
b) Introduction
c) Illustration
d) Explanation

9. In your final outline,
a) write a paragraph on each point.
b) include all details for illustrations.
c) use single words for points.
d) state each point in a short sentence.

10. Which problem is stated as a principle?
a) Doubt
b) The effects of doubt
c) Thomas doubted Jesus.
d) Doubt is a bad habit.

Essay Test Topics Write 50-100 words on each of these goals that you studied in this chapter.

Example 1: Creating the Problem and Solution Parts of a Sermon (Method A)

Goal: *Summarize how to develop the problem and solution parts of a sermon using Method A.*

Example 2 and Practice Creating the Problem and Solution Parts of a Sermon Using Method A

Goal: *Create the problem and solution parts of an expository sermon using Method A ($P_1P_2-S_1S_2$).*

Chapter 11:
Present the Problem Before the Solution (Method B)

Introduction

I. **Problem 1: God subtracts from the negligent.**

   A. **Explanations:**
      1. Biblical Setting:
      2. Causes:

   B. **Illustrations:**

   C. **Applications:**

II. **Solution 1: God adds to the diligent.**

   A. **Explanations:**
      1. Biblical Setting:
      2. Causes:

   B. **Illustrations:**

   C. **Applications:**

Figure 11.1

In Method B, each Problem is followed at once by its Solution (P_1S_1–P_2S_2–P_3S_3).

In contrast, in Method A, we grouped all of the Problems together, and all of the Solutions together (P_1P_2–S_1S_2).

Four common questions about Problems and Solutions

Question 1: — Does a preacher always need to present two problems?

Answer: — No. Sometimes one is enough, as in our sermon on conquering worry (Phil. 4:6-8). Or there may be three or more problems you want to present.

A young preacher once asked an old preacher, "How many principles or points should a sermon have?" The wise old man thought for a moment. Then he smiled and answered, "At least one!"

Question 2: — Should the number of problems always match the number of solutions?

Answer: — No. One solution might solve two problems. Or there might be several solutions to solve one problem. For example, in our sermon on overcoming worry, we gave three keys in the solution (Phil. 4:6-8).

Question 3: — Do I need to always write *principle* before I state a problem or solution?

Answer: — No. We have used the word *principle* to help teach you. Soon, we will stop reminding you to state your problems and solutions as principles. Also, if you find it too hard to always state a main point as a principle, state it as a fact or truth. Then you will still be able to explain, illustrate, and apply it.

Question 4: — How can I make the key parts of my outline stand out more?

Answer: — Some preachers underline key points or illustrations with colored pens.

Q 1 ↗ *Answer the 4 common questions on Problems and Solutions.*

In the Problem, you make people thirsty. The Problem is like leading people through a dry, hot desert. But in the *Solution, you offer your listeners a cool, refreshing drink of water.

Lessons:

30 Two Examples of Presenting Problems and Solutions With Method B
Goal: *Contrast Method A and Method B of preparing an expository sermon.*

31 Practice Preparing Problems and Solutions Using Method B
Goal: *Prepare an expository sermon using Method B (P_1S_1–P_2S_2–P_3S_3).*

Two Examples of Presenting Problems and Solutions With Method B

Goal: *Contrast Method A and Method B of preparing an expository sermon.*

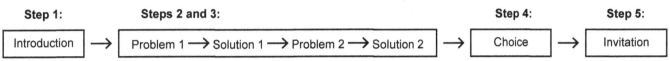

Step 1:	Steps 2 and 3:		Step 4:	Step 5:
Introduction →	Problem 1 → Solution 1 → Problem 2 → Solution 2	→	Choice	→ Invitation

Figure 11.2 In Method B, each Problem is followed at once by its Solution.

In chapter 10 we studied Method A. There, we sometimes presented two problems together, or several solutions together. In Method B each Problem is followed at once by its Solution (Figure 11.2). Use whichever method fits the passage best. The main thing is to preach biblical solutions to the problems people face. And always preach about the Problem before the Solution. Plow before you plant! Notice that we continue to explain, illustrate, and apply each Pproblem and each Solution. (Sometimes it is possible to mix illustrations and applications together, if both are from the present. This is true because a modern illustration applies the truth at once.)

A. First example of the Problem and Solution Parts of a sermon (Matt. 1:1-17)

> **Problem 1:** Racial prejudice is like a wall between people.
>
> **Solution 1:** Jesus came to break down the walls of prejudice.
>
> -
>
> **Problem 2:** Some put a wall between men and women—they treat women as inferior to men.
>
> **Solution 2:** Jesus came to break down the wall between men and women.
>
> -
>
> **Problem 3:** Sin is like a wall that separates God and man.
>
> **Solution 3:** Jesus came to break down the wall of sin (Luke 19:10).

Figure 11.3 Outline of the sermon: Jesus Came to Break Down 3 Types of Walls (Matt. 1:1-17)

Q 2 *Summarize the 3 reasons why Matthew included the sinful women in the family tree of Jesus.*

> **Title:** Jesus Came to Break Down 3 Types of Walls
>
> **Text:** Matthew 1:1-17
>
> **Introduction:**
>
> Matthew wrote to show the Jews that Jesus was their Messiah. So he began his Gospel with the genealogy or family tree of Jesus. To convince the Jews, it was important to show that Jesus was the son of Abraham and David.
>
> We are not surprised to see the names of the Jewish men in Matthew 1. But what surprises us are the names of the four sinful women in the family tree of Jesus. In biblical times a Jewish man thanked God for three things each morning: that he was not born a Gentile, a slave, or a woman.[1] So it amazes us to see the names of five women—especially four sinful women—in the family tree of Christ.
>
> Why did Matthew mention Tamar, Rahab, Ruth, and Bathsheba in the lineage of Jesus? These are not only women; they are sinful women! Why did Matthew drag them from the closets of sin? Why did he march them across a page of Scripture? One famous Bible teacher guides us to three wonderful lessons we can learn from this diseased family tree.[2]

Figure 11.4 Title and Introduction to the sermon: Jesus Came to Break Down 3 Types of Walls (Matt. 1:1-17)

Q 3 *Why was there a wall of prejudice between Israel and Moab?*

Q 4 *Give an example of prejudice in your culture.*

Q 5 *How did Jesus help break down the wall of prejudice between Israel and Moab?*

Q 6 *Give an example of a wall of prejudice in your culture that Jesus is breaking down.*

I. **Problem 1: (Principle) Racial prejudice is like a wall between people.**
   A. **Explanations:**
      1. **Biblical Setting:** Ruth was a woman from Moab. The Moabites were the children of Lot and his daughter (Gen. 19:30-37). The nation of Moab was southeast of Judah and east of the Dead Sea.
      2. **Biblical Setting:** The hard feelings between Israel and Moab began after the Exodus. Balak was the king of Moab (Num. 22:4). Balak hired a prophet named Balaam to try to curse Israel. It is not possible to curse those God chooses to bless. But Balaam taught the Moabites to cause Israel to commit sexual sins. And sin brings the judgment of God on any people. Men of Israel committed sexual sins with women of Moab (Rev. 2:14). From that time on, Israel considered Moab to be an enemy.
      3. The Law of Moses forbade the Moabites to mix with the Israelites (Deut. 23:3).
   B. **Illustrations and applications:**
      1. In some places there is prejudice between blacks and whites.
      2. In Rwanda the tribes of the Hutus and Tutsis have shown hatred for each other.
      3. In India many have a strong prejudice against levels or classes of society.

II. **Solution 1: (Principle) Jesus came to break down the walls of prejudice.**
   A. **Explanations:**
      1. **Biblical Setting:** Jesus could not have been a priest in the days of Ezra. Why? Because our Lord had Ruth, a woman from Moab, as a relative. Yet the Holy Spirit guided Matthew to include Ruth of Moab in the family tree of Jesus. This shows us that God wants us to forgive the sins of the past. We should not hate people today, no matter what wrongs others did in the past. Jesus was willing to have His name beside Ruth, a woman from Moab.
   B. **Illustrations:**
      1. In biblical times, the Jews hated the Samaritans because they were only partly Jewish. But Jesus showed love to the Samaritan woman at the well (John 4).
      2. Ephesians 2:14 says that Jesus broke down the wall of hostility between Jews and Gentiles.
      3. He healed the servant of a Roman soldier (Matt. 8:5-13).
      4. He cast out a demon from the daughter of a woman from Canaan (Matt. 15:21-28).
      5. Jesus guides us to love and disciple people in all nations (Matt. 28:19-20).
   C. **Applications:**
      1. God wants the Jews to love the Germans; the blacks to love the whites.
      2. Search your own heart. Do you have prejudice against anyone because of education, race, gender, age, tribe, economic or social status? Jesus wants to save you from the sins of prejudice!
      3. How can we forgive or love those for whom we feel prejudice? As we pray and follow Jesus, His love will flow through us.

Figure 11.5   The first Problem (P₁) and Solution (S₁) explained, illustrated, and applied in the sermon: Jesus Came to Break Down 3 Types of Walls (Matt. 1:1-17)

III. Problem 2: (Principle) Some put a wall between men and women—they treat women as inferior to men.

  A. Explanations:

    1. **Biblical Setting:** As we stated in the Introduction, in the days of Jesus, a Jewish man thanked God each morning that he was not born as a woman.

    2. In those days, a man could divorce his wife for putting too much salt in the food!

  B. Illustrations and applications:

    1. In countries like Pakistan and Bangladesh, about 85% of the women cannot read because they have never been allowed to go to school.

    2. In some places men buy young girls and force them to serve as sexual slaves.

    3. In many countries a woman is expected to give all of her love to one man—her husband. But the husband shares his love with many women.

    4. In many places the man eats the best food and leaves the rest for the woman. Only the man's name is on the title deed to property.

    5. In many places a woman works harder than her husband. If she complains, he beats her.

Q 7 *How would Jesus like to see the rights of women raised in your culture?*

IV. Solution 2: (Principle) Jesus came to break down the wall between men and women.

  A. Explanations:

    1. **Biblical Setting:** Jesus included the names of five women in His family tree. He is the Savior of both men and women!

    2. God did not create woman from man's foot, to walk on her. Rather, He made her from man's rib, a place at his side and near his heart.

  B. Illustrations and applications:

    1. The Bible teaches that a man should only have one wife, and that a man should love his wife as he loves himself (Eph. 5:28).

    2. In Christ, all believers are equal. In Him, *"There is neither Jew nor Greek, slave nor free, male nor female, for you are all one in Christ Jesus"* (Gal. 3:28).

    3. A husband should love his wife as Christ loved the Church and gave Himself for her (Eph. 5:25).

    4. Men should give women the same rights and privileges God desires them to have. This includes the right to vote, to receive and give education, to own property, and to be treated with kindness and respect. The Golden Rule that Jesus taught applies to men and women.

Figure 11.6   The second Problem (P_2) and Solution (S_2) explained, illustrated, and applied in the sermon: Jesus Came to Break Down 3 Types of Walls (Matt. 1:1-17)

Q 8 ⟋ *In Matthew 1:1-17, how does Jesus relate to those famous for sin?*

V. Problem 3: Sin is like a wall that separates God and man.

   A. Explanations:

     1. **Biblical Setting:** Romans 3:23 includes all of us with Tamar, Rahab, Ruth, and Bathsheba.

     2. The Bible defines sin as lawlessness—rebelling against God (1 John 3:4).

   B. Illustrations and applications:

     1. If anyone says he has never sinned, he is a liar (1 John 1:10).

     2. There are great sinners like Saul of Tarsus, who called himself the chief of sinners (1 Tim. 1:15 KJV).

     3. There are small sinners like Timothy who was saved as a child (2 Tim. 1:5; 3:15).

VI. Solution 3: Jesus came to break down the wall of sin (Luke 19:10).

   A. Explanations:

     1. **Biblical Setting:** Tamar became an ancestor of Jesus because she committed adultery with Judah, her father-in-law (Gen. 38). What a way to qualify for a genealogy! Rahab was a harlot from Jericho (Josh. 2:1). She became the great-grandmother of King David. Bathsheba's name reminds us of David's terrible sin (2 Sam. 11). The king murdered her husband, Uriah, and committed adultery with her. Her womb that carried a child created by adultery, later carried Solomon, a relative of Jesus. Our sin does not make Jesus dirty!

     2. His name is called Jesus—Savior—because He will save His people from their sins (Matt. 1:21).

   B. Illustrations:

     1. Jesus cast seven demons out of Mary Magdalene and saved her.

     2. He forgave and saved national traitors like Matthew.

   C. Application:

     1. Jesus came to save all of us who have sinned. It does not matter whether our sins are few or many, great or small, we all need Jesus to save us.

Q 9 ⟍ *How can a person get past the wall between God and sinners?*

Figure 11.7   The third Problem (P₃) and Solution (S₃) explained, illustrated, and applied in the sermon: Jesus Came to Break Down 3 Types of Walls (Matt. 1:1-17)

We have worked through a sermon on Matthew 1:1-17. Now, we can shorten and revise our outline (Figure 11.8).

Title: Jesus Came to Break Down 3 Types of Walls   **Date:** _____   **Place:** _____

Text: Matthew 1:1-17

Introduction: We are surprised to see the names of the four women in the family tree of Jesus.

Continued on next page

I. **Problem 1: Racial prejudice is like a wall between people.**
    A. **Explanations:**
        1. **Biblical Setting:** Ruth was a woman from Moab.
        2. **Biblical Setting:** The hard feelings between Israel and Moab began after the Exodus.
        3. The Law of Moses forbade the Moabites to mix with the Israelites (Deut. 23:3).
    B. **Illustrations and applications:**
        1. In some places there is prejudice between blacks and whites.
        2. In Rwanda the tribes of the Hutus and Tutsis have shown hatred for each other.
        3. In India many have a strong prejudice against levels or classes of society.

II. **Solution 1: Jesus will enable us to conquer prejudice.**
    A. **Explanations:**
        1. **Biblical Setting:** Jesus was willing to have his name beside Ruth, a woman from Moab.
    B. **Illustrations:**
        1. Jews hated Samaritans, but Jesus showed love to the Samaritan woman at the well (John 4).
        2. Ephesians 2:14 says that Jesus broke down the wall of hostility between Jews and Gentiles.
        3. He healed the servant of a Roman soldier (Matt. 8:5-13).
        4. He cast out a demon from the daughter of a woman from Canaan (Matt. 15:21-28).
        5. Jesus guides us to love and to disciple people in all nations (Matt. 28:19-20).
    C. **Applications:**
        1. God wants the Jews to love the Germans; the blacks to love the whites.
        2. Do you have prejudice against anyone because of education, race, gender, age, tribe, economic or social status? Jesus wants to save you from the sins of prejudice!
        3. How can we forgive or love those for whom we feel prejudice?

III. **Problem 2: Some put a wall between men and women—they treat women as inferior to men.**
    A. **Explanations:**
        1. **Biblical Setting:** Jewish men thanked God each morning that that they were not born a woman.
        2. In those days, a man could divorce his wife for putting too much salt in the food!
    B. **Illustrations and applications:**
        1. In countries like Pakistan and Bangladesh, about 85% of the women cannot read.
        2. In some places men buy young girls and force them to serve as sexual slaves.
        3. In many countries a woman is expected to give all of her love to her husband, but the husband...
        4. In many places the man eats the best food; and only the man's name is on the title deed to property.
        5. In many places a woman works harder than her husband. If she complains, he beats her.

IV. **Solution 2: Jesus came to break down the wall between men and women.**
    A. **Explanations:**
        1. **Biblical Setting:** The names of five women in Christ's family tree show that He saves men and women!
        2. God did not create woman from man's foot, to walk on her, but from his rib, a place near his heart.
    B. **Illustrations and applications:**
        1. A man should love his wife as he loves himself (Eph. 5:28).
        2. In Christ, all believers are equal. In Him, all are one in Christ (Gal. 3:28).
        3. A husband should love his wife as Christ loved the Church and gave Himself for her (Eph. 5:25).
        4. The Golden Rule that Jesus taught applies to men and women! (Voting, education, property, kindness)

Continued on next page

V. Problem 3: Sin is like a wall that separates God and man.
  A. Explanations:
      1. **Biblical Setting:** Romans 3:23 includes all of us with Tamar, Rahab, Ruth, and Bathsheba.
      2. The Bible defines sin as lawlessness—rebelling against God (1 John 3:4).
  B. Illustrations and applications:
      1. If anyone says he has never sinned, he is a liar (1 John 1:10).
      2. There are great sinners like Saul of Tarsus—the chief of sinners (1 Tim. 1:15 KJV).
      3. There are small sinners like Timothy who was saved as a child (2 Tim. 1:5; 3:15).

VI. Solution 3: Jesus came to break down the wall of sin (Luke 19:10).
  A. Explanations:
      1. **Biblical Setting:** Tamar, Rahab, Ruth, and Bathsheba
      2. His name is called Jesus—Savior—because He will save His people from their sins (Matt. 1:21).
  B. Illustrations:
      1. Jesus cast seven demons out of Mary Magdalene and saved her.
      2. He forgave and saved national traitors like Matthew.
  C. Application:
      1. Jesus came to save all of us who have sinned. It does not matter whether our sins are few or many, great or small, we all need Jesus to save us.

**Figure 11.8   Shortened, revised outline of the sermon:
Jesus Came to Break Down 3 Types of Walls (Matt. 1:1-17)**

B. Second example of the Problem and Solution Parts of a sermon (Matt. 2:1-18)

Let us look at another example. This one comes from Matthew 2:1-18. Note that most of this sermon is based on our course *The Life & Teachings of Christ.*[1] As in example one, each Problem is followed at once by its Solution. As always, we will explain, illustrate, and apply each main point.

Problem 1: Some, like Herod, oppose God (Matt. 2:3-8; 16-18).

Solution 1: Wise men join God's team (Matt. 2:1-2).

Problem 2: God subtracts from the negligent (Matt. 2:3-6).

Solution 2: God adds to the diligent (Matt. 2:1-11).

Problem 3: Some people only worship with words (Matt. 2:7-8).

Solution 3: Wise men worship Jesus with their words and their wealth (Matt. 2:10-11).

Figure 11.9   Outline of the sermon: Attitudes Toward Jesus (Matt. 2:1-18)

Q 10 ✗ *What are 2 illustrations below on the problem of opposing Jesus?*

Title: Attitudes Toward Jesus

Text: Matthew 2:1-18

Introduction: (Choose an introduction fitting to your culture.)

I.   **Problem 1: (Principle) Some, like Herod, oppose God (Matt. 2:3-8; 16-18).**

   A. **Explanations:**

      1. **Biblical Background and Setting:** Who was Herod? Herod the Great was not a Jew, but the Romans appointed him as king. He ruled over the districts of Judea, Galilee, Iturea, and Trachonitis. Herod rebuilt the great temple in Bethlehem.

      2. When Herod heard that the king of the Jews was born, he was disturbed. All of Jerusalem was disturbed with him. They knew Herod would try to kill the new king. In time, Herod killed all the baby boys under 2 years of age near Bethlehem.

      3. Causes of the Problem: Herod opposed Jesus for personal reasons like greed, selfishness, and jealousy. He hated anyone who might take away part of his power. What he hated most was sharing! Herod did not care what blessings Jesus might bring. Herod's only concern was that Jesus might take away some of his kingdom. Herod cared only about himself. His favorite name was Herod.

   B. **Illustrations and Applications:**

      1. History records that Herod murdered his wife, his mother-in-law, three of his sons, his brother-in-law, his uncle, many other adults, and even babies. He feared that they might want to share something that was his. The Roman Caesar, Augustus, said it was safer to be Herod's pig+ than his son!

      2. Herod was as greedy as a hungry dog with only one bone!

      3. Pharaoh is an example of one who opposed God. He refused to listen to Moses, the preacher God sent to him.

      4. The Pharisees opposed Jesus. Cause: they envied the honor that people gave Him (Mark 15:10).

      5. The attitude of Herod lives on in some leaders. There was once a presbyter who supervised several churches. He was very jealous of his position. When a young pastor graduated from Bible school, the older pastor sent him to pastor a church far away from any city. He did not want the younger pastor to become influential or successful. Like King Herod, he cared more about himself than the good of the people. Leaders like Herod oppose Jesus.

II. **Solution 1: (Principle) Wise men join God's team (Matt. 2:1-2).**

   A. **Explanations:**

      1. The Magi were smarter than Herod. They realized that God created the stars, the world, and all people. They recognized that man is weak and God has all power.

   B. **Illustrations:**

      1. In most cases, there is a team that wins and a team that loses. The Bible teaches us that God's team wins. Wise people do not oppose God. Rather, they become members of His team.

      2. Herod opposed God for his years on earth. He could not defeat God's plan by killing the young, male babies around Jerusalem. In the end, Herod died and faced God as his judge.

      3. Nebuchadnezzar once opposed God, until God took away his mind for 7 years. Then, he learned to become a part of God's team, and honor God (Dan. 4:1-37).

   C. **Applications:**

      1. Each of us must decide whether to oppose God, or join His team.

      2. Each of us must choose—to build our own kingdom, or to build God's kingdom. Will you be like Herod, or the Wise Men?

Figure 11.10 **The first Problem (P₁) and Solution (S₁) explained, illustrated, and applied in the sermon: Attitudes Toward Jesus (Matt. 2:1-18)**

+ In Greek, some words for pig and son sound alike; pig is *hueios* and son is *huios*.

III. Problem 2: (Principle) God subtracts from the negligent (Matt. 2:3-6).

   A. Explanations:

   1. **Biblical Background and Setting:** Herod called together the chief priests and teachers of the Law. These Jews knew what the Scriptures said about the Jewish King or Messiah. Herod asked them where Christ was born. They told him that the new King would be born in Bethlehem (Matt. 2:3-6).

   2. Bethlehem was a small town only 5 miles from Jerusalem—the home of the chief priests. But the priests did not care. They were not willing to walk or ride this short distance to see if their new King was born.

   3. Causes of the Problem: (Matt. 13:14-15). Why did the chief priests and Jewish teachers ignore Jesus at His birth? Their ears were deaf to spiritual truth. Their eyes were blind to the light of the new star. A new king had been born, but this meant nothing to them. They had calluses on their hearts (Matt. 13:15). The Spirit was speaking, but they could not hear Him. They could not see new truth because they had neglected old truth. God subtracts from those who neglect.

Q 11 ➤ Explain why the servant of Matthew 25:24-30 lost his talent and was judged.

   B. Illustrations:

   1. We lose what we do not use. If we do not use the skill of speaking a language, we will lose it. If we do not use the ability to play a musical instrument, we will lose it. If we do not obey what we know is right, we will lose the ability to know truth from error. God subtracts from those who neglect.

   2. The mole is an animal that lives under the ground. He has eyes but cannot see, because he stopped using his eyes. God subtracts from those who neglect.

   3. Many members of cults today were once members of churches. They ignored the truth, and now follow after lies (Rom. 1:21-25). God subtracts from those who neglect.

   4. Matthew 25:24-30—the servant who neglected his talent lost it.

   C. Applications:

   1. If we neglect today's spiritual privileges, we must face God's judgment tomorrow. Those who ignore what the Holy Spirit says today may not be able to hear Him tomorrow.

Transition sentences: We have looked at two bad attitudes toward Jesus in Matthew 2. Herod opposed Jesus, and the chief priests ignored Jesus. Now let us look at the good attitude of the Wise Men.

IV. Solution 2: (Principle) God adds to the diligent (Matt. 2:1-11).

   A. Explanations:

   1. **Biblical Background and Setting:** Who were the Wise Men? They are sometimes called *Magi—a word linked with "magic." They came to Israel from the East, perhaps from a country like Persia (modern Iran). These men were Gentiles who probably did not have the Scriptures. Their theology was mixed up. It seems that they thought the stars were connected to the lives of people. They had a little light mixed with a lot of darkness. Still, they walked in the light they had to seek God. He sent them a special star to guide them to the Savior.

   2. The Wise Men walked faithfully in the little light that they had. Tradition says they rode camels through the night, while the chief priests were sleeping. Riding at night was hard work and tiring. But starlight led them to more light—to Jesus, the Light of the world, born in a manger. God subtracts from the *negligent, but adds to the diligent.

   B. Illustrations:

   1. Those who study well and pass one level in school may go on to the next grade or level.

   2. Luke 19:11-19 teaches that God adds to those who are faithful.

   3. Proverbs 4:18-19

Q 12 ➤ Under C Applications, point 2, state something we should not neglect today.

   C. Applications:

   1. We should follow the example of the Wise Men and walk in the light we have. When the Spirit calls us to repent, witness, forgive, or do good deeds, we should obey Him—not ignore Him.

   2. We should listen to our conscience—a light God has placed inside us.

Figure 11.11   The second Problem (P₂) and Solution (S₂) explained, illustrated, and applied in the sermon: Attitudes Toward Jesus (Matt. 2:1-18)

V. Problem 3: (Principle) Some people only worship with words (Matt. 2:7-8).

  A. Explanations:

    1. **Biblical Setting:** Herod said he wanted to worship Jesus. But he was just talking, and not sincere.

  B. Illustrations and Applications:

    1. Matthew 15:8 says some honor God with their lips, but their hearts are far from Him. They refused to honor God with their money, by helping their old parents.

    2. Matthew 7:21-23 describes those who say they love God, but do not obey Him.

VI. Solution 3: (Principle) Wise men worship Jesus with their words and their wealth (Matt. 2:10-11).

  A. Explanations:

    1. **Biblical Background and Setting:** Unlike Herod, the Wise Men did not try to keep all of their wealth for themselves. Rather, they gave gifts to the new king. They gave gold, incense (perfume often burned in a home or temple), and myrrh (a costly perfume often used in burials).

  B. Illustrations:

    1. Worship and giving should be in harmony. What we say with our tongues we should show with our treasure. Otherwise, we are like the man who played his guitar in one key, but sang in another.

    2. The greatest commandment is to worship God with all of our heart (Matt. 22:36-38). Jesus said that our treasure and our heart are in the same place (Matt. 6:21). So to worship God with our hearts, we must worship Him with our money.

    3. What would you think of a person who wore a sandal on one foot and a boot on the other? Shoes should match. Likewise, our giving should match our talking.

  C. Applications:

    1. The hands we raise in praise should also reach into our pockets to give tithes and offerings.

    2. It does not matter how much we give, if it is our best. Sometimes God is as pleased with copper as He is with gold (Mark 12:41-44).

Figure 11.12   **The third Problem (P₃) and Solution (S₃) explained, illustrated, and applied in the sermon: Attitudes Toward Jesus (Matt. 2:1-18)**

Q 13 ↗
Summarize the 2 illustrations that show that words should match money.

We have worked through the sermon on Matthew 2:1-18. Now, we can shorten and revise our outline (Figure 11.13).

Title: Attitudes Toward Jesus   **Date:** _____ **Place:**_____

Text: Matthew 2:1-18

Introduction:

I.   **Problem 1: Some, like Herod, oppose God (Matt. 2:3-8; 16-18).**

   A. **Explanations:**
   1. **Biblical Background and Setting:** Who was Herod?
   2. When Herod heard that the king of the Jews was born, he was disturbed.
   3. Causes of the Problem: Herod opposed Jesus for personal reasons like greed.

   B. **Illustrations and Applications:**
   1. History records that Herod murdered his own family members.
   2. Herod was as greedy as a hungry dog with only one bone!
   3. Pharaoh is an example of one who opposed God. He refused to listen to Moses.
   4. The Pharisees opposed Jesus. Cause: they envied the honor that people gave Him (Mark 15:10).
   5. The attitude of Herod lives on in some leaders.

II. **Solution 1: Wise men join God's team (Matt. 2:1-2).**

   A. **Explanations:**
   1. The Magi were smarter than Herod.

   B. **Illustrations:**
   1. In most cases, there is a team that wins and a team that loses.
   2. In the end, Herod died and faced God as his judge.
   3. Nebuchadnezzar once opposed God, until God took away his mind for 7 years (Dan. 4:1-37).

   C. **Applications:**
   1. Each of us must decide whether to oppose God, or join His team.
   2. Will you be like Herod, or the Wise Men?

III. **Problem 2: God subtracts from the negligent (Matt. 2:3-6).**

   A. **Explanations:**
   1. **Biblical Background and Setting:** The chief priests knew where Jesus would be born (Matt. 2:3-6).
   2. The chief priests were not willing to travel 5 miles to see if their new King was born.
   3. Causes of the Problem: (Matt. 13:14-15) God subtracts from those who neglect.

   B. **Illustrations:**
   1. We lose what we do not use: a language, a musical instrument, truth.
   2. The mole has eyes but cannot see. God subtracts from those who neglect.
   3. Many members of cults today were once members of churches (Rom. 1:21-25).
   4. Matthew 25:24-30—the servant who neglected his talent lost it.

   C. **Applications:**
   1. Those who ignore what the Holy Spirit says today may not be able to hear Him tomorrow.

Transition sentences: We have looked at two bad attitudes toward Jesus in Matthew 2. Herod opposed Jesus, and the chief priests ignored Jesus. Now let us look at the good attitude of the Wise Men.

IV. **Solution 2: God adds to the diligent (Matt. 2:1-11).**

   A. **Explanations:**
   1. **Biblical Background and Setting:** Who were the Wise Men or Magi?
   2. The Wise Men walked faithfully in the little light they had. Starlight led them to more light.

   B. **Illustrations:**
   1. Those who study well and pass one level in school may go on to the next grade or level.
   2. Luke 19:11-19 teaches that God adds to those who are faithful.
   3. Proverbs 4:18-19

   C. **Applications:**
   1. When the Spirit calls us to repent, witness, forgive, or do good deeds, we should obey Him.
   2. We should listen to our conscience—a light God has placed inside us.

V. **Problem 3: Some people only worship with words (Matt. 2:7-8).**

A. **Explanations:**
1. **Biblical Setting:** Herod said he wanted to worship Jesus. But he was just talking, and not sincere.

B. **Illustrations and Applications:**
1. Matthew 15:8 says some honor God with their lips. They refused to honor their old parents.
2. Matthew 7:21-23 describes those who say they love God, but do not obey Him.

VI. **Solution 3: Wise men worship Jesus with their words and their wealth (Matt. 2:10-11).**

A. **Explanations:**
1. **Biblical Background and Setting:** The Wise Men gave gold, incense, and myrrh.

B. **Illustrations:**
1. Worship and giving in harmony. One man played his guitar in one key, but sang in another.
2. The greatest commandment is to worship God with all of our heart (Matt. 22:36-38). Jesus said that our treasure and our heart are in the same place (Matt. 6:21).
3. What would you think of a person who wore a sandal on one foot and a boot on the other?

C. **Applications:**
1. The hands we raise in praise should also reach into our pockets to give tithes and offerings.
2. It does not matter how much we give, if it is our best. Sometimes God is as pleased with copper as He is with gold (Mark 12:41-44).

Figure 11.13   Shortened, revised outline of the sermon: Attitudes Toward Jesus (Matt. 2:1-18)

Lesson 31 Practice Preparing Problems and Solutions Using Method B
Goal: *Prepare an expository sermon using Method B (P_1S_1–P_2S_2–P_3S_3)*

The part that follows will help students develop and prepare. If you are studying this course by yourself, complete it and present it to a friend, family member, or small group. It will be good practice for you. Expand the outline to fit your needs.

Your presentation should be 10-15 minutes. In a classroom, teachers may limit students to a specific amount of time so many students can preach. Perhaps there was not time for all of the students to preach in earlier class periods. If so, allow the ones who did not preach to go first now. Video these sermons if possible. Students will benefit greatly from watching themselves on video outside of class. Change and adapt the outline that follows to your needs. For example, the text you choose may have two principles instead of three.

Student	Problem/Solution with Method B (P_1S_1/P_2S_2/P_3S_3)	Date
1.		
2.		
3.		
4.		
5.		
6.		
7.		
8.		
9.		
10.		

Figure 11.14   Schedule for students to preach 10-15 minutes in class (Teachers will tell students when to preach.)

Title: _____   **Date:** _____ **Place:** _____

Text: _____

Introduction

I.   **Problem 1:**

    A. Explanations:

      1. **Biblical Setting:**

      2.

    B. Illustrations:

      1.

      2.

      3.

    C. Applications:

      1.

      2.

      3.

II. **Solution 1:**

    A. Explanations:

      1.

      2.

    B. Illustrations:

      1.

      2.

      3.

    C. Applications:

      1.

      2.

      3.

III. **Problem 2:**

    A. Explanations:

      1. **Biblical Setting:**

      2.

    B. Illustrations:

      1.

      2.

      3.

    C. Applications:

      1.

      2.

      3.

IV. **Solution 2:**

    A. Explanations:

      1.

      2.

    B. Illustrations:

      1.

      2.

      3.

    C. Applications:

      1.

      2.

      3.

Figure 11.15   Practice preaching the Problem and Solution (Method B).

Test Yourself: Circle the letter by the *best* completion to each question or statement.

1. Explaining a Solution is like
a) digging in the sand.
b) leading people to the desert.
c) offering a drink of cold water.
d) pouring cold water on the ground.

2. An outline that uses Method B might look like:
a) $P_1S_1–P_2S_2$
b) $P_1S_1–P_2P_3$
c) $P_1P_2–S_1S_3$
d) $S_1P_1–P_2S_2$

3. What should you do to each Problem?
a) Explain it and apply it to the past.
b) Use a transition.
c) Explain and illustrate it.
d) Explain, illustrate, and apply it.

4. Solutions should be stated as
a) principles.
b) phrases.
c) questions.
d) suggestions.

5. When you present a Solution,
a) show that the Solution solves the Problem.
b) explain how to put the Solution into action.
c) deal with the questions of the listeners.
d) do all of the above.

6. A sermon should have
a) at least 1 principle.
b) 2 or more principles.
c) exactly 3 principles.
d) no more than 3 principles.

7. Which 2 parts may be combined at times?
a) Principle, Explanation
b) Transition, Principle
c) Solution, Choice
d) Illustration, Application

8. Which is an application?
a) In biblical times, Jewish men prayed daily.
b) Racial prejudice is a big problem.
c) Jesus lifts up the place of women.
d) Ask God to help you love all people.

9. In the Solution Step, your points might start with
a) "Reasons why…"
b) "Keys to overcoming…"
c) "Problems with…"
d) "Positive results of…"

10. In Method B, each problem is followed by
a) its solution.
b) an illustration.
c) another problem.
d) an application.

 Essay Test Topics Write 50-100 words on each of these goals that you studied in this chapter.

Two Examples of Presenting Problems and Solutions With Method B

Goal: *Contrast Method A and Method B of preparing an expository sermon.*

Practice Preparing Problems and Solutions Using Method B

Goal: *Prepare an expository sermon using Method B ($P_1S_1–P_2S_2–P_3S_3$).*

Chapter 12:
The Choice

Introduction

In this step, the speaker takes the listeners into the future. He shows them that today's choice will lead to either a good result or a bad result. This was a favorite method of Jesus, as Matthew 25:14-30 illustrates.

[14] *"Again, it will be like a man going on a journey, who called his servants and entrusted his property to them.* [15]*To one he gave five talents of money, to another two talents, and to another one talent, each according to his ability. Then he went on his journey.* [16]*The man who had received the five talents went at once and put his money to work and gained five more.* [17]*So also, the one with the two talents gained two more.* [18]*But the man who had received the one talent went off, dug a hole in the ground and hid his master's money.* [19]*After a long time the master of those servants returned and settled accounts with them."*

Future Good Result: [20] *"The man who had received the five talents brought the other five. 'Master,' he said, 'you entrusted me with five talents. See, I have gained five more.'* [21]*His master replied, 'Well done, good and faithful servant! You have been faithful with a few things; I will put you in charge of*

many things. Come and share your master's happiness!' [22]*The man with the two talents also came. 'Master,' he said, 'you entrusted me with two talents; see, I have gained two more.'* [23]*His master replied, 'Well done, good and faithful servant! You have been faithful with a few things; I will put you in charge of many things. Come and share your master's happiness!'"*

Figure 12.1   A choice today always leads to a good or bad result in the future.

Future Bad Result: [24] *"Then the man who had received the one talent came. 'Master,' he said, 'I knew that you are a hard man, harvesting where you have not sown and gathering where you have not scattered seed.* [25]*So I was afraid and went out and hid your talent in the ground. See, here is what belongs to you.'* [26]*His master replied, 'You wicked, lazy servant! So you knew that*

I harvest where I have not sown and gather where I have not scattered seed? [27]*Well then, you should have put my money on deposit with the bankers, so that when I returned I would have received it back with interest.* [28]*Take the talent from him and give it to the one who has the ten talents.* [29]*For everyone who has will be given more, and he will have an abundance. Whoever does not have, even what he has will be taken from him.* [30]*And throw that worthless servant outside, into the darkness, where there will be weeping and gnashing of teeth'"* (Matt. 25:14-30).

Lessons:

 Explanation and Examples of Step IV—The Choice
Goal: *Illustrate the positive, negative, and contrast methods of the Choice Step.*

 Practice Preparing Step IV—The Choice
Goal: *Use the contrast method to create Step IV of a sermon.*

Explanation and Examples of Step IV—The Choice

Goal: *Illustrate the positive, negative, and contrast methods of the Choice Step.*

In the Problem Step, we gave reasons why something was a problem. We illustrated each reason at least twice. In the Solution Step, we showed how to solve the problem. There, we stated principles and illustrated them. In the *Choice Step, we show what the result will be if listeners accept or reject God's solution. This will strengthen people's desire to accept the solution to the problem.

Q 1 ⟩ *Summarize what to do in each of these steps: the Problem, the Solution, the Choice.*

In Step IV, you take the listeners mentally into the future. You should be realistic, but use language that touches the senses. That is, you should use words to help the listeners' imagination. They need to imagine seeing, hearing, feeling, tasting, and smelling the future. In this chapter, we will teach you how to touch their senses. Your listeners will sense a future situation based on the choice they make about your message.

Q 2 ⟩ *In Step IV, the preacher guides listeners to consider the _____.*

In Step IV—The Choice, you take your listeners into a future situation. Let us look at three different ways to prepare the Choice Step.

Q 3 ⟩ *Explain: In the Choice Step, the preacher must touch the senses.*

A. Positive: Describe the future good result.

Select a definite situation in the future. Picture your listeners there. Describe them enjoying safety, peace, honor, pleasure, joy, and satisfaction. They are happy because they chose to accept God's solution to the problem.

Jesus emphasized a future good result in Matthew 19. The rich young ruler had refused to forsake all to follow Christ. Peter asked, *"What then will there be for us?"* (Matt. 19:27). Jesus wanted to encourage Peter and the other disciples. They had made the difficult choice of following Him. So the Master took them into the future. He did this by using words to paint a picture of that future:

Q 4 ⟩ *How did Jesus emphasize a future good result in Matthew 19:28-29?*

> [28]*Jesus said to them, "I tell you the truth, at the renewal of all things, when the Son of Man sits on his glorious throne, you who have followed me will also sit on twelve thrones, judging the twelve tribes of Israel.* [29]*And everyone who has left houses or brothers or sisters or father or mother or children or fields for my sake will receive a hundred times as much and will inherit eternal life"* (Matt. 19:28-29).

Jesus helped His followers feel the honor they would receive in the future. He guided them to think about the thrones they would sit upon. Jesus showed the future good result of the choice the disciples were making. Emphasizing the future good result encourages people to make hard decisions in the present. We might not have the strength to carry the cross *today* if we think only about its weight. But thinking about the joy ahead (future) inspires and motivates us. How was Jesus able to choose the cross? He thought of the future good result.

Q 5 ⟩ *What helped Jesus endure the cross?*

> *Let us fix our eyes on Jesus, the author and perfecter of our faith, who **for the joy set before him** endured the cross, scorning its shame, and sat down at the right hand of the throne of God* (Heb. 12:2).

A preacher wanted his people to give an offering to help a missionary. He spoke about the problem and the solution. Then, he came to Step IV—The Choice. He said, "I am asking you to help a missionary who will minister to people you will never see. But in heaven, we will find this missionary and ask him to show us those people. One by one you will meet them. They will thank you for sharing your wealth. And Jesus will say 'Well done' for being a faithful steward of the money He gave you. In heaven, you will be thankful for the people you helped on earth."

Q 6 ⟩ *How did a preacher use the Choice Step to help his people give?*

Q 7 ⟍ *For what purpose did God give Ezekiel a vision of a future temple?*

Q 8 ⟍ *Why do you think God has given us a beautiful picture of the New Jerusalem and a new heaven and earth (Rev. 21–22)?*

Q 9 ⟍ *What future bad result did John the Baptist emphasize (Matt. 3:7, 10)?*

Q 10 ⟍ *For what purpose did Jesus tell the parable of a fig tree?*

Q 11 ⟍ *What bad result did Jesus predict if His listeners rejected Him (Luke 19:41-44)?*

Q 12 ⟍ *What future, bad result does Jesus speak of in Revelation 2:16?*

Q 13 ⟍ *What contrast of the future did Isaiah describe (Isa. 1:18-20)?*

Ezekiel ministered to the Jews in captivity. Nebuchadnezzar had conquered thousands of them and carried them away to Babylon. Their city and temple were destroyed. The Jews were discouraged. Ezekiel rebuked Israel for the problem of sin. He told them that the solution was to repent and obey God. And he painted a mental picture of the future. In Ezekiel 40–48 he told about a glorious temple. This caused the Jews to lift up their heads. Describing the future gave them new hope and strength. God gave Ezekiel this vision of the future for a purpose. It was to encourage the Jews to make the right decisions.

B. Negative: Describe a future bad result.

Sometimes you may want to emphasize a future bad result instead of a future good result. To do this, picture your hearers in a bad future setting. Describe them feeling guilt, shame, regret, sorrow, fear, failure, and such. Why are they having such feelings? They rejected God's solution to the problem.

Emphasizing a future bad result helps people make the right choice. John the Baptist warned his listeners to flee from the wrath to come. He spoke of an ax and a fire of judgment (Matt. 3:7, 10). People may change direction when you describe the bad future where their road is leading.

> *6Then he told this parable: "A man had a fig tree, planted in his vineyard, and he went to look for fruit on it, but did not find any. 7So he said to the man who took care of the vineyard, 'For three years now I've been coming to look for fruit on this fig tree and haven't found any. Cut it down! Why should it use up the soil?' 8'Sir,' the man replied, 'leave it alone for one more year, and I'll dig around it and fertilize it. 9If it bears fruit next year, fine! If not, then cut it down'"* (Luke 13:6-9).

Jesus described a future bad result in Luke 19:41-44. He wanted to show His listeners what would happen in the future if they did not accept Him. It is good for a preacher to weep like Jesus when he predicts future sorrow.

> *41As he approached Jerusalem and saw the city, he wept over it 42and said, "If you, even you, had only known on this day what would bring you peace—but now it is hidden from your eyes. 43The days will come upon you when your enemies will build an embankment against you and encircle you and hem you in on every side. 44They will dash you to the ground, you and the children within your walls. They will not leave one stone on another, because you did not recognize the time of God's coming to you"* (Luke 19:41-44).

C. Contrast future good and bad results.

The final way to develop Step IV is to use contrast. This is the most powerful way to develop the Choice Step. Jesus used it often. Picture your listeners in a future setting. First show the good result that will come to those who accept the solution offered by the Bible. Then show the bad result that will fall on those who reject the solution.

We will consider five examples of the contrast method.

1. Deuteronomy 28:1-24:   People must choose to be blessed or cursed.

Future good result: *1"If you fully obey the Lord your God and carefully follow all his commands I give you today, the Lord your God will set you high above all the nations on earth. 2All these blessings will come upon you and accompany you if you obey the Lord your God: 3You will be blessed in the city and blessed in the country. 4The fruit of your womb will be blessed, and the crops of your land and the young of your livestock—the calves of your herds and the lambs of your flocks. 5Your basket and your kneading trough will be blessed. 6You will be blessed when you come in and blessed when you go out. 7The Lord will grant that the enemies who rise up against you will be defeated before you. They will come at you from one direction but flee from you in seven. ⁸The Lord will send a blessing on your barns and on everything you put your hand to. The Lord your God will bless you in the land he is giving you. ⁹The Lord will establish you as his holy people, as he promised you on oath, if you keep the commands of the Lord your God and walk in his ways. ¹⁰Then all the peoples on earth will see that you are called by the name of the Lord, and they will fear you. ¹¹The Lord will grant you abundant prosperity—in the fruit of your womb, the young of your livestock and the crops of your ground—in the land he swore to your forefathers to give you. ¹²The Lord will open the heavens, the storehouse of his bounty, to send rain on your land in season and to bless all the work of your hands. You will lend to many nations but will borrow from none. ¹³The Lord will make you the head, not the tail. If you pay attention to the commands of the Lord your God that I give you this day and carefully follow them, you will always be at the top, never at the bottom. ¹⁴Do not turn aside from any of the commands I give you today, to the right or to the left, following other gods and serving them"* (Deut. 28:1-14).

Q 14 ↘ How is Leviticus 26 like Deuteronomy 28?

Future bad result: ¹⁵*"However, if you do not obey the Lord your God and do not carefully follow all his commands and decrees I am giving you today, all these curses will come upon you and overtake you: ¹⁶You will be cursed in the city and cursed in the country. ¹⁷Your basket and your kneading trough will be cursed. ¹⁸The fruit of your womb will be cursed, and the crops of your land, and the calves of your herds and the lambs of your flocks. ¹⁹You will be cursed when you come in and cursed when you go out. ²⁰The Lord will send on you curses, confusion and rebuke in everything you put your hand to, until you are destroyed and come to sudden ruin because of the evil you have done in forsaking him. ²¹The Lord will plague you with diseases until he has destroyed you from the land you are entering to possess. ²²The Lord will strike you with wasting disease, with fever and inflammation, with scorching heat and drought, with blight and mildew, which will plague you until you perish. ²³The sky over your head will be bronze, the ground beneath you iron. ²⁴The Lord will turn the rain of your country into dust and powder; it will come down from the skies until you are destroyed"* (Deut. 28:15-24). [Turn to Deuteronomy 28 to read 45 more verses that describe the terrible, future result of disobeying God!]

2. Matthew 7:24-27: Some build on the rock and some build on the sand.

Q 15 ↗ Contrast the future bad and good at the close of the Sermon on the Mount (Matthew 5–7).

Future good result: ²⁴*"Therefore everyone who hears these words of mine and puts them into practice is like a wise man who built his house on the rock. ²⁵The rain came down, the streams rose, and the winds blew and beat against that house; yet it did not fall, because it had its foundation on the rock"* (Matt. 7:24-25).

Future bad result: ²⁶*"But everyone who hears these words of mine and does not put them into practice is like a foolish man who built his house on sand. ²⁷The rain came down, the streams rose, and the winds blew and beat against that house, and it fell with a great crash"* (Matt 7:26-27).

As Matthew 7:24-27 shows, Jesus used the method of Step IV near the close of His message. He took His listeners into a future setting. Christ used language that touched the senses of His listeners. The Lord's language made the situation very real. A person could almost feel the rain falling and the wind blowing. The listeners experienced the crash of the house that fell and felt the sorrow of this loss. In contrast, the listeners felt the joy of those who were safe after a bad storm.

Q 16 ↗ How did Jesus use language that touched the senses in Matthew 7:24-27?

3. Matthew 25:1-13: Some are wise and some are foolish.

Future good result: ¹*"At that time the kingdom of heaven will be like ten virgins who took their lamps and went out to meet the bridegroom. ²Five of them were* *foolish and five were wise. ³The foolish ones took their lamps but did not take any oil with them. ⁴The wise, however, took oil in jars along with their lamps. ⁵The bridegroom was a long time in coming, and they all became drowsy and fell asleep. ⁶At midnight the cry rang out: 'Here's the bridegroom! Come out to meet him!' ⁷Then all the virgins woke up and trimmed their lamps. ⁸The foolish ones said to the wise, 'Give us some of your oil; our lamps are going out.' ⁹'No,' they replied, 'there may not be enough for both us and you. Instead, go to those who sell oil and buy some for yourselves.' ¹⁰But while they were on their way to buy the oil, the bridegroom arrived. The virgins who were ready went in with him to the wedding banquet. And the door was shut"* (Matt 25:1-10).

Future bad result: ¹¹*"Later the others also came. 'Sir! Sir!' they said. 'Open the door for us!' ¹²But he replied, 'I tell you the truth, I don't know you.' ¹³Therefore keep watch, because you do not know the day or the hour"* (Matt. 25:11-13).

4. Matthew 24:45-51:   Faithful servants will be rewarded, but wicked servants will be condemned.

Future good result: ⁴⁵*"Who then is the faithful and wise servant, whom the master has put in charge of the servants in his household to give them their food at the proper time? ⁴⁶It will be good for that servant whose master finds him doing so when he returns. ⁴⁷I tell you the truth, he will put him in charge of all his possessions"* (Matt. 24:45-47).

Future bad result: ⁴⁸*"But suppose that servant is wicked and says to himself, 'My master is staying away a long time,' ⁴⁹and he then begins to beat his fellow servants and to eat and drink with drunkards. ⁵⁰The master of that servant will come on a day when he does not expect him and at an hour he is not aware of. ⁵¹He will cut him to pieces and assign him a place with the hypocrites, where there will be weeping and gnashing of teeth"* (Matt. 24:48-51).

Q 17 ↗ *Summarize the contrast method of Step IV.*

We are studying how to use the contrast method in the Choice Step (Step IV). We are preparing our listeners to make a decision. In Step V, we will *invite* them to choose. But first we want them to see how important their choice is. Today's choice always leads to good or bad results in the future.

Scripture	Contrast
Matt. 8:11-12	Believers and unbelievers
Matt. 13:47-50	The wicked and the righteous
Matt. 24:40-42	Two men; two women
Matt. 25:14-30	Faithful servants and the lazy servant
Matt. 25:31-46	The sheep and the goats
1 Cor. 4:21	A whip and a gentle spirit
2 Thess. 1:5-10	Sinners and saints when Christ returns
Rev. 13:16-18; 14:1	The mark of the beast and the mark of Christ
Rev. 17–20; 21–22	The fall of Satan, Babylon, and her citizens; The rise of Christ; the New Jerusalem, and her citizens

Figure 12.2   More examples using a future contrast of bad and good results

Q 18 ↖ *What kind of emotions do you think each of the following people felt (Matt. 25:1-13)?*

a) The wise virgins: _____.

b) The foolish virgins: _____.

We could cite many more examples! The prophets, Jesus, and the apostles used contrasts to influence their listeners to make good choices. The contrast method is a powerful sermon tool! It brings people to a point of decision near the end of a sermon. It quickly summarizes what the results will be if people accept or reject a biblical solution. But we must always leave the choice to the listeners.

5. Step IV: Listeners must choose to think good thoughts or to worry

We have given four examples to illustrate the contrast method of the Choice Step. All of these were examples in the Bible. For our final example, we will prepare the Choice Step of our sermon on *worry*. Recall that earlier we created the Problem and Solution Steps for a sermon on *worry*. Review the outline in Figure 10.7. Then, study Figure 12.3. There, we use the contrast method to develop the Choice Step of our sermon on *worry*.

Transition sentence: **Not everyone will respond in the same way to this message on worrying.**

IV. The Choice: **You choose what your future will be like by the way you respond to God's Word.**

   A. *Future good result:*
      1. **Illustration:**   A Christian can practice praying his problems, giving thanks for blessings, and thinking good thoughts. When he does these things, a wonderful thing happens. God's **peace** comes. Philippians 4:7 pictures the peace of God standing like a soldier, guarding the believer's heart and mind against worry. Pray your problems. Give thanks. Think good thoughts. These three things bring God's peace to protect your mind, like a guard protects a house.
      2. **Illustration:**   Many here today have worried a lot in the past. But this message has brought a new beginning to you. I imagine you, several years in the future, sleeping in your bed. Your arms are folded peacefully over your chest. Even in your sleep, there is a big smile on your face. You have told the children an evening Bible story and then prayed together. They are having happy dreams. You sleep peacefully and awake refreshed. You sing throughout the day as you work. Your joyful, peaceful life inspires those around you. Other people enjoy being with you and come to you for counsel. You have learned the secret of defeating worry and living in victory. Today was one of the best days of your life.

   B. *Future bad result:*
      1. **Illustration:**   Others of you may choose to continue worrying. I see myself, a few years in the future, standing in a hospital room. I am standing beside the bed of one of you who heard the words of this sermon. You have lost a lot of weight. The lines on your face make you look much older than you are. An operation is scheduled to remove an ulcer in your stomach. No one in your family is happy. Several are crying; sorrow fills the air. Your children are never at church because your religion does not appeal to them. Why are these things happening to you? You refused to make a decision to stop worrying. You did not let God help you. Even in that terrible state, God will love you. Your pastor will still understand and love you. But your life *could* be different. I will still come to visit you if you reject this sermon today and continue to worry. But I may have to visit you in a hospital if you do not change.

Figure 12.3
The Choice Step (contrast method) for the sermon: Trade Your Worries for Peace
(Phil. 4:6-8)

> **Transition sentence:**   Not everyone will respond in the same way to this message on worrying.
>
> **IV. The Choice:**   You choose what your future will be like by the way you respond to God's Word.
>   **A.** *Future good result:*
>   1. Philippians 4:7 pictures the peace of God standing like a soldier to guard against worry.
>   2. Peace, joy, happiness, respect, honor, and a good influence on family and others are ahead for those who conquer worry.
>   **B.** *Future bad result:*
>   1. Weariness, unrest, sorrow, shame, health problems, and even the hospital are ahead for those who choose to worry.

Figure 12.4   Shortened outline of Step IV of a sermon to prevent worry

Q 19 ✎ *Which do you think is better to present last—the good result or the bad result?*

When using the contrast method, some preachers prefer to present the negative result first. Then they can move to Step V (The Invitation) in a positive, encouraging manner. But we should reflect on the biblical examples in this chapter. Jesus first stated the positive result, and then the negative. Perhaps He presented the negative, bad result last so that people would turn from future trouble.

Ending Step IV with the bad, future result is like putting leprosy in front of someone and asking, "Do you want this?" Only a person with a hard heart will answer, "Yes, give me the disease." It is good to end Step IV with the bad result. However, this is not the end of your sermon. You still have Step V—The Invitation to close with an encouraging word.

Lesson 33

Practice Preparing Step IV—The Choice
Goal: *Use the contrast method to create Step IV of a sermon.*

Q 20 ✎ *Use the contrast method to create Step IV— The Choice for a sermon you prepared in chapter 10.*

Now it is your turn to practice. In chapter 10, you worked on Steps II and III of a sermon on Romans 6:23 (Figure 10.15). Use the contrast method to prepare Step IV— The Choice. (Teacher, this would be a good exercise to do together with students in class.)

> **Title:** _____
>
> **Text:** _____
>
> **Transition:** _____
>
> **IV. The Choice:**
>   **A.** *Future good result:*
>
>
>
>   **B.** *Future bad result:*

Figure 12.5
Practice using the contrast method to create Step IV of a sermon on Romans 6:23.

The chart that follows is for scheduling students to preach in class. If you are studying this course by yourself, preach your Choice Step to a friend or family member. It will be good practice for you. Expand the outline to fit your needs. Your presentation should be 3 to 5 minutes long.

Student	Choice	Date
1.		
2.		
3.		
4.		
5.		
6.		
7.		
8.		
9.		
10.		

Figure 12.6   Schedule for students to preach the Choice Step in 3-5 minutes.
(Teachers will tell students when to preach.)

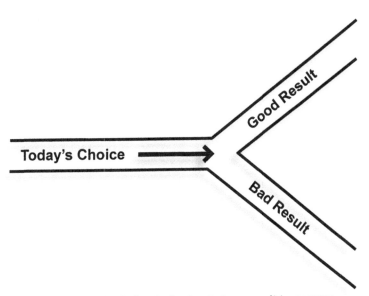

Figure 12.7   A choice today leads to a result tomorrow.
Help your listeners choose wisely.

Test Yourself: Circle the letter by the ***best*** completion to each question or statement.

1. In the Choice Step, the preacher should
a) state the problem.
b) repeat his main points.
c) describe the future.
d) choose a Scripture text.

2. What is a key to describing results?
a) Use history.
b) Use emotion.
c) Use names.
d) All of these are important.

3. In his last days, which method did Moses use?
a) Positive results
b) Contrasting results
c) Negative results
d) God's results

4. Which of these shows negative results?
a) Endure persecution to strengthen your faith.
b) Pray for God to help your enemies.
c) Reject Christ and face judgment.
d) If your hand sins, cut it off.

5. Which example shows contrasting results?
a) The wise and foolish builders
b) The cities of Sodom and Capernaum
c) The calling of Matthew and John
d) The Law and the Prophets

6. In the Beatitudes, Jesus emphasizes
a) positive results.
b) negative results.
c) similar results.
d) contrasting results.

7. When you describe results to people, you
a) ignore their emotions.
b) influence them to make a choice.
c) make a decision for them.
d) force them to repent.

8. Which shows a positive result?
a) Ezekiel's prophecy of the temple
b) Jesus' prophecy of the temple
c) Daniel's prophecy of the temple
d) Jeremiah's prophecy of the temple

9. What is the most powerful way to develop the Choice Step?
a) Positive results
b) Contrasting results
c) Negative results
d) Immediate results

10. What method did Jesus use when He spoke of the future destruction of Jerusalem?
a) Negative result
b) Positive result
c) Contrast
d) Comparison

Essay Test Topics Write 50-100 words on each of these goals that you studied in this chapter.

Explanation and Examples of Step IV—The Choice

Goal: *Illustrate the positive, negative, and contrast methods of the Choice Step.*

Practice Preparing Step IV—The Choice

Goal: *Use the contrast method to create Step IV of a sermon.*

Chapter 13:
The Invitation

Introduction

Shakespeare, a famous English writer, wrote, "All is well that ends well." This is especially true of a good sermon.

It is possible to omit Step IV—The Choice in a sermon—once in a while. But NEVER close a sermon without inviting people to respond to your message. Preach every sermon to cause change:

- to solve a problem,
- to meet a need,
- to make something or someone better.

And after you preach to change something, invite people to make an immediate decision—right then and there.

Q 1 ➤ *Not giving an invitation at the end of a sermon is like _____.*

Closing a sermon without an *invitation is foolish. It is like getting fish into a net, and then just dropping the net and letting them escape. Always pull in the net! Never close a sermon without giving people the opportunity to make a choice right then and there.[1]

Figure 13.1   Always pull in the net at the end of your sermon.

Lessons:
Explanation and Examples of Step V—The Invitation

Goal A: *Summarize the 5 rules of an invitation.*
Goal B: *Explain ways to invite people to respond and how to plan time at the altar.*
Goal C: *Prepare the Invitation Steps for 2 sermons.*

Practice Presenting Steps I–V of a Complete Sermon

Goal: *Write and preach a complete expository sermon using the Five-Step Method.*

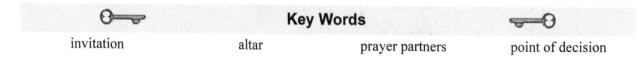

Key Words

invitation   altar   prayer partners   point of decision

Explanation and Examples of Step V—The Invitation

Goal A: *Summarize the 5 rules of an invitation.*
Goal B: *Explain ways to invite people to respond and how to plan time at the altar.*
Goal C: *Prepare the Invitation Steps for 2 sermons.*

A. The five rules of the Invitation

Preachers should follow five basic rules for the Invitation Step. These are: be prepared, be brief, be specific, be personal, and be bold. Let us look at each of these five rules.

1. Be prepared. Plan carefully the words of Step V.[2] Make the Invitation a part of your outline. Do not assume that you will find the right words to use without planning. If you do not plan, you may commit one of two common errors. These errors are: ending too quickly, and ending too weakly.

Ending too quickly: Do not end your message so suddenly that you shock or surprise your hearers. They may feel like they are in a car that ran out of gas on the way up a mountain.

Ending too weakly: Do not close your message with wandering, aimless speech. This will wear out your people. They may think you are like a lost guide looking for the way home!

Often, listeners leave a church confused and tired because of the preacher's poor invitations. Do not be like these preachers. People should make a decision in Step V. This is your final appeal. You must plan it well. Do not destroy all of the effort you have put into the first four steps. People will either walk to the *altar to change, or walk out the back door unchanged. Do not fail at this important moment.

2. Be brief. The final step is not the time to present new ideas or new truths. It is not the time to plow new ground. Neither is it time to re-plow ground you have already covered. In other words, the Invitation is not a summary of your message. Instead, this is the time to complete what you set out to do. Finish it! End the sermon as powerfully as you started it. Generally, the Invitation should be about ten percent of the length of your message. For a 30-minute sermon, the Invitation might be 3 minutes or less. However, a preacher should always follow the leading of the Spirit. Some preachers give longer invitations than others. Do what works for you!

Preachers who do not develop Step II (The Problem) often take too long during the Invitation Step. Why? They are not preaching to solve a specific problem. They do not know where they are leading people. Such preachers do not have clear goals for their Invitation at the end of their sermon. When you fail to plan, you plan to fail!

A young boy heard an unprepared preacher say repeatedly, "In conclusion . . ." during his sermon. Finally, the child asked his father, "What does 'in conclusion' mean?" The tired father replied, "Nothing, son. Absolutely nothing!" What is the point of this story? A preacher should stand up, speak up, and then hush up.

3. Be specific. State your Invitation so clearly that no one can doubt what you want. In the Introduction, you kept the "cat" in the bag (see chapter 11). Now it should be out of the bag! People should know exactly why you brought the cat. Even children should understand what you are inviting people to do.

Q 2 ⟍ *Explain the 5 steps of a sermon.*

Q 3 ⟍ *Name 2 common errors that preachers make when they fail to plan the Invitation Step.*

Q 4 ⟍ *Explain this statement: "The invitation is neither the time to plow new ground nor the time to re-plow old ground."*

Q 5 ⟍ *Contrast the Introduction and the Invitation.*

Q 6 ⟋ *How does the statement, "Preachers who aim at nothing usually hit it," relate to the Invitation?*

State exactly what you want people to do. Preachers who aim at nothing usually hit just that—nothing! Ask yourself, What response do I want the most? Then be sure you ask the people for it!

In Lake Victoria in East Africa, fishermen catch several types of fish. The Nile perch is a very large fish. Many of them are longer than a man's leg. Some of these fish weigh more than two hundred kilograms (440 pounds)! The net used to catch these fish is made with large holes. This fish is so big that it cannot swim through the holes.

There is another kind of fish in Lake Victoria called the omena. The omena is smaller than a person's little finger, but it is a very good fish to eat. Fishermen must use a net made with small holes to catch this tiny fish.

At the Invitation Step, do not use a large Nile perch net if you are trying to catch the small omena. Use a spiritual "net" (Invitation) that is designed to catch the spiritual fish you want. Therefore, do not give a general altar call. It is important to be specific.

A man was once hunting deer with a gun. His family needed meat. Suddenly, a herd of deer ran past him. In his excitement, the man forgot to aim at a specific animal. He just shot in the direction of the herd. They all ran off—frightened but unharmed. He hit nothing! This is what usually happens to people who do not have a specific aim.

Two pastors wanted their members to contact people who had visited their churches. One pastor emphasized the need and solution well. The people agreed with him. They were willing to help. But this pastor did not set a definite time for this ministry. The next Sunday he was disappointed because no visitor had been contacted. The other pastor preached a similar message. However, he asked for volunteers to meet at the church on Saturday at 2 p.m. Several raised their hands and agreed to come. This preacher was successful because he was specific. Both men hit what they aimed at.

Q 7 ⟋ *What do we mean by "being personal" during the Invitation?*

4. **Be personal.**   Talk to each individual, not to the entire crowd. In Step V, each listener should be asking himself, What does this sermon have to do with me? Each person should feel you are talking to him or her. Try to look briefly at the eyes of each person during the Invitation Step. Lower your voice. Talk slowly, as you do when you talk with a friend about a serious matter.

Suppose you deliver a sermon entitled "Three Men Who Died at Calvary." You are preaching Christ: the One on the middle cross. The repentant thief is on His left. The unrepentant thief is on His right. The final words of your Invitation could be:

"Each man and woman stands today in the place of one of these two thieves. We are either repentant or unrepentant. We are either forgiven or unforgiven. We are either saved or lost. In which place are you today?"[3]

5. **Be bold: request a decision.**   Give an invitation, not an apology. *Ambassadors do not apologize when they deliver a message from their king or leader. And preachers should not apologize when they deliver a message from their heavenly King.[4]

Charles H. Spurgeon became a famous preacher. When he was a young man, he felt guilty for his sins. He went from one church to another, wanting to know how he could be forgiven. One Sunday evening, he struggled through a violent storm. Because of the bad weather, he was forced to give up his plan to attend a certain church some distance away. Instead, Spurgeon turned down a side street where he found a small church. Only fifteen people had come that night to worship. Even the pastor had not been able to come because of the storm. In his place, a man from the congregation stood to preach. This layman chose as his text Isaiah 45:22: *"Turn to me and be saved, all you ends of the earth; for I am God, and there is no other."*

This lay preacher knew very little about preaching. His sermon consisted mostly of repeating the text in different ways. Finally, the man could say no more about the passage.

He looked at the young Spurgeon sitting in the back of the church and spoke directly to him. "Young man, you look very miserable. You will never stop being miserable—in life or in death—if you do not do as this text says. If you will simply look to Jesus, you will be saved." Then he shouted, "Young man, look to Jesus!"

At that moment, Spurgeon stopped dwelling on his own guilt and began trusting in Christ for salvation. His sorrow left. Spurgeon was filled with joy, for he knew that his sins were forgiven. Forgiveness came because he looked to Christ alone for salvation. The preacher requested a decision and got it.[5] At times, a good Invitation can overcome a sermon that is poorly preached.

A Roman general was once sent by Caesar to confront a rebellious leader. Caesar's general found the rebel and told him to surrender. The rebel replied, "I'll think about it." The Roman general used his sword to draw a circle on the ground around the rebel. The general then told the man, "Make up your mind before you step out of the circle."

Q 8 *What is the point in the story about the general and the rebel?*

A preacher cannot force people to act. He must never be rude. But his duty is to bring people to a *point of decision. Their decision may be to call for the preacher at a more convenient time. Still, the preacher should ask each listener to decide something.

A man stood in the fruit market admiring the fruit. He really liked a certain pineapple. The seller bragged on the golden fruit before naming the price. Then he picked up the pineapple and placed it in the customer's hands. This wise seller had learned from experience that this would keep the customer's attention. Now the customer had the pineapple. Now he had to decide.

The man bought the pineapple! The seller brought the man to a moment of decision. Similarly, a preacher should bring each listener to a moment of spiritual decision. The Invitation must place the matter in the listener's hands and leave it there as the sermon closes.

A Bold Invitation by Spurgeon: "God has spoken to you tonight. There will never be a better opportunity to have your sins forgiven than tonight. Tomorrow you will have less time than today. Tomorrow you will have more sin and less time to get right with God. Tomorrow you will have a harder heart because of more sin. Furthermore, God may never call you to repent again. Come now. I am waiting for you."[6]

Q 9 *In which 3 ways did we illustrate the rule: "Be bold: request a decision"?*

B. The altar service: How to invite people

How should you give the Invitation? All you need is something to bring listeners to a moment of decision. Use a question, a quotation, or a verse from a song.[7] Use a story or any type of challenging illustration.

You can encourage each person to respond in various ways, by asking:
- "Come forward and pray at the altar."
- "Raise your hand as a sign of commitment or decision."
- "Kneel and pray where you are seated."
- "Write your name on a piece of paper to volunteer for something."
- "Write your name and an amount on a piece of paper to make a financial promise."

The type of response you ask for depends on what you want.

Q 10 *List three possible responses to a preacher's invitation.*

The Invitation Step in the sermon on worrying could be something like this:

Each of us has battled the problem of worry. You know you have worried, and God knows it. Right now, your heavenly Father is reaching His hand down to help you. You may feel you want to make a decision to stop worrying. Today, you can begin praying your problems, counting your blessings, and thinking positive thoughts. Raise your hand up toward God as an expression of your decision. (Pause)

I want those who raised their hands to stand up, come forward, and pray together. Come now! Perhaps someone here is not a Christian and wants to commit his life to Christ. Come forward now and ask us to pray with you for your salvation.

Figure 13.2   Step V—Invitation for a sermon to prevent worry

In this book we have created all of the Five Steps for a sermon to prevent worry. The shortened outline follows.

Q 11 ✎ *Could you preach the sermon on worry that is outlined in Figure 13.3? Explain.*

Introduction:

A small boy asked his mother, "Are warts really caused by worrying?"

I.   **The Problem: The Bible gives several reasons why you should not worry (Phil. 4:6).**

   A. **Explanations:**
      1. **Biblical Background:** Philippi was a city in Europe.
      2. **Biblical Background:** Acts 16 tells us about Paul's ministry in Philippi.
      3. **Biblical Setting:** Paul wrote from a prison in Rome, about A.D. 62/63.
      4. Explain Philippians 4:6—*"Do not be anxious about anything."*

   B. **Illustrations and Applications:**
      1. Quote: Jesus said we should not worry because it does not help us (Matt. 6:27).
      2. Comparison: Worrying is like digging to get out of a pit.
      3. Contrast: Knitting produces something good. But worrying is not like knitting.
      4. Story: Amnon's thoughts made him sick (2 Sam. 13:1-2). Likewise, worry will cause cavities in your teeth and ulcers in your stomach.
      5. Story: One young man in Bible School worried so much that he went bald.

Transition: Paul gives us 3 keys to overcoming the problem of worry.

II. **The Solution #1: Give your problems to God in prayer (Phil. 4:6).**

   A. **Explanations:**
      1. Explain what it means to obey Philippians 4:6—*"present your requests to God."*

   B. **Illustrations and Applications:**
      1. "Pray your problems to God."
      2. Imagine a man with a heavy chair he wants to sell.

III. **The Solution #2: (Principle) Give thanks for your blessings (Phil. 4:6).**

   A. **Explanations:**
      1. Explain Philippians 4:6—*"with thanksgiving".*
      2. Count your blessings instead of your problems.

   B. **Illustrations and Applications:**
      1. Psalm 103
      2. A father worried about money to buy shoes for his children.

IV. **The Solution #3: (Principle) Think good, positive thoughts (Phil. 4:8).**

   A. **Explanations:**
      1. Explain Philippians 4:8—*"think about such things"* instead of worrying.

   B. **Illustrations and Applications:**
      1. Fill a bucket with rice to keep rocks out. Fill your mind with good thoughts to keep worry out.
      2. Paul and Silas sang in jail at Philippi, instead of worrying (Acts 16:25). Sing instead of worrying.

V. **The Choice: You choose what your future will be like by the way you respond to God's Word.**

   A. *Future good result:*

      1. Philippians 4:7 pictures the peace of God standing like a soldier to guard against worry.

      2. Peace, joy, happiness, respect, honor, and a good influence on family and others are ahead for those who conquer worry.

   B. *Future bad result:*

      1. Weariness, unrest, sorrow, shame, health problems, and even the hospital are ahead for those who choose to worry.

The Invitation

   Right now, your heavenly Father is reaching His hand down to help you. You may feel you want to make a decision to stop worrying. Raise your hand up toward God as an expression of your desire to stop worrying.

Figure 13.3 Five-Step outline of a sermon to prevent worry

C. At the altar

A pastor must plan good altar services. As he begins his Invitation, he should ask the worship leader or team to come forward with the musicians. Music is very important during the altar time.

- The musicians should have songs ready that fit the theme of the altar call.
- They should be sensitive to the leading of the Holy Spirit.
- Their music should not be too loud, or it will discourage people from praying.
- They must be ready to sing and play instruments.
- They should continue this ministry of music while people pray at the altar or at their seats.

Do not cut short this part of the service. Altar services allow people to apply sermons to their lives while they are in God's presence. You can save hours of counseling by planning good altar services.

People will come forward to make various decisions. Some pastors like to lead those who come forward into a special room or private place to pray. You and the *prayer partners you have trained should pray with those who come forward. There are several things you must teach your prayer partners.

- Teach prayer partners to be specific—to ask those at the altar for what they are praying.
- Teach prayer partners to explain the steps to receiving Jesus Christ as Savior and Lord.
- Teach prayer partners to explain the importance of water baptism and joining the local church.
- Teach prayer partners to explain how to be baptized in the Spirit.
- Teach prayer partners to record the names and addresses of visitors and new converts before they leave the service.
- Teach prayer partners to give biblical literature to those they pray with.
- Teach prayer partners to follow up on those they pray with. That is, they should contact these people week by week to continue praying with them, and disciple the new converts.

A pastor must follow up on his sermons. He should find out whether people need more help. He may learn about people's needs by talking with them at church and visiting them in their homes.

Q 12 *How will the worship leader and musicians know when to begin singing at the Invitation?*

Q 13 *What are 5 things a pastor must teach prayer partners?*

Q 14 *What question will prayer partners ask those who come to the altar?*

D. Practice Preparing Step V—The Invitation

Q 15 ✎ *Create Step Five—The Invitation for the sermon on Romans 6:23 that you created in chapter 10.*

Now it is time for you to create the Invitation Step for sermons you have worked on in this course.

Q 16 ✎ *Create Step Five—The Invitation for the sermon you created in chapter 11, Figure 11.15.*

Practice Presenting Steps I–V of a Complete Sermon
Lesson 35
Goal: *Write and preach present a complete expository sermon using the Five-Step Method.*

Each student who completes this course must write and orally present a sermon using the Five-Step Method. Those taking this course outside of a class should preach the sermon in a church or group setting. For those studying in a class, we have planned this class period for oral sermons. There is only enough time for two or three students to preach in one class period. But a class could meet some extra times for students to preach. All students who do not preach in class should preach their sermons in a church or group setting. After each sermon in class, the teacher and students should discuss the sermon. There is an evalutaion form on the next page to help discuss a sermon in light of the things we have studied in this course.

Every sermon has strengths and weaknesses. When you discuss another person's sermon, always try to identify at least three strengths for each weakness you think you see. The authors of this course pray that it has been helpful to you. May the God who called you lead you in the paths of righteousness, fill your heart with love and compassion, and anoint your messages to His people.

The chart that follows is to schedule students to preach in class.

Student	Sermon	Date
1.		
2.		
3.		
4.		
5.		
6.		
7.		
8.		
9.		
10.		

Figure 13.4   Schedule for students to preach sermons in class (Teachers will tell students when to preach.)

Q 17 ✎ *From Appendix E, preach the sermon, "Thoughts About Thought." Preach it to other students or in a local church.*

(Teachers may want to copy the form on the next page and hand it out for students to use in class.)

Attention Students: In Appendix E you will find a powerful sermon called:

Thoughts About Thought.[8]

This sermon is included for two reasons. *First,* as a sample for students to practice preaching. *Second,* it is one of the most helpful, powerful, life-guiding sermons the authors know about.

PLEASE take time to read this sermon. It may become one of your favorites.

Sermon Evaluation Form

Student Preacher: _____

Listener: _____

Date: _____

Part 1:   Structure

Step I: The Introduction

Did it capture your attention? _____

Did it move you toward the subject? _____

Step II: The Problem(s)

Was it a real problem? _____

Did the main points explain why it was a problem? _____

Did the illustrations convince you that the problem was both real and serious? _____

Step III: The Solution(s)

Was it biblical? _____

Was it practical? _____

Was it clear? _____

Was each point illustrated well? _____

Step IV: The Choice

Did it bring you to a point of decision? _____

Step V: The Invitation

What did the preacher ask you to do? _____

Part 2:   Delivery

(Grade each of the following items, using grades of A, B, C, D, or F)

___confidence	___manners	___gestures	___eyes
___neatness	___voice	___hands	___passion
___posture	___speaking	___pace	

Part 3:   Illustrations

A. Check the types of illustrations the preacher used:

___comparison	___parable	___riddle	___testimony
___contrast	___poem	___song	___visual aid
___drama	___proverb	___statistics	
___event	___quotation	___story	

B. Check only those that apply to the preacher. He or she was:

___accurate	___honest	___prepared	___anointed
___creative	___modest	___sincere	___wise
___bold	___focused	___single-minded	
___discreet	___personal	___spiritual	

Part 4:   Summary:

Was the preacher true to the text? _____

Was he true to the context? _____

Comments to encourage the preacher (Use the back of the page if necessary.)

_____

_____

Test Yourself: Circle the letter by the ***best*** completion to each question or statement.

1. What is a key to the Invitation?
a) Careful planning
b) Dramatic movements
c) A soothing voice
d) Loud music

2. During the Invitation,
a) summarize main points.
b) repeat your Introduction.
c) request a decision.
d) introduce new truths.

3. A common Invitation for a 30-minute sermon should be
a) about 1 minute.
b) about 3 minutes
c) about 5 minutes
d) about 10 minutes.

4. When you give your Invitation,
a) be loud.
b) be happy.
c) be specific.
d) be on guard.

5. What should prayer partners explain to new converts?
a) The Beatitudes
b) The Second Coming
c) Water baptism
d) Fasting

6. Why is time at the altar important?
a) It closes the service.
b) It allows people to apply sermons.
c) It helps people get to know one another.
d) It helps people learn new songs.

7. How does a pastor learn about people's needs?
a) Talking with them
b) Preaching sermons
c) Reading books
d) Asking other people

8. If you preach a sermon about forgiveness,
a) you do not need an Invitation.
b) ask people to go and witness.
c) ask people to go think about it.
d) ask people to respond in some way.

9. What is Step V of a sermon?
a) The Problem
b) The Solution
c) The Choice
d) The Invitation

10. Which part of the sermon must always be there?
a) The Choice
b) The Consecration
c) The Invitation
d) The Apostolic Blessing

 Essay Test Topics Write 50-100 words on each of these goals that you studied in this chapter.

Explanation and Examples of Step V—The Invitation

Goal: *Summarize the 5 rules of an invitation.*

Goal: *Explain ways to invite people to respond and how to plan time at the altar.*

Goal: *Prepare the Invitation Steps for 2 sermons.*

Practice Presenting Steps I–V of a Complete Sermon

Goal: *Write and preach a complete expository sermon using the Five-Step Method.*

Appendix A:
150 Bible Stories

Bible stories are the world's most popular stories. Characters and events from the Bible are used by many people to illustrate what is currently happening in their own world. Poets and writers have referred to Bible stories for hundreds of years. Much can be learned about both people and God from reading Bible stories. There are many stories from Scripture that you could add to those that follow.

FROM THE BEGINNING

STORIES OF THE PATRIARCHS

DELIVERANCE FROM EGYPT

IN THE WILDERNESS

INTO THE PROMISED LAND

KINGS OF ISRAEL

The Rich Young Ruler . . . . Matt. 19:16-24;
. . . . Mark 10:17-30; Luke 18:18-30
Jesus Heals a Man Born Blind . . . . John 9:1-34
The Parable of the Good Samaritan . . . . Luke 10:25-37
The Lost Son . . . . Luke 15:11-32
Lazarus Raised to Life . . . . John 11:1-44

THE LAST WEEK

The Triumphal Entry . . . Matt. 21:1-11; Mark 11:1-10;
. . . . Luke 19:29-44; John 12:12-19
Jesus Cleanses the Temple . . . . Matt. 21:12-13;
. . . . Mark 11:15-18; Luke 19:45-48
Jesus Curses the Fig Tree . . . . Matt. 21:18-19;
. . . . Mark 11:12-14
Jesus' Authority Questioned . . . . Matt. 21:23-27;
. . . . Mark 11:27-33; Luke 20:1-8
Jesus Teaches in the Temple . . . . . Matt. 21:28–23:39;
. . . . Mark 12:1-44; Luke 20:9–21:4
Jesus Anointed . . . . Matt. 26:6-13;
. . . . Mark 14:3-9; John 12:2-11
The Plot Against Jesus . . . . Matt. 26:3-5, 14-16;
. . . . Mark 14:10-11; Luke 22:3-6
The Last Supper . . . . . Matt. 26:17-29; Mark 14:12-25;
. . . . Luke 22:7-20; John 13:1-38

Jesus Comforts the Disciples . . . . John 14:1–16:33
Gethsemane . . . . Matt. 26:36-46;
. . . . Mark 14:32-42; Luke 22:40-46
Jesus' Arrest and Trial . . . . Matt. 26:47–27:26;
. . . . Mark 14:43–15:15;
. . . . Luke 22:47–23:25; John 18:2–19:16
Jesus' Crucifixion and Death . . . . Matt. 27:27-56;
. . . Mark 15:16-41; Luke 23:26-49; John 19:17-30
The Burial of Jesus . . . Matt. 27:57-66; Mark 15:42-47;
. . . . Luke 23:50-56; John 19:31-42

AFTER THE RESURRECTION

The Empty Tomb . . . . Matt. 28:1-10; Mark 16:1-8;
. . . . Luke 24:1-12; John 20:1-10
Mary Magdalene Sees Jesus in the Garden . . . .
. . . . Mark 16:9-11; John 20:11-18
Jesus Appears to the Two Going to Emmaus . . . .
. . . . Mark 16:12-13; Luke 24:13-35
Jesus Appears to 10 Disciples . . . . Mark 16:14;
. . . . Luke 24:36-43; John 20:19-25
Jesus Appears to the 11 Disciples . . . . . John 20:26-31
Jesus Talks With Some of His Disciples . John 21:1-25
Jesus Returns to His Father in Heaven   Mark 28:16-20;
. . . . Luke 16:19-20; John 24:44-53

Appendix B:
The Miracles of Jesus

" ... believe the miracles, that you may learn and understand that the Father is in me, and I in the Father" (John 10:38).

Throughout His ministry, Jesus performed many great, miraculous signs which caused people to either become very angry or to believe in Him. Some miracles are included in more than one Gospel.

	Matthew	Mark	Luke	John
Water Turned Into Wine				2:1-11
Crowd in Galilee	4:23-35			
Catch of Fish			5:1-11	
Man With Leprosy	8:2-3	1:40-42	5:12-13	
Roman Centurion's Servant	8:5-13		7:1-10	
Peter's Mother-in-law	8:14-15	1:30-31	4:38-39	
Many at Sunset	8:16-17	1:32-39	4:40-41	
Calming of the Storm	8:23-27	4:35-41	8:22-25	
Two Men From Gadara	8:28-34	5:1-17	8:27-35	
Paralyzed Man	9:2-7	2:3-12	5:18-25	
Raising Jairus' Daughter	9:18-19, 23-25	5:22-24, 35-42	8:41-42, 49-56	
Woman With Bleeding	9:20-22	5:25-34	8:43-48	
Two Blind Men	9:27-31			
Man Dumb and Possessed	9:32-33			
Crowd in Galilee	9:35			
Man With a Shriveled Hand	12:9-13	3:1-5	6:6-10	
Man Blind, Dumb, Possessed	12:22		11:14	
Few in Nazareth		6:1-6		
Feeding 5,000 People	14:13-21	6:32-44	9:10-17	6:1-13
Walking on Water	14:22-33	6:47-51		6:16-21
Touching His Clothes	14:34-36	6:53-56		
Canaanite Woman's Daughter	15:21-28	7:24-30		
A Multitude	15:29-31			
Feeding 4,000 People	15:32-38	8:1-9		
Boy With Epilepsy	17:14-18	9:17-27	9:38-43	
Coin in Fish's Mouth	17:24-27			
Crowds in Judea	19:1-2			
Two Blind Men	20:29-34			
Many in Jerusalem	21:14			
Fig Tree Withered	21:18-22	11:12-14, 20-25		
Man Possessed in Synagogue		1:23-26	4:33-35	
Deaf Mute		7:31-37		
Blind Man at Bethsaida		8:22-26		
Bartimaeus; One Blind Man		10:46-52	18:35-43	
Raising Widow's Son at Nain			7:11-15	

	Matthew	Mark	Luke	John
Crippled Woman			13:10-13	
Man With Dropsy			14:1-4	
Ten Lepers			17:11-19	
The High Priest's Servant			22:49-51	
Official's Son at Capernaum				4:46-54
Sick Man at Pool of Bethesda				5:1-9
The Man Born Blind				9:1-6
Raising Lazarus				11:1-44
Another Catch of Fish				21:1-11

Appendix C:
The Parables of Jesus

"He taught them many things by parables…" (Mark 4:2).

	Matthew	Mark	Luke
The Wise and Foolish Builders	7:24-27		6:46-49
New Cloth on Old Garment	9:16	2:21	5:36
New Wine in Old Wineskins	9:17	2:22	5:37-39
The Sower	13:3-23	4:2-20	8:4-15
The Weeds	13:24-30, 36-43		
The Mustard Seed	13:31-32	4:30-32	13:18-19
The Yeast	13:33		13:20-21
The Hidden Treasure	13:44		
The Pearl	13:45-46		
The Net	13:47-50		
The Lost Sheep	18:12-14		15:3-7
The Unmerciful Servant	18:21-35		
The Workers in the Vineyard	20:1-16		
The Two Sons	21:28-32		
The Tenants	21:33-45	12:1-12	20:9-19
The Wedding Banquet	22:1-14		
The Fig Tree	24:32-35	13:28-29	21:29-31
The Ten Virgins	25:1-13		
The Talents	25:14-30		
The Sheep and Goats	25:31-46		
The Growing Seed		4:26-29	
The Day and Hour Unknown		13:34-37	
Two Debtors			7:41-43
The Good Samaritan			10:25-37
The Good Gifts			11:5-13
The Rich Fool			12:16-21
Watchfulness			12:35-48
The Fruitless Fig Tree			13:6-9
The Humbled Wedding Guest			14:7-11
The Great Banquet			14:15-24
The Lost Coin			15:8-10
The Lost Son			15:11-32
The Shrewd Manager			16:1-15
The Rich Man and Lazarus			16:19-31
The Master and the Servant			17:7-10
The Persistant Widow			18:1-8
The Pharisee and the Tax Collector			18:9-14
The Ten Minas (Pounds)			19:11-27

Appendix D:
360 Topics

A
Abstinence
Accusers
Adultery
Alcoholism
Angels
Anger
Antichrist
Anti-Semitism
Apathy
Apostasy
Armageddon
Asceticism
Astrology
Atheists

B
Babies
Babylon
Backbiting
Backsliding
Baptism, Holy Spirit
Baptism, water
Belief
Bible
Blasphemers
Blood
Bondage
Boredom
Buddhism
Burdens
Buying

C
Capital punishment
Catholicism
Cell groups
Children
Christ
Christian living

Church
Cigarettes
Cities
Communication
Communism
Complaining
Conformity
Confusion
Conscience
Consecration
Contentment
Conversion
Courage
Courtship
Covenants
Covetous
Criticism
Cross
Cruelty
Cults

D
Darkness
Dead Sea
Death
Debts
Deceit
Decision
Dedication
Demons
Devil
Devotional life
Discipleship
Discouragement
Diseases
Dishonesty
Disobedience
Divorce
Doubt
Drug abuse

E
Earthquakes
Eating
Ecology
Economy
Education
Encouragement
Endurance
Energy
Envy
Equal rights
Eternity
Euthanasia
Evangelicals
Evangelism/
    witnessing
Evil
Evil spirits
Evolution

F
Faith
Faithfulness
Falling away
False christs
False prophets
Family
Family devotions
Famines
Father
Fear
Fellowship
Finances
Fire
Flattery
Forgetfulness
Forgiving
Form of godliness
Fortune telling
Freedom/liberty

Friendship

G
Gambling
Giving
Glorifying God
God
Gospel
Gossip
Government
Guidance

H
Happiness
Hastiness
Hatred
Hearing
Heart
Heaven
Hebrew language
Hell
Hinduism
Holy Spirit
Home
Homosexuality
Honesty
Hope/hopelessness
Hospitality
Human rights
Humility
Husband
Hypocrisy

I
Idolatry
Ignorance
Immorality
Immortality
Inflation
Influence

Injustice
Integrity
Islam
Israel (nation)

J
Jealousy
Jerusalem
Jesus Christ
Jews
Joy
Judging
Judgment
Justice

K
Kindness
Kings
Knowledge

L
Language
Lawlessness
Laymen
Laziness
Leadership
Learning
Legalism
Leisure
Liberal theology
Life
Light
Lightning
Listening
Loneliness
Love
Lukewarmness
Luxury
Lying

M

Mark of the Beast
Marriage
Martyrs
Memory
Men
Mental illness
Middle age
Middle East
Millennium
Miracles
Missions
Mistakes
Mockers
Money
Moon
Morality
Mother
Motivation
Mountains
Movies
Murder
Murmuring
Music

N

Names
Nations
Neglect
Neighbors
New Year

O

Obedience
Old age
Ordinances, Church
Overcoming

P

Parents
Pastor
Patience
Peace
Persecution

Perseverance
Pestilence
Planting
Pleasure
Population
Pornography
Poverty
Prayer
Preacher
Prejudice
Preparedness
Pride
Prison
Procrastination
Profanity
Progress

Q

Quality
Quantity
Quietness

R

Rapture
Reading
Rebellion
Recklessness
Religion
Re-marriage
Repentance
Reputation
Rest
Restlessness
Resurrection
Reverence
Revival
Rewards
Rich
Rivers
Rumors

S

Sabbath
Sacrifice

Salvation
Satan
School
Scoffers
Seas and oceans
Second Coming
Seeing
Self-centeredness
Self-confidence
Self-righteousness
Service
Sex
Signs and wonders
Silence
Sin
Singleness
Skill
Sky
Slavery
Sleep
Small things
Sorrow
Soul-winning
Space age
Spiritism
Stars
Stealing
Step families
Stewardship
Storms
Stubbornness
Students
Submission
Success
Suffering
Suicide
Sun
Sunday
Sunday school
Superstitions
Surrender
Swearing

T

Talking
Teachers
Tears
Technology
Television
Temple
Temptation
Tension
Terrorism
Thankfulness
Theater
Thieves
Thinking
Thoughtfulness
Thoughts
Time
Tithing
Tongue
Tongues, speaking in
Trade
Traitors
Transcendental
    meditation
Travel
Treaties
Trees
Trials/troubles
Trust
Truth

U

Unbelief
Unholy
UFO
United Nations
Unity
Universe
Unjust
Unrepentant
Unthankful

V

Vengeance/revenge

Violence
Vision

W

Walking with God
War
Watchfulness
Water
Wealth
Weapons
Weather
Welfare
Wife
Will of God
Winds
Wine
Wisdom
Witchcraft
Women
Women's liberation
Work/labor
World/earth
Worldliness
Worldly separation
Worry
Worship
Wrath

Y

Yielding to God
Youth

Z

Zeal

Appendix E:
Thoughts About Thought (A Sample Sermon)

Sample Sermon   A sermon follows which is titled "Thoughts About Thought." It is included for two reasons. *First,* as a sample for students to practice preaching. *Second,* it is one of the most helpful, powerful, life-guiding sermons the authors know about.

Title: Thoughts About Thought[8]

Text: 2 Corinthians 10:5

Introduction: How many different thoughts are possible in only one hour? 100? 1,000? How many thoughts are possible in a day? A week? A month? A year? Thoughts can be so many! They swarm like bees. They fly in flocks like birds. They are like links of a chain—one leads to another.

Thoughts are like grains of sand. A single grain does not matter. But a ton of sand is made up of single grains! Because our thoughts are many, we must make them our friends. Then, they will escort us to heaven. But if our thoughts are our enemies, they will become a mighty army that drags us down to hell.

I.   **The Problem: Bad thoughts are worse than some people realize.**

   A. **God knows our thoughts.**
      1. God sees our thoughts within us (Ps. 94:11).
      2. I once saw a glass beehive. You could see all the bees inside it. Likewise, God sees our thoughts.

   B. **God tells us that meditating on evil thoughts is sinful.**
      1. Welcoming thoughts of lust is adultery (Matt. 5:27-28).
      2. Feeding thoughts of hate is murder (1 John 3:15).

   C. **Welcoming evil thoughts leads to the bondage of sin.**
      1. A match will not light dry charcoal. But soak charcoal in kerosene, and a match will light it. Likewise, sin will one day burst into flame in the life of a person whose mind is soaked with evil thoughts.
      2. Evil thoughts are the nest in which the eggs of sin hatch.
      3. An arrow leaves no trail as it flies through the air. In contrast, dwelling on evil thoughts leaves a slimy trail like a snail does.
      4. Nurse evil thoughts and they will grow into a giant that will conquer you.
      5. It was not a demon that led King David to commit adultery with Bathsheba. It was his own thoughts that he refused to rule.
      6. Pornography, sinful books and magazines, and worldly movies or videos lower your resistance to temptation. They move you step by step to sin.
      7. As surely as John the Baptist prepared the way for Jesus, welcoming evil thoughts prepares the way for sin.

Transition: Many have believed the devil's lie that we cannot control our thoughts. But the truth is that we can live a life of mental freedom and victory. Here are four keys to having pure thoughts:

II.   **The Solution: You can live a life of freedom and victory in your thoughts.**

   A. **Depend on God to help you.**
      1. All of us need a Savior to save us from our sins (Matt. 1:21; Rom. 3:23; 6:23).
      2. Allow the Spirit to control you. Submit your mind and will to Him (Rom. 8:9-14).
      3. Walk in the Spirit (Gal. 5:16-26).

B. Be aware of your thoughts.

1. You can know what is in your pocket by emptying its contents on the table in front of you. Likewise, you can keep your thoughts out in front of you. Be watchful. Be aware of what you are thinking.

2. A person who owns a store keeps an inventory—a list of what is in his store. Likewise, you must keep a constant inventory of what you allow to stay in your heart and mind.

C. Let the Spirit train you to hate what God hates.

1. I was talking with a man once when a pretty woman walked by. His eyes followed every step she took. He seemed hypnotized by her body and movements. Finally, he returned from his mental safari. I said to him, "It looks like you have a problem." He answered, "Oh, I cannot help that. Besides, it was just a thought!"

2. We cannot keep from being tempted. Even Jesus was tempted by evil thoughts. Thoughts fly to us as swiftly as birds. You cannot keep a crow from flying over your head. But you can prevent it from building a nest in your hair! You cannot prevent a thief from coming to your door, but you do not have to invite him in!

3. A person turns a piece of candy over in his mouth because he likes it. Likewise, a person turns an evil thought over in his mind because he likes it. In contrast, we spit out what we do not like. We reject food that we hate, and we reject thoughts that we hate. As we learn to hate evil thoughts, we will reject them as quickly as Jesus rejected Satan's suggestions.

4. Loving what is right is only half of our walk with God. We must hate evil (Heb. 1:9).

5. Psalm 97:10 says *"Let those who love the Lord hate evil, for he guards the lives of his faithful ones and delivers them from the hand of the wicked."*

6. *"To fear the Lord is to hate evil; I hate pride and arrogance, evil behavior and perverse speech"* (Prov. 8:13).

7. *"Hate evil; love good"* (Amos 5:15).

8. *"Hate what is evil; cling to what is good"* (Rom. 12:9).

9. [15]*"Do not love the world or anything in the world. If anyone loves the world, the love of the Father is not in him.* [16]*For everything in the world—the cravings of sinful man, the lust of his eyes and the boasting of what he has and does—comes not from the Father but from the world"* (1 John 2:15-16).

10. *"But you have this in your favor: You hate the practices of the Nicolaitans, which I also hate"* (Rev. 2:6). To fellowship with God, we must learn to love what He loves and hate what He hates.

11. When a mother decides to wean a nursing child, a battle takes place. The child has become used to the warm milk, and the pleasant feelings of resting on its mother's breast. But after only a few days of protesting, the child will learn to be content with other food. Likewise, if you have developed the habit of savoring sinful thoughts, your fleshly man will cry like a baby when you try to wean it. But as you stand firm in Christ and your desire to hate what He hates, the voice of the flesh will become quieter and quieter. As you daily choose to hate evil thoughts, they will pass by you like birds. You will not give an evil thought a second thought! Temptations to a pure mind are like matches thrown into a barrel of water.

12. Your will is like a guard to your mind. When a temptation comes to your mind the first time, it must knock at the door of your mind. But if you decide to welcome the evil thought, it will not knock the next time. Instead, it will boldly rush into your mind, because your will is not guarding the door. So it is important to choose to hate evil thoughts and reject them.

13. Be like Joseph—flee from sin as you would flee from a poisonous snake (Gen. 39:10-12).

D. Love, welcome, practice, and cultivate good thoughts.

1. Rizpah became tired trying to keep the birds away (2 Sam. 21:10). Likewise, a person could wear himself out trying to chase away every evil thought. The easy way to keep dirty things out of a bucket is to fill it with good things. Once the Savior has cleansed your mind, do your part to think good thoughts. It is impossible to think a bad thought and a good thought at the same time!

2. Fill your mind with good thoughts. How? Read and meditate on the Bible. Pray and sing. Listen to worship music or preaching at church, on the radio, television, cassettes, or CDs. Fellowship with other godly people and talk about godly things. When you seek entertainment, such as books, radio, television, or such, it is important that you reject evil things and approve only what is good. It would be self-defeating to have

devotions in the mornings and then watch bad movies in the evenings! Refuse to watch any movies that use the Lord's name in vain or show nudity. Fill your heart, mind, and soul with good things. Hate what God hates, and love what God loves.

III. The Choice: Two roads are before you today. Only you can decide which one you will travel.

A. *Future good result:* If you choose the road of good thoughts, you choose to walk beside God. A year from now, you will be so different. You will be experiencing peace instead of guilt. You will have freedom instead of bondage. You will be walking away from shame and heading towards honor. Others will rise up and bless you because you honor God in your private thoughts. Your good example will influence your family and many others.

B. *Future bad result:* If you decide to indulge sinful thoughts, you will become a slave to your thoughts—a prisoner of your own imagination. Little by little, you will slide down the slippery slope of sin. Thoughts that once would have embarrassed you will no longer alarm you. Your appetite for spiritual things will become weaker. You will make the decision to welcome evil thoughts in private. But the day will come when everyone knows the road you chose to travel. If you travel the road to destruction, one day you will arrive at that destination. Your name can easily be added to the long list of those whose names and reputations have been shamed.

The Invitation

A. If you are on the wrong road, you can find the right one today. Perhaps your thoughts are out of control. You are in bondage, and at times in agony and torment to the thoughts that come to you. There is another road for you to walk. Regardless of the lies the devil has told you, he cannot keep you as a prisoner against your will. Jesus forgives, cleanses, and empowers those who ask Him for help. The Savior's work is to set the captive free, whether the bondage is great or small.

B. God is speaking to people at this very moment. What is your decision? Raise your hand if you want Jesus to help you. Stand up immediately. Come boldly to the front. Strong believers will pray with you. As you come forward, tell us your need so we can pray together. Come as we begin to sing.

Definitions

The right-hand column lists the chapter in the textbook in which the word is used.

Chapter

altar—any place of prayer at which a person kneels to seek God; often at the front of a church — 13

ambassador—any person who seeks to build good relationships between God and others — 13

anointing—the presence of the Holy Spirit in and upon a person's life — 4

Athens—capital city of present-day Greece; ancient center of philosophy, culture, and democracy. Visited by Paul on his second missionary journey — 9

blameless—without guilt — 1

candid—honest, open, sincere, frank — 2

character—the sum of qualities that make up a person; who you really are — 1

Choice Step—the fourth step of a sermon; the step in which a preacher takes listeners into the future, showing them the result of their response to a biblical message — 12

clarify—to explain or make more clear — 6

condescend—to lower or humble oneself; to stoop down — 2

conviction—a deep feeling, firm belief, confidence, or faith — 3

cross-reference—a note that lists other related topics to research or Scriptures to look up — 7

delivery—the way or manner in which a person preaches a sermon — 3

devotions—times of personal prayer and worship, Bible study, and fellowship with God — 2

diligent—hard working and faithful — 11

domineering—proud, bossy, or forceful; ruling over others — 1

drama—a skit or play in which people act, pretending to be someone or something else — 5

episkopos—based on a Greek word for overseer, bishop, pastor, or steward — 1

ethos—a person's character, behavior, or lifestyle — 1

exegete—to discover and explain the meaning of a biblical passage — 8

expository sermon—a message with main points from one passage of Scripture — 8

filler words—unnecessary, wasted words that a nervous person repeats to avoid silence — 3

gestures—body movements used to emphasize or explain something, or to express feelings or ideas — 3

historical context—the background, setting, circumstances, and events that surround a biblical book — 2

homiletics—the study of preparing and preaching biblical messages — 1

illustrations—stories, testimonies, statistics, etc. that let light into the mind and soul — 5

indent—to move in or under; in an outline, sub-points are indented. — 8

indirect—not direct, bold, or obvious; coming from the side rather than the front — 6

introduction—the first part of a sermon, used to gain attention and favor — 8

invitation—the step in which a preacher welcomes listeners to accept a biblical message and respond to it — 13

literary context—the written verses, paragraphs, and pages that surround a verse in the Bible — 2

logical—in harmony with the way people think; mentally acceptable — 9

Scripture List

Bibliography

Adams, Jay. *Preaching With Purpose*. Grand Rapids, Michigan: Baker Book House, 1983.

Arredondo, Lani. *How to Present Like a Pro*. New York, New York: McGraw-Hill, 1991.

Barclay, William. *The Daily Study Bible: Galatians and Ephesians*. Rev. ed. Philadelphia, Pennsylvania: The Westminster Press, 1976.

_____. *The Daily Study Bible: Matthew*. Rev. ed. Vol. 1. Philadelphia, Pennsylvania: The Westminster Press, 1975.

_____. *The Daily Study Bible: Matthew*. Rev. ed. Vol. 2. Philadelphia, Pennsylvania: The Westminster Press, 1975.

Barnes, Albert. *Notes on the New Testament*. Vol. 13. Grand Rapids, Michigan: Baker Book House, 1985.

Barrett, David. "Status of Global Mission, 2000, in Context of 20th and 21st Centuries," *International Bulletin of Missionary Research* (January 2000).

Bisagno, John R. *Principle Preaching—How to Create and Deliver Purpose Driven Sermons for Life Applications*. Nashville, Tennessee: Broadman & Holman Publishers, 2002.

Bounds, E. M. *Powerful and Prayerful Pulpit*. Grand Rapids, Michigan: Baker Book House, 1993.

Braga, James. *How to Prepare Bible Messages*. Portland, Oregon: Multnomah Press, 1981.

Buttrick, David. *Homiletics: Moves and Structures*. Philadelphia, Pennsylvania: Fortress Press, 1987.

Cushman, Ralph S. "The Secret," *Spiritual Hilltops*. http://www.angelfire.com/ia/andycat/literaturepg.html [Accessed 11/03].

Davis, James O. *The Preacher's Summit*. Springfield, Missouri: Cutting Edge Books, 2001.

Douglas, J. D., ed. *The New Bible Dictionary*. Grand Rapids, Michigan: Wm. B. Eerdmans Publishing Co., 1978.

Fant, Clyde E. *Preaching for Today*. New York, New York: Harper & Row, 1977.

Fasi, S. S. *Swahili Sayings*. Nairobi, Kenya: Kenya Literature Bureau, 1980.

Getz, Gene. *The Measure of a Man*. Glendale, California: Regal Books Division, G/L Publications, 1976.

Gingrich, F. Wilbur. *Shorter Lexicon of the Greek New Testament*. Chicago, Illinois: University of Chicago Press, 1965.

Griffin, Em. *The Mind Changers*. Wheaton, Illinois: Tyndale House Publishers, 1983.

Guest, Edgar A. "Sermons We See." In *The Light of Faith*. Chicago, Illinois: The Reily & Lee Co., 1926.

Harding, Joe. *Have I Told You Lately?* Pasadena, California: Church Growth Press, 1982.

Harris, Ralph W., ed. *The Complete Biblical Library: The New Testament Study Bible,* Galatians–Philemon. Vol. 8. Springfield, Missouri: World Library Press, Inc., 1994.

Hastings, Robert J. *Illustrations*. Nashville, Tennessee: Broadman Press, 1971.

Holmes, Oliver Wendell, Jr. as quoted in http://www.businessmotivator.com [Accessed 11/03].

http://www.gborocollege.edu/prescorner/plain.html [Accessed 1/04].

http://www.globaled.ausaid.gov.au/secondary/casestud/economics/1/glob-inc.html [Accessed 6/17/03].

Hull, William E. "The Contemporary World and the Preaching Task," Michael Duduit, ed. *Handbook of Contemporary Preaching*. Nashville, Tennessee: Broadman & Holman Publishers, 1992.

Hutchcraft, Ronald. "Relating the Gospel to a Secular Society," Lewis A. Drummond, ed. *Equipping for Evangelism: North American Conference for Itinerant Evangelists*. Minneapolis, Minnesota: World Wide Publications, 1996.

Kaiser, Walter C., Jr. *Toward an Exegetical Theology—Biblical Exegesis for Preaching and Teaching*. Grand Rapids, Michigan: Baker Book House, 1981.

Klein, William W., Craig L. Blomberg, and Robert L. Hubbard, Jr. *Introduction to Biblical Interpretation*. Dallas, Texas: Word Publishing, 1993.

Larsen, David. *The Evangelism Mandate—Recovering the Centrality of Gospel Preaching.* Wheaton, Illinois: Crossway Books, 1992.

MacPhearson, Ian. *The Art of Illustrating Sermons.* Grand Rapids, Michigan: Baker Book House, 1976.

McGhee, Quentin. *The Life & Teachings of Christ (Teacher's Guide).* 4th ed. Springfield, Missouri: RDM 2005.

Menzies, William W. and Robert P. Menzies. *Spirit and Power.* Grand Rapids, Michigan: Zondervan Publishing House, 2000.

Neely, Lois. *Fire in His Bones: The Official Biography of Oswald J. Smith.* Wheaton, Illinois: Tyndale House Publishers, Inc., 1982.

Olford Stephen F. and David L. Olford. *Anointed Expository Preaching.* Nashville, Tennessee: Broadman & Holman Publishers, 1998.

Partridge, Eric. *Famous Quotations.* Bombay, India: D. B. Taraporevala & Sons & Co., 1958.

Perry, Lloyd M. *Biblical Preaching for Today's World.* Chicago, Illinois: Moody Press, 1973.

Pettry, W. Ernest. *Preaching and Teaching.* Springfield, Missouri: Global University, 1981.

Quayle, William A. *The Pastor-Preacher.* New York, New York: Eaton and Mains, 1910.

Robinson, Haddon W. *Biblical Preaching.* 2nd ed. Grand Rapids, Michigan: Baker Academic, 1980, 2001.

_____. *Making a Difference in Preaching.* Grand Rapids, Michigan: Baker Book House, 1999.

Verderber, Rudolph F. *The Challenge of Effective Speaking.* Belmont, California: Wadsworth Publishing Co., 1985.

Secretary-General of the United Nations, speech to World Food Summit (June 2002). http://www.escwa.org.lb/information/press/articles/10june02.html [Accessed 11/03].

Spurgeon, Charles H. *John Ploughman's Talks.* Ann Arbor, Michigan: Baker Book House, 1976.

_____. *Lectures to My Students on the Art of Preaching.* Great Britain: Marshall, Morgan and Scott, 1986.

_____. *Spurgeon At His Best.* Grand Rapids, Michigan: Baker Book House, 1988.

_____. *The Soul Winner.* Grand Rapids, Michigan: Wm. B. Eerdmans Publishing Co., 1963.

Stamps, Donald C., gen. ed. *The Full Life Study Bible,* NIV. Grand Rapids, Michigan: Zondervan Publishing House, 1975.

Stott, John R. *Between Two Worlds—The Art of Preaching in the Twentieth Century.* Grand Rapids, Michigan: Wm. B. Eerdmans Publishing Co., 1982.

Sugden, Edward H., ed. *Wesley's Standard Sermons.* Vol. 1. London, England: Epworth Press, 1921.

Traina, Robert A. *Methodical Bible Study.* Grand Rapids, Michigan: Zondervan Publishing House, 2002.

Vander Ark, Nellie A. *Devotions for Teachers.* Grand Rapids, Michigan: Baker Book House, 1978.

Virkler, Henry A. *Hermeneutics—Principles and Processes of Biblical Interpretation.* Grand Rapids, Michigan: Baker Book House, 1981.

Wheeler, Elmer. *How to Sell Yourself to Others.* New York, New York: Prentice Hall, 1952.

Whitesell, Faris D. *Sixty-Five Ways to Give an Evangelistic Invitation.* Grand Rapids, Michigan: Kregel Publications, 1984.

Wiersbe, Warren W. *Preaching and Teaching With Imagination: The Quest for Biblical Preaching.* Wheaton, Illinois: Victor Books, 1994.

Wingren, Gustaf. *The Living Word.* Philadelphia, Pennsylvania: Fortress Press, 1960.

Wood. George O. "Expository Preaching." Trask, Thomas E., Wayde I. Goodall, and Zenas J. Bickett, eds. *The Pentecostal Pastor.* Springfield, Missouri: Gospel Publishing House, 1997.

Wood, George O. "How Expository Preaching Helps the Church." *Enrichment Magazine (*Summer 1996).

Endnotes

Chapter 1

1 W. Ernest Pettry, *Preaching and Teaching* (Springfield, Missouri: Global University, 1981), p. 35.

2 Dr. Larry Lacour, Professor at Oral Roberts University, comments in a doctor of ministry class, 1986.

3 Rudolph F. Verderber, *The Challenge of Effective Speaking* (Belmont, California: Wadsworth Publishing Co., 1985), n. p.

4 F. Wilbur Gingrich, *Shorter Lexicon of the Greek New Testament* (Chicago, Illinois: University of Chicago Press, 1965), p. 177.

5 Donald C. Stamps, gen. ed., *The Full Life Study Bible,* NIV (Grand Rapids, Michigan: Zondervan Publishing House, 1975), Titus 1:7 note, p. 1904.

6 Stamps, *The Full Life Study Bible,* NIV, Titus 1:7 note, p. 1904.

7 Gene Getz, *The Measure of a Man* (Glendale, California: Regal Books Division, G/L Publications, 1976), p. 19.

8 Stamps, *The Full Life Study Bible,* NIV, 1 Timothy 3:1-2 note, p. 1882.

9 Albert Barnes, *Notes on the New Testament,* vol. 13 (Grand Rapids, Michigan: Baker Book House, 1985), pp. 300-301.

10 Edgar A. Guest, "Sermons We See" (Poem), *The Light of Faith* (Chicago, Illinois: The Reily & Lee Co., 1926), n. p.

11 Nellie A. Vander Ark, *Devotions for Teachers* (Grand Rapids, Michigan: Baker Book House, 1978), pp. 79-80.

Chapter 2

1 Adapted from Ralph S. Cushman, "The Secret," *Spiritual Hilltops,* http://www.angelfire.com/ia/andycat/literaturepg.html [Accessed 11/03].

2 William A. Quayle, *The Pastor-Preacher* (New York: Eaton and Mains, 1910), p. 261.

3 James O. Davis, *The Preacher's Summit* (Springfield, Missouri: Cutting Edge Books, 2001), Section VIII, p. 4.

4 E. M. Bounds, *Powerful and Prayerful Pulpit* (Grand Rapids, Michigan: Baker Book House, 1993), p. 20.

5 Charles H. Spurgeon, *Spurgeon At His Best* (Grand Rapids, Michigan: Baker Book House, 1988), p. 142.

6 Edward H. Sugden, ed., *Wesley's Standard Sermons,* vol. 1 (London, England: Epworth Press, 1921), pp. 31-32.

7 William W. Menzies and Robert P. Menzies, *Spirit and Power* (Grand Rapids, Michigan: Zondervan Publishing House, 2000), p. 64.

8 William W. Klein, Craig L. Blomberg, and Robert L. Hubbard, Jr., *Introduction to Biblical Interpretation* (Dallas, Texas: Word Publishing, 1993), pp. 161-172.

9 Pettry, pp. 66-67.

10 Pettry, p. 45.

11 Lloyd M. Perry, *Biblical Preaching for Today's World* (Chicago, Illinois: Moody Press, 1973), p. 162.

12 Clyde E. Fant, *Preaching for Today* (New York, New York: Harper & Row, 1977), p. 41.

13 Fant, p. 105.

14 Fant, p. 41.

15 Dr. George O. Wood likes to emphasize this truth.

16 Terry Johnson (missionary to Brazil), e-mail story concerning his father's ministry in Brazil, 4 August, 2003.

Chapter 3

1 Charles H. Spurgeon, *Lectures to My Students on the Art of Preaching* (Great Britain: Marshall, Morgan and Scott, 1986), p. 115.

2 Lani Arredondo, *How to Present Like a Pro* (New York: McGraw-Hill, 1991), pp. 77-79.

3 Spurgeon, *Lectures,* p. 290.

4 Spurgeon, *Lectures,* p. 114.

5 Spurgeon, *Lectures,* p. 114.

6 Spurgeon, *Lectures,* p. 273.

7 Jimmy Beggs (missionary to Kenya), interviewed by Quentin McGhee on preaching, Nairobi, Kenya, 1985.

Chapter 4

1 J. D. Douglas, ed., "Anointing," *The New Bible Dictionary* (Grand Rapids, Michigan: Wm. B. Eerdmans Publishing Co., 1978), p. 39.

2 Douglas, "Messiah," p. 818.

3 Stephen F. Olford and David L. Olford, *Anointed Expository Preaching* (Nashville, Tennessee: Broadman & Holman Publishers, 1998), pp. 220-222.

4 Jim Hall (missionary to the inner city USA), interviewed by Quentin McGhee at Global University, June 2003.

5 Davis, Section VIII, p. 16.

6 Lois Neely, *Fire in His Bones: The Official Biography of Oswald J. Smith* (Wheaton, Illinois: Tyndale House Publishers, Inc., 1982), p. 295.

Chapter 5

1 Oliver Wendell Holmes, Jr., as quoted in www. businessmotivator.com [Accessed 11/03].

2 Eric Partridge, *Famous Quotations* (Bombay, India: D. B. Taraporevala & Sons & Co., 1958), p. 1.

3 Ian MacPhearson, *The Art of Illustrating Sermons* (Grand Rapids, Michigan: Baker Book House, 1976), p. 32.

4 David Barrett, "Status of Global Mission, 2000, in Context of 20th and 21st Centuries," *International Bulletin of Missionary Research* (Jan. 2002), p. 25.

Chapter 6

1 MacPhearson, p. 32.

2 Adapted from the Holy Bible, New International Version (Grand Rapids, Michigan: Zondervan Bible Publishers, 1973, 1978, 1984), p. 19 (of the 1973 version).

3 MacPhearson, p. 40.

4 Warren W. Wiersbe, *Preaching and Teaching With Imagination: The Quest for Biblical Preaching* (Wheaton, Illinois: Victor Books, 1994), p. 297.

Chapter 7

1 Rev. Edith Gibbs, mother of Dr. Carl Gibbs. This lady has been ordained for 50 years. She likes to give one illustration from her life and experience for each point.

2 Robert J. Hastings, *Illustrations* (Nashville, Tennessee: Broadman Press, 1971), p. 13.

3 Fant, 32-33.

4 Haddon W. Robinson, *Biblical Preaching,* 2nd ed. (Grand Rapids, Michigan: Baker Academic, 1980, 2001), p. 157.

5 http://www.gborocollege.edu/prescorner/plain.html [Accessed 1/04].

6 Joe Harding, *Have I Told You Lately?* (Pasadena, California: Church Growth Press, 1982), pp. 65-67.

Chapter 8

1 David Buttrick, *Homiletics: Moves and Structures* (Philadelphia, Pennsylvania: Fortress Press, 1987), p. 37.

2 Haddon W. Robinson, *Making a Difference in Preaching* (Grand Rapids, Michigan: Baker Book House, 1999), p. 20.

3 John R. Stott, *Between Two Worlds—The Art of Preaching in the Twentieth Century* (Grand Rapids, Michigan: Wm. B. Eerdmans Publishing Co., 1982), pp. 125-126.

4 George O. Wood, "Expository Preaching," Trask, Thomas E., Wayde I. Goodall, and Zenas J. Bickett, eds. *The Pentecostal Pastor* (Springfield, Missouri: Gospel Publishing House, 1997), p. 83.

5 Wood, "Expository Preaching," p. 83

6 George O. Wood, "How Expository Preaching Helps the Church," *Enrichment Magazine* (Summer 1996); pp. 26-30.

7 James Braga, *How to Prepare Bible Messages* (Portland, Oregon: Multnomah Press, 1981), p. 53.

8 John R. Bisagno, *Principle Preaching—How to Create and Deliver Purpose Driven Sermons for Life Applications* (Nashville, Tennessee: Broadman & Holman Publishers, 2002), p. 3.

9 Klein, Blomberg, and Hubbard, p. 422.

10 Klein, Blomberg, and Hubbard, p. 411.

11 Robert A. Traina, *Methodical Bible Study* (Grand Rapids, Michigan: Zondervan Publishing House, 2002), p. 241.

12 Bisagno, p. 5.

13 Bisagno, p. 3.

14 Henry A. Virkler, *Hermeneutics—Principles and Processes of Biblical Interpretation* (Grand Rapids, Michigan: Baker Book House, 1981), p. 212.

15 Walter C. Kaiser, Jr., *Toward an Exegetical Theology—Biblical Exegesis for Preaching and Teaching* (Grand Rapids, Michigan: Baker Book House, 1981), p. 152.

16 Kaiser, p. 151.

17 Wood, "Expository Preaching," pp. 87-93.

18 Bisagno, pp. 14-16.

19 Virkler, p. 213.

20 Virkler, pp. 220-221.

21 William Barclay, *The Daily Study Bible: Galatians and Ephesians,* rev. ed. (Philadelphia, Pennsylvania: The Westminster Press, 1976), p. 173.

22 Rev. Steve Eutsler encouraged us to emphasize this guideline. We are indebted to him for his input and expertise.

23 Chris Lewis, Sermon on Joshua 8 at James River Assembly of God, February 2005.

24 Bisagno, p. 4.

25 Stott, p. 225.

26 Kaiser, p. 157.

27 Wood, "Expository Preaching," p. 90.

28 Stott, p. 226.

29 Stott, p. 224.

30 Ronald Hutchcraft, "Relating the Gospel to a Secular Society," Lewis A. Drummond, ed., *Equipping for Evangelism: North American Conference for Itinerant Evangelists* (Minneapolis, Minnesota: World Wide Publications, 1996), p. 60.

31 Jay Adams, *Preaching With Purpose* (Grand Rapids, Michigan: Baker Book House, 1983), n. p.

32 Mike McClaflin, missionary to Kenya, shared this story about himself in a sermon in East Africa, about 1983.

Chapter 9

1 Elmer Wheeler, *How to Sell Yourself to Others* (New York, New York: Prentice Hall, 1952), n.p.

2 Em Griffin, *The Mind Changers* (Wheaton, Illinois: Tyndale House Publishers, 1983), pp. 102-103.

3 William E. Hull, "The Contemporary World and the Preaching Task," Michael Duduit, ed., *Handbook of Contemporary Preaching* (Nashville, Tennessee: Broadman & Holman Publishers, 1992), p. 571.

4 Gustaf Wingren, *The Living Word* (Philadelphia, Pennsylvania: Fortress Press, 1960), p. 211.

5 http://globaled.ausaid.gov.au/secondary/casestud/economics/1/glob-inc.html [Accessed 6/17/2003].

6 Barrett, p. 25.

7 The Secretary-General of the United Nations, speech to World Food Summit (June 2002). http://www.escwa.org.lb/information/press/articles/10june02.html [Accessed 11/03].

Chapter 10

1 Klein, Blomberg, and Hubbard, p. 410.

2 Oral Roberts, an evangelist, has taught many people to pray their problems.

3 This story is from Quentin McGhee.

4 William Barclay, *The Daily Study Bible: Matthew,* vol. 1, rev. ed. (Philadelphia, Pennsylvania: The Westminster Press, 1975), pp. 1-4.

5 William Barclay, *The Daily Study Bible: Matthew,* vol. 2, rev. ed. (Philadelphia, Pennsylvania: The Westminster Press, 1975), p. 308.

Chapter 11

1 Barclay, *Matthew,* vol. 1, p. 17.

2 Barclay, *Matthew,* vol. 1, pp. 16-18.

3 Quentin McGhee, *The Life & Teachings of Christ,* 3rd ed. (Springfield, Missouri: RDM, 2005), Teacher's Guide, n.p.

Chapter 13

1 David Larsen, *The Evangelism Mandate—Recovering the Centrality of Gospel Preaching* (Wheaton, Illinois: Crossway Books, 1992), p. 99.

2 Faris D. Whitesell, *Sixty-Five Ways to Give an Evangelistic Invitation* (Grand Rapids, Michigan: Kregel Publications, 1984), p. 22.

3 Braga, p. 236.

4 Charles H. Spurgeon, *The Soul Winner* (Grand Rapids, Michigan: Wm. B. Eerdmans Publishing Co., 1963), p. 84.

5 Braga, p. 23.

6 Spurgeon, *The Soul Winner,* p. 84.

7 Whitesell, page unknown.

8 Adapted from a sermon by C. H. Spurgeon in *John Ploughman's Talks* (Ann Arbor, Michigan: Baker Book House, 1976), pp. 50-53.